SCIENTIFIC DATING IN ARCHAEOLOGY

Studying Scientific Archaeology

Studying Scientific Archaeology is a series of titles from Oxbow Books. The series produces books on a wide variety of scientific topics in archaeology aimed at students at all levels. These examine the methods, procedures and reasoning behind various scientific approaches to archaeological data and present case studies or extended examples to demonstrate how data is used and interpretations are arrived at.

In particular we aim that they should demonstrate how scientific analyses contribute to our wider understanding of past human behaviour, technology and economy. The series title reflects an inclusivity in the volumes in the sense of encouraging readers in practical research rather than just presenting collected papers as statements of work completed.

Our aim is that these titles will come to feature as recommended reading for university courses, providing a sound basis for the appreciation and application of scientific archaeology.

Already published in this series

French, C. 2015. *A handbook of geoarchaeological approaches for investigating landscapes and settlement sites*

Hardy, K. & Kubiak-Martens, L. (eds), 2016. *Wild Harvest: plants in the hominin and pre-agrarian human worlds*

Allen, M. J. 2017. *Molluscs in Archaeology: methods, approaches and applications*

Wickham-Jones, C. 2018. *Landscape Beneath the Waves: the archaeological investigation of underwater landscapes*

Griffiths, S. (ed.) 2022. *Scientific Dating in Archaeology*

Gearey, B. & Chapman, H. 2022. *An Introduction to Peatland Archaeology and Palaeoenvironments*

French, C. 2022. *Human Transformations of the Earth*

SERIES EDITORS: Michael J. Allen and Terry O'Connor

STUDYING SCIENTIFIC ARCHAEOLOGY No. 5

Scientific Dating in Archaeology

edited by
Seren Griffiths

with contributions by
Martin Bridge, Ben Gearey, Sam Harris, Tom Higham,
Richard Staff and Abi Stone

OXBOW | books
Oxford & Philadelphia

Published in the United Kingdom in 2022 by
OXBOW BOOKS
The Old Music Hall, 106–108 Cowley Road, Oxford, OX4 1JE

and in the United States by
OXBOW BOOKS
1950 Lawrence Road, Havertown, PA 19083

© Oxbow Books and the individual contributors 2022

Paperback Edition: ISBN 978-1-78925-562-1
Digital Edition: ISBN 978-1-78925-563-8 (epub)

A CIP record for this book is available from the British Library

Library of Congress Control Number: 2022942570

All rights reserved. No part of this book may be reproduced or transmitted in any form or by any means, electronic or mechanical including photocopying, recording or by any information storage and retrieval system, without permission from the publisher in writing.

Printed in the United Kingdom by Short Run Press

Typeset in India by Lapiz Digital Services, Chennai.

For a complete list of Oxbow titles, please contact:

UNITED KINGDOM	UNITED STATES OF AMERICA
Oxbow Books	Oxbow Books
Telephone (01865) 241249	Telephone (610) 853-9131, Fax (610) 853-9146
Email: oxbow@oxbowbooks.com	Email: queries@casemateacademic.com
www.oxbowbooks.com	www.casemateacademic.com/oxbow

Oxbow Books is part of the Casemate Group

Front cover: Adam Stanford for Cadw, Crown Copyright
Back cover: Left image: copyright Norfolk County Council. Right image: copyright Clive Bonsall

Contents

Contributors vii
Conventions used viii
Acknowledgements ix

1. Introduction 1
   Seren Griffiths
   Scientific dating and archaeological thought 4
   The structure of this volume 7

2. Radiocarbon 9
   Seren Griffiths and Thomas Higham
   History of development and importance in the history
      of archaeological thought 9
   Underlying principles 13
   Measurement 15
   Offsets 18
   Quality indicators: being a critical consumer 24
   Case studies 26
   Chapter conclusions 39

3. Dendrochronology 43
   Martin Bridge and Seren Griffiths
   History of methodological development 44
   Underlying principles 46
   Measurement 47
   Sample selection 50
   Quality indicators: being a critical consumer 51
   Wiggle matching 53
   Case studies 54
   Chapter conclusions 61

4. Luminescence: Optically Simulated Luminescence and Thermoluminescence 63
   Seren Griffiths and Abi Stone
   Principles and methodological developments 65
   Measurement 70
   Applied sampling considerations 72

    Quality indicators: being a critical consumer 77
    Case studies 79
    Chapter conclusions 91

5. Archaeomagnetic dating 95
    Sam Harris and Seren Griffiths
    History of development 99
    Age calculation and calibration 104
    Quality indicators: being a critical consumer 107
    Case studies 108
    Chapter conclusions 113

6. Ecofactual chronologies 119
    Seren Griffiths and Ben Gearey
    Thinking about ecofactual chronologies 119
    Sampling for proxy chronologies 120
    Analytical definition of palaeo-environmental events 124
    Constructing models 124
    Case studies 125
    Chapter conclusions 132

7. On site: designing and implementing chronometric sampling strategies 135
    Seren Griffiths
    Applications of scientific dating in the field 135
    Approaches to designing chronometric sampling strategies 135
    Practical considerations of different methods in the field 142
    Ensuring quality 142
    Sampling considerations by method 147
    Chapter conclusions 152

8. Analysing datasets: Bayesian inference and archaeological
    chronometric data 153
    Seren Griffiths and Richard Staff
    Approaches to archaeological chronometric data and Bayesian modelling 154
    Case studies 165
    Chapter conclusions 189

9. Scientific dating and narrative 193
    Seren Griffiths
    'Science facts' and archaeological narratives 195
    Warrants, reversibility, close observation and Big Data 196
    Chronological knowledge structure and sequence 198
    Chapter conclusions 200

Appendix: Code for selected case studies in Chapter 8 203

Contributors

MARTIN BRIDGE is Lecturer in Dendrochronology at the Institute of Archaeology at University College London. Martin applies tree-ring studies to the dendrochronological dating of historic timbers, and to explore the impact of climate, woodland management and natural pests on tree ecology. He has worked internationally, including on wreck sites such as the *Mary Rose*, and the Newport ship.

BEN GEAREY is Lecturer in Environmental Archaeology in the Department of Archaeology at University College Cork. Ben has research interests in terms of palaeoecology, wetland archaeology and alluvial geoarchaeology. He is interested in integrating chronometric data using multi-proxies for paleoenvironmental reconstruction.

SEREN GRIFFITHS is Reader in Public Heritage and Archaeological Science at Manchester Metropolitan University. She currently leads two international research projects (funded by the Arts and Humanities Research Council and the Irish Research Council) looking at chronology in the 4th and 3rd millennium cal BC, and Big Data. She was a BBC New Generation Thinker (2020–21) and the Golson Lecturer at Australian National University (2018–19). She has worked across the UK and on research projects internationally.

SAM HARRIS is a specialist in archaeomagnetic dating. He has recently completed a Historic Environment Scotland funded PhD at the University of Bradford on archaeomagnetism in the Neolithic. He was previously a Palaeomagnetism Technician at Lancaster University, where he worked on projects in the UK, Sweden, Ukraine, Poland and the Svalbard archipelago.

TOM HIGHAM was until recently Professor of Archaeological Science at the Research Laboratory for Archaeology and the History of Art at the University of Oxford and is now Professor of Scientific Archaeology at the University of Vienna. Tom focuses on radiocarbon and especially pretreatment techniques. He recently led a large international research project increasing the precision of dating in the Middle and Upper Palaeolithic of Eurasia.

RICHARD STAFF is a Leverhulme Trust Early Career Research Fellow in Quaternary Geochronology at the Scottish Universities Environmental Research Centre. Richard specialises in radiocarbon dating and radiocarbon calibration, with expertise in Bayesian chronological modelling. His research focuses on the production of chronologies for palaeoenvironments, especially for lake sediments.

ABI STONE is Senior Lecturer in Physical Geography at the University of Manchester. Abi focuses on Quaternary environmental change, geochronology, hydrogeology and geomorphology. Her research focuses on the application of Optically Stimulated Luminescence dating and including the development of portable readers. She has worked internationally on geological and archaeological research projects.

Conventions used

We have used the chronological conventions 'AD' and 'BC' for date ranges throughout the volume, rather than 'CE' or 'BCE'. These are commonly used conventions in Britain, from which most of our case studies come. The 2020 northern hemisphere atmospheric radiocarbon calibration datasets (Reimer et al. 2020) is used throughout unless otherwise specified. Locations of sites are reported using latitude and longitude in WGS84. We use the Courier font to distinguish Chronological Query Language v2 terms from the OxCal computer program (Bronk Ramsey 1995; 1998; 2001; 2008; 2009) from similar archeologically meaningful terms.

Bronk Ramsey, C. 1995. Radiocarbon calibration and analysis of stratigraphy: the OxCal program. *Radiocarbon* 3(2), 425–30
Bronk Ramsey, C. 1998. Probability and dating. *Radiocarbon* 40(1), 461–74
Bronk Ramsey, C. 2001. Development of the radiocarbon calibration program OxCal. *Radiocarbon* 43(2A), 355–63.
Bronk Ramsey, C. 2008. Radiocarbon dating: revolutions in understanding. *Archaeometry* 50, 249–75 [doi:10.1111/j.1475-4754.2008.00394.x]
Bronk Ramsey, C. 2009. Bayesian analysis of radiocarbon dates. *Radiocarbon* 51(1), 337–60
Reimer, P., Austin, W., Bard, E., Bayliss, A., Blackwell, P., Bronk Ramsey, C., Butzin, M, Cheng, H., Edwards, R., Friedrich, M., Grootes, P., Guilderson, T., Hajadas, I., Heaton, T., Hogg, A., Hughen, K., Kromer, B., Manning, S., Muscheler, R., Palmer, J., Pearson, C., van der Plicht, J., Reimer, R., Richards, D., Scott, E., Southon, J., Turney, C., Wacker, L., Adolphi, F., Büntgen, U., Capano, M., Fahrni, S., Fogtmann-Schultz, A., Friedrich, R., Köhler, P., Kudsk, S., Miyake, F., Olsen, J., Reinig, F., Sakamoto, M., Sookdeo, A. and Talamo, S. 2020. The IntCal20 northern hemisphere radiocarbon age calibration curve (0–55 cal. kBP). *Radiocarbon* 62(4), 725–57

Acknowledgements

This volume is indebted to work the of a wide range of specialists, this includes: Alison Arnold, Alistair Barclay, Clive Bonsall, Tim Darvill, Jeffery S. Dean, Anne Dodd, Ben Ford, Kirsten Jones, Paul Linford, Fraser Sturt and Manca Vinazza. Pat English gave permission to use the image of Glyn Daniel. Cathy Batt, Richard Bradley, Caitlin Buck, Ian Bailiff, Ben Edwards and Tim Murray made very helpful comments on earlier drafts of chapters. This volume was produced during the 2020–2021 global pandemic, and the people at Oxbow Books have been very, very patient, especially Jessica Hawxwell and Julie Gardiner. Especial thanks to Mike Allen and Terry O'Connor for being invited to produce the volume. Seren would like to think Gill Hey, Alex Bayliss, Matthew Spriggs and Berthold Schoene for supporting her career at key moments, and everyone else she has worked with, who have generally been lovely.

1. Introduction

Seren Griffiths

Radiocarbon dating heralded a revolution in archaeology. For the first time archaeologists were able to make use of *independent* chronological evidence. Until this point they had to rely on time reckoning that was highly indebted to what they thought they knew about the past. The independence of chronometric methods resulted in a fundamental shift in both intellectual approaches in archaeology and how archaeology is practised.

Traditional ways of time reckoning used a suite of 'relative' chronological evidence. Relative dating techniques included the construction of typological sequences where changes in styles of material culture (such as pottery) were interpreted as evidence for the passage of time. These schemes represent the culmination of decades of work by many researchers. Evidence from material culture was combined with other relative chronological information, including from the stratigraphic sequences observed at individual sites, to create synthetic, abstracted models of change over time: 'culture historic' models.

These abstracted 'culture historic' models defined groups of material culture and site types over large regions. Prior to the invention of scientific dating techniques the temporal currency of these culture historic packages had to be estimated by archaeologists, so that material culture and chronological sequences were closely linked together in archaeological reasoning. The British Neolithic is one such culture historic package, defined by material culture and given a relative temporal currency, so that the British Neolithic preceded the British Bronze Age culture historic package. Such relative schemes are very powerful approaches in our thinking about the past. However, an obvious issue with such relative models is that they are heavily indebted to archaeologists' understandings of the past. Material culture, whether individual types of artefact or culture historic packages, needs to be interpreted. Relative chronological schemes are in this sense both situated and highly structuring intellectual devices.

Beyond relative dating, in periods with written records, textual sources such as books or inscriptions can provide chronological evidence of a very different type. However, there may also be problems with these types of sources as the basis for building chronologies. Textual sources may be biased in terms of the histories that are told.

The importance of the introduction of radiocarbon measurements in the 1950s was therefore in the *independence* of these age estimates from the kinds of limitations inherent in relative dating and textual sources. The importance of the development of scientific dating techniques was that they provided a check against the elaborate typo-chronologies archaeologists had previously developed to structure their histories. As we shall discuss over this volume there are actually many issues to consider in the production and analysis of chronometric data and we need to think critically about the 'data journeys' that measurements go through in the process of chronology building.

The importance of independent time reckoning meant that worldwide archaeology really started again in the 1950s. This was the conclusion of the eminent Cambridge University prehistorian Glyn Daniel (Fig. 1.1) when reviewing his career in 1981 on a BBC Radio Four *Desert Island Discs* programme. For Daniel, radiocarbon was the greatest single development in the history of archaeology, it

> … revolutionised archaeology…because it had an absolute framework, and we could no longer say 'Oh, I wonder how old Stonehenge is?' … [and]… try and tie things up with Egypt and with Greece… (Daniel 13 November 1981).

The radicalness of this revolution may be impossible to appreciate if you did not live through it. In 1981, some 30 years after the development of radiocarbon, Daniel's voice still registered the impact that scientific dating had. The personal impact on eminent

Figure 1.1. Glyn Daniel at West Kennet in 1974. The then Cambridge students Matthew Spriggs (subsequently Professor of Archaeology at Australian National University) and Daniel Miller (subsequently Professor of Anthropology at University College London) can be seen in the background. Copyright: Pat English.

archaeologists cannot be over-estimated. In Britain, Daniel was confronted with his life's work (e.g. Daniel 1962) being rather publicly upended. Orser and Patterson (2004, 4) suggest that the impact on V.G. Childe may have contributed to his suicide.

Radiocarbon was revolutionary because it demonstrated that archaeological thinking was flawed. Not only was what we thought about the past wrong but also *how* we thought about the past could be problematic. Daniel's mention of Greece or Egypt

Figure 1.2. A map illustrating in Daniel's (1941) 'passage grave culture' (of which Bryn Celli Ddu is an example) and the proposed routes of 'colonisation', based on apparent similarities in cultural groupings (identified by numbers). Radiocarbon measurements provided independent evidence for the first time that many such schemes were misleading and reflected the concerns of 19th and 20th century European societies more than any 'Passage Grave culture'. Copyright: Seren Griffiths.

makes reference to some of these pre-scientific dating practices (Fig. 1.2). In Europe, pre-radiocarbon, cross-links between historical king-lists or Classical references anchored 'prehistoric' pasts in absolute years. All these cross-links, correlations and logical leaps provided chronological sequences for their archaeological evidence. However, it meant that some inherent biases also travelled with these approaches. In Europe, pre-radiocarbon ideas about 'civilisation' and 'development' meant that many researchers understood evidence for social change in some kind of *ex orient lux* diffusion from societies listed in Classical texts. Radiocarbon demonstrated that this kind of approach tells us more about European elite tastes in the 19th and early 20th centuries – the times these models were developed – than societies in the 4th or 3rd millennium BC.

In that quote about Stonehenge Daniel was identifying the importance of radiocarbon in terms of our *sequences*; chronologies provide the temporal axis against which we assemble the evidence from material culture, sites and landscapes. If we get our sequences right, we may be able to sift out meaningful patterns for the societies that we are researching.

However, radiocarbon was revolutionary not because it changed the sequence of archaeological facts, but because it challenged the intellectual *structure* of archaeology (Griffiths 2017). Chronologies are not just a timeline. Chronological structures actually condition how we think about the past and this is especially true for societies which did not produce written texts. The creation of chronologies frames the types of histories we develop and the stories of which people we tell. In Australia, Tim Murray notes that from the 1960s onwards it '… is not an overstatement to assert that radiometric dating has to all intents and purposes created the … archaeology of Australia' (Murray 2016, 189).

Chronologies also intersect with the contemporary practice of archaeology. Who produces these data, how they are controlled, and how they are assembled can be powerful and political. We can see this in the popular reporting of archaeological discoveries, when claims for the oldest example of some form of material culture, site or behavioural trait are made. There is a latent power in chronologies and in chronology building, in who controls what narratives about which pasts. Chronologies are therefore not neutral sequences against which we assemble evidence and chronological data – as 'science facts' (Chapter 9) – can have a peculiar power in archaeological narratives.

Scientific dating and archaeological thought

Glyn Daniel's identification of the 1950s as the restart of archaeology provides a convenient reference point for the history of scientific dating. However, taken more broadly, systematic attempts to build chronologies have a much longer history, with important related developments in palaeontology and geology. In this sense it is possible to include Charles Lyell's (e.g. Lyell 1830) important work identifying the principles of geology – including ideas about superimposition and the formation of deposits – as of foundational value to archaeological scientific dating. Equally important was the recognition of the 'Deep Time' age of the world, the identification of problems with Classical sources and the Bible, and the development of alternative explanations for 'antediluvian' assemblages of cave fauna.

Classical sources had provided an approach to the subdivision or 'periodisation' of time which was subsequently developed in 19th century early archaeological work. The legacy of these ideas still plays a critical role, especially in prehistory. Classical writers such as Lucretius described successive ages of stone and wood, copper and bronze, and iron. These material culture groups were understood not simply in functional terms; the technological prowess and the social virtue of an age were matched. A 'decline' in materials was accompanied by decline in the morals of the human world as we became more distant from the Titans of the earliest times. In contrast to this entropic slant to social change, more recent European approaches have often privileged the *development* of societies as time elapses and materials become more 'complex'. This was formalised in C.J. Thomsen's Three-Age System in 1824–5 (Gräsland 1987, 19), with the Stone, Bronze and Iron Ages revised in the 1860–70s to accommodate the Palaeolithic, Mesolithic and Neolithic or equivalent terms (Lubbock 1865; Worsaae 1866; Westropp 1872).

The processes of validation that established these chronological schemes were complex and detailed. They required extensive knowledge of geographically wide ranging evidence. Without independent dating evidence, material culture occupied a double location in these kinds of temporal models. Things were here simultaneously subjects of inquiry (in terms of their spatial and temporal distribution and in terms of their social importance and meaning in specific contexts) *and* they were also proxies for the passage of time.

In terms of philosophy of science, we can think about this phase of archaeological thought as an example of the Second Science paradigm – the establishment of theoretical approaches through the creation of models and generalisation (Hey *et al.* 2009). The ordering of such large groups of materials was such a significant task and was achieved incrementally by researchers such as Oscar Montelius who developed his ages in Sweden (e.g. Montelius 1885). In Britain, we see the codification of material culture reach its most sophisticated expression in the work of V. Gordon Childe (e.g. 1932) though these approaches continued into the 1950s, for example with the work of Stuart Piggott (1954).

Culture historic terms – as the legacy of the first theoretical approaches in archaeology – are foundational concepts and are still widely used. As noted above, such concepts can bring with them the technological or developmental preconceptions which were implicit in their development even though archaeology now has the advantage of independent chronometric data. Such latent concepts include an inevitably linear model of 'development' against time. Some of these latent ideas can be unhelpful or 'bad to think with' when attempting to evaluate critically independent scientific dating measurements. In coming to terms with the first radiocarbon revolutions, and as early as 1968, Glyn Daniel was arguing that '… the old labels should be abolished and people should talk in chronological periods … but I expect that we shall go on using terms like Neolithic and Bronze Age' (Daniel 1968, 346). The enduring nature of these terms after the development of independent scientific dating shows the power of convenient labels. However, they also show an unwillingness to engage with messy, nuanced and regionally variable narratives that scientific chronologies could offer us.

There are more profound issues with culture historic terms that owe much to 19th century European colonialism and the westward expansionism of people of European descent across North America. It was in these contexts that social anthropologists classified human societies in terms of 'complexity' and 'development'. So, Edward Tylor (1871) and Lewis Morgan (1877) saw contemporary human societies as defined in terms of social evolution. If Charles Lyell's (1863) geological work had provided a space for 'prehistory', that space was subsequently filled with highly problematic ways of thinking about people that derive from this 19th century context. The subtitle of John Lubbock's 1865 volume *Pre-historic Times, as Illustrated by Ancient Remains, and the Manners and Customs of Modern Savages*, illustrates the kinds of ideas latent in these terms.

Concepts like 'prehistory' – and the culture historic terms that populate it – then derive from a highly specific, ethnocentric approach to past (cf. McNiven and Russell 2009, 429); as John Mulvaney (1990, 157) noted, to '… a people without writing, history need not be written down'. The problems with these terms are further highlighted when they are exported outside the European context of their initial development. When terms that derive from European studies are applied to other places with their own unique circumstances and very different trajectories of social change, we are creating concealed, problematic comparisons. Thinking about a southern African 'Iron Age' that butts up against European Colonial contact (Mitchell 2002) creates all kinds of difficulties when compared with a European 'Iron Age' of a very different type and timescale.

What these kinds of comparisons also highlight is that contemporary definitions of many culture historic groups have been revised and qualified so much as to make their utility as heuristic devices almost redundant. The British 'Neolithic', for example, has been variously defined by the presence of domesticated plants and animals (e.g. Childe 1940), characterised by different pottery-defined groups (e.g. Piggott 1954) or associated with the introduction of a new body of beliefs (e.g. Thomas 1999).

The apparent neutrality of some temporal terms is matched by the way that chronological data are often accepted uncritically in discussions. Despite the pervasive centrality of chronometric data to our research, chronology and the 'data journeys' (Wylie 2020; Chapter 9) which chronological data go through have often been regarded as relatively unproblematic aspects of the archaeological process. Lewis Binford, speaking in 1984 (in Taylor 2000, 15, my emphasis), reflected the positivism of the time, and the idea that chronologies are theoretically neutral, when he stated that the introduction of radiocarbon dating:

> … has certainly changed the activities of archaeologists, so that now, in many ways for the first time, they direct their methodological investments toward *theory building rather than towards chronology building*.

Similar responses to the introduction of radiocarbon amongst the wider archaeological community are reported by Renfrew. Archaeological science generally, and radiocarbon measurements specifically, were seen in the post-Second World War period as a new independent arbiter of a whole range of archaeological knowledge claims. All our interpretative problems would be resolved in this brave new world of radiocarbon, so that '… all that was needed was a couple of ounces of charcoal … and *science would do the rest*' (Renfrew 1976, 53; my emphasis).

Throughout this volume we will stress that chronological data are as situated as any other type of archaeological evidence. 'Prehistory' and associated culture historic terms are not neutral and we need to think critically about how we deploy them and what they do in our narratives. Chronological data do not speak for themselves and data are absolutely not neutral. As with relative chronologies, chronologies built with independent scientific dating evidence are construed as part of a process. New evidence or understandings are assimilated into extant intellectual frameworks because of the degree of cogency this evidence has with those frameworks. So, when new scientific chronological data are produced, they are evaluated against both the sequence of other data associated with relevant comparanda, but also within the over-arching structure of our archaeological knowledge framework (Griffiths 2017). If, following Matthew Johnson (2020), theory is the order we put facts in, then an essential part of an archaeological 'fact' is its chronological and spatial definition; this gives chronometric data a peculiar status in archaeology as 'science facts' (Chapter 9).

The 1950s radiocarbon revolution redefined the nature of the facts that underpin our discipline. In this sense, the first radiocarbon revolution is probably the only paradigm shift archaeology has been through, through the full implications of this revolution may not have been fully played out (Chapter 9). Certainly, relatively few researchers have critically considered the ways that scientific dating is integrated into archaeology at in the widest sense. This volume provides an holistic approach to scientific dating from the application in the field, to the analysis of datasets, and critical consideration of chronological sequences and structures.

The structure of this volume

Scientific dating is, therefore, far more than 'simply' a method of time reckoning. It is deeply interconnected with other aspects of archaeological practice and is theoretically loaded in ways which are often under-recognised. The production, consumption and publication of chronometric data can be a highly political component of archaeological practice.

The next chapters detail different scientific dating measurements: radiocarbon (Chapter 2), dendrochronology (Chapter 3), archaeomagnetic (Chapter 4), and luminescence (Chapter 5). As we shall see in these chapters, an understanding of first principles *and* the archaeological context of chronology construction is essential to evaluate all scientific data. Following these chapters, we start to think about how we can apply these methods, discussing sampling for palaeoenvironmental reconstruction using multi-proxy evidence (Chapter 6). We apply these fundamental principles in a systematic approach to chronology building from the project planning and site sampling stages onwards using our 'A, B, C, D' approach to scientific dating in Chapter 7. Chapter 8 looks at Bayesian modelling and discusses analysis using the computer programme OxCal. In the last chapter, we discuss different approaches to writing archaeological narratives more broadly, and how we need to consider chronometric data as part of the wider practice and philosophy of archaeology.

Bibliography

Childe, V.G. 1932. Chronology of prehistoric Europe: a review. *Antiquity* 6, 410–18
Childe, V.G. 1940. *Prehistoric Communities of the British Isles.* London: Chambers
Daniel, G. 1962. *The Idea of Prehistory.* London: Watts
Daniel, G. 1968. *The First Civilizations: the archaeology of their origins.* London: Thames and Hudson
Daniel, G. 1981. *Desert Island Discs.* First broadcast Friday 13 November 1981 [https://www.bbc.co.uk/programmes/p009mtkm]
Gräsland, B. 1987. *The Birth of Prehistoric Chronology. Dating Methods and Dating Systems in Nineteenth-Century Scandinavian Archaeology.* Cambridge: Cambridge University Press
Griffiths, S. 2017. We're all Cultural Historians now: revolutions in understanding archaeological theory and scientific dating. *Radiocarbon* 59(5), 1347–57 [doi:10.1017/RDC.2017.20]
Hey, T., Tansley S. and Tolle, K. 2009. Jim Grey on eScience: a transformed scientific method. In T. Hey, S. Tansley and K. Tolle (eds), *The Fourth Paradigm: data-intensive scientific discovery*, xvii–xxxi. Redmond WA: Microsoft Research
Lubbock, J. 1865. *Pre-historic Times, as Illustrated by Ancient Remains, and the Manners and Customs of Modern Savages.* London: Williams and Norgate
Lyell, C. 1830. *Principles of Geology: being an attempt to explain the former changes of the Earth's surface, by reference to causes now in operation.* London, John Murray
Lyell, C. 1863. *The Geological Evidences of the Antiquity of Man, with Remarks on Theories of the Origin of the Species by Variation.* London: Murray
Johnson, M. 2020. *Archaeological Theory: an introduction* (3rd edn). Hoboken NJ: Wiley-Blackwell
Mitchell, P. 2002. *The Archaeology of Southern Africa.* Cambridge: Cambridge University Press
McNiven, I. and Russell, L. 2009. Towards a postcolonial archaeology of Indigenous Australia. In R. Bentley, H. Maschner and C. Chippendale (eds), *Handbook of Archaeological Theories*, 423–47. Lanham MD: AltaMira
Montelius, O. 1885. *Sur la Chronologie de l'Age du Bronze, Spécialement dans la Scandinavie.* Paris: Matériaux pour l'Histoire Primitive de l'Homme. 19e année, 3e série, Tome II, 3–8
Morgan, L. 1877. *Ancient Society.* New York: Holt
Mulvaney, J. 1990. Afterword: the view from the window. In S. Janson and S. MacIntyre (eds), *Through White Eyes*, 155–67. St Leonards: Allen and Unwin
Murray, T. 2016. The New Archaeology and the archaeology of Australia. In G. Delley, M. Díaz-Andreu, F. Djindian, V. Fernández, A. Guidi and M-A. Kaeser (eds), *History of Archaeology: International Perspectives*, 187–93. Oxford: Archaeopress
Orser, C. and Patterson, T. 2004. Introduction. V. Gordon Childe and the foundations of Social Archaeology. In T. Patterson and C. Orser (eds), *Foundations of Social Archaeology. Selected Writings of V. Gordon Childe*, 1–23. Lanham MD: AltaMira
Piggott, S. 1954. *The Neolithic Cultures of the British Isles: a study of the stone-using agricultural communities of Britain in the second millennium BC.* Cambridge: Cambridge University Press
Renfrew, C. 1976. *Before Civilization: the radiocarbon revolution and prehistoric Europe.* Harmondsworth: Penguin
Taylor, R. 2000. The contribution of radiocarbon dating to New World archaeology. *Radiocarbon* 42(1), 1–21
Thomas, J. 1999. *Understanding the Neolithic.* London: Routledge
Tylor, E. 1871. *Primitive Culture.* London: Murray
Westropp, H. 1872. *Pre-historic Places; or, introductory essays on pre-historic archaeology.* London: Bell and Daldy
Wylie, A. 2020. Radiocarbon dating in archaeology: triangulation and traceability. In S. Leonelli and N. Tempini (eds), *Data Journeys in the Sciences*, 285–301. Dordrecht: Springer Open
Worsaae, J. 1866. The Antiquities of South Jutland or Sleswick. *Archaeological Journal* 23, 21–40

2. Radiocarbon

Seren Griffiths and Thomas Higham

Radiocarbon dating is the most commonly applied scientific dating method in archaeology. Its ubiquity results from several factors. First, radiocarbon measurements can be made on a wide range of material types which are often preserved on archaeological sites. Samples that are routinely measured include wood charcoals, waterlogged or charred plant remains and bone, though measurements are also made on lots of other, more specialist samples. Radiocarbon is also widely used because it can be applied across the world, to the entirety of the Holocene period and into the preceding Pleistocene period. This means that chronologies can be built using radiocarbon measurements for the time periods in which most archaeologists work. Another compelling aspect is the relative affordability in comparison with the cost of many other scientific dating methods. Finally, the principles that provide the basis for radiocarbon age calculations are well-understood. Measurements can be reproduced and the resultant age estimates can be demonstrated to be accurate. Over 70 years of research and development into radiocarbon methods has significantly improved measurement precision. It is this combination of wide-ranging applicability, relative affordability and demonstrable accuracy, together with good routine measurement precision that makes radiocarbon the most commonly use scientific dating method.

History of development and importance in the history of archaeological thought

The ideas behind the radiocarbon technique were probably first outlined publicly by Willard Libby in 1948 (Taylor 1987) but the process of developing the technique for application in archaeology took 16 years, between 1933 and 1949 (Taylor 1978, 3), when Libby and his collaborator James Arnold published the first measurements on known age samples (Arnold and Libby 1949).

The application of radiocarbon measurements to archaeological samples is arguably the single most important development in the history of archaeological thought. Libby is certainly the only person to have been awarded a Nobel prize (in 1960) for contributions to science associated with archaeology. As the first method to produce independent chronologies with wide-ranging geographical application, radiocarbon provided a means to verify – or to challenge – the existing relative chronologies developed out of cross-dating and seriation in many different parts of the world.

It was this independence that made the radiocarbon technique revolutionary. Radiocarbon chronologies provided archaeologists with the potential to move beyond typological straightjackets. It also contributed to a new valorisation of science and a positivism that framed the intellectual development of the discipline in the post-Second World War years (cf. Renfrew 1976).

The introduction of the technique was one of four key developments in the radiocarbon method (Bronk Ramsey 2008; Bayliss 2009). These are:

- the initial development of the method;
- the recognition of the need for calibration;
- the development and application of Accelerator Mass Spectrometry (which reduced sample size requirements) and;
- the development of Bayesian statistical analysis techniques (Buck *et al.* 1991; Chapter 8).

These developments have all been presented as 'revolutions'. However, both in terms of the scope for rethinking the discipline and the impact on archaeological approaches, the first introduction of the method had by far the most significant impact. We are currently living through the impact of the fourth, Bayesian, revolution and it remains to be seen what the implications of Bayesian approaches will be on archaeology (see Chapter 9).

The dated event, and the archaeological event of interest

One of the key ideas in this book is that scientific chronologies are constructed from a series of measurements that can be thought of as 'dated events'. Dated events are actually not points in time but scientific observations or measurements. How meaningful these dated events are in terms of addressing specific archaeological research questions depends on the *association* with what we can define as 'the archaeological event of interest'. In order to make meaningful chronologies, regardless of which measurement technique we are working with, we need measurements that represent very clearly defined dated events and very clearly understood associations between the measurements and the archaeological event that we are actually interested in. In radiocarbon, there are a number of issues than can confuse the definition of the dated event. These can include the measurement of a 'bulk sample' of entities of different ages, the presence of contamination and the measurement of a sample with an inbuilt age offset.

The next stage in building robust chronologies is to consider the association between the dated event and any archaeological event of interest. Having identified what our dated event represents, in order to think about association we need to think about the sample and the physical processes on an archaeological site including stratigraphic associations, deposit formation and taphonomy. We then need to think about how we are defining the specific archaeological event that we are interested in and our research aims more broadly. For each scientific dating method there may be different underlying principles that we need to consider when thinking about the definition of the dated event and the association between this measurement and the archaeological record. We explore systematic approaches to defining dated events and archaeological events of interest in Chapter 8 as part of the development of chronometric sampling strategies on site.

The importance in chronology building of thinking critically about the physical association of dated samples was identified by the hugely influential Dutch archaeologist H.T. Waterbolk. Waterbolk (1971, 16) identified four broad classes of sample association which we have adapted here:

- **Class one**. The sample *is* the object of interest. A direct measurement on these kinds of samples should have a very strong association with the archaeological event of interest. If the research question is when an individual died, a direct measurement on the human skeletal remains – accounting for diet-derived offsets and tissue turnover rates (see below) – should resolve the research question. Another example might be measurement on a charred food crust on a pottery vessel; here the measurement should provide a direct estimate for the presence of the food (though possibly not the creation of the pot).
- **Class two**. There is a *functional relationship* between the sample and the archaeological event of interest. Samples that fall into this class may include, for example, a placed deposit rich in short-life charred plant remains in a ditch fill sequence before the primary silting. In this case, if the research question is 'when was the ditch excavated?' we can see that there is an association. However, we can also see that the archaeological event of interest (digging the ditch) does not have the same temporal definition as the dated event (the death of the plants). In this example, measurements on the plant remains may provide a *terminus ante quem* based on the stratigraphic relationships. Equally the charred plant remains could have been harvested on exactly the same day that the ditch was dug. In any case, the nature of the deposit, the plant remains assemblage, and the position in the fill sequence suggest a very close association with the excavation of the ditch. Samples with good functional associations that are often used for radiocarbon measurements include short-life charcoals from hearth deposits, where the interpretation is that the plant remains represents fuel for the hearth. Tools such as antler mattocks or short-life materials used as hafts for axes or daggers should also provide estimates for the use of the artefacts (but possibly not their original manufacture).
- **Class three**. Archaeological observations *suggest a relationship* between a potential sample and the archaeological event in question. For example, a pit fill rich in faunal remains, pottery and metalwork might suggest that the assemblage was deposited together as a result of specific anthropogenic activity. Considering the nature of the species profile might help explore the taphonomy of the assemblage as a whole. A skeletal element from a burrowing animal, which is the only one of its kind in an assemblage, might not provide a robust radiocarbon measurement for the formation of the rest of the assemblage. Evidence for anthropogenic selection might also suggest an assemblage has been deliberately deposited, for

example if an assemblage of faunal remains is dominated by the same elements of pig bone. In this case a measurement on one of the pig bones might provide a useful estimate for the timing of deposition of the skeletal assemblage but it might not provide a good estimate for other aspects of the site (for example for the timing of use of metalwork also included in the feature). The association here depends on archaeological interpretation of the processes associated with the infilling of the feature.
- **Class four**. There is the *possibility* that a sample is associated with the archaeological event of interest. Waterbolk uses the example of a sample from an organic-rich occupation deposit. An isolated, hand-recovered fragment of charcoal may provide an accurate estimate for the formation of the parent deposit. However, there is also the strong possibility that such a sample is residual or intrusive. Interpretation of measurements on such types of sample can be very difficult because there is no clear association between the dated event, and the archaeological of interest.

In order to build robust chronologies, the association between each potential chronometric sample and the archaeological event of interest needs to be assessed in these terms. We have updated and refined Waterbolk's terms by focusing on the association to identify:

- **direct measurements**. This type of measurement should mean that the dated event is the same as the archaeological event of interest (e.g. skeletal element from a burial = date of tissue formation; charred food crust on pottery = use of pottery; bark edge of log coffin = felling of tree for coffin);
- **measurements with a functional relationship** with the event of interest (e.g. measurement on articulated bone provides a good terminus ante quem for the infilling of a feature; measurement on *in situ* dumped deposit provides a good estimate for the use of a structure);
- **measurement with probable association** with the event of interest (e.g. material from mixed fill of rubbish pit may provide an estimate for the presence of other material recovered from the feature);
- **measurement which could be associated** with the event of interest (e.g. measurement on hand-recovered fragment of charcoal from inhumation; measurement on isolated bone fragment from occupation layer; measurement on charcoal fragment from otherwise sterile ditch fill).

In every research question, assessing the nature of any association provides an important step in the processes of critical chronological building. As might be apparent from the list above even in the case of 'direct' measurements there is the need for archaeological interpretation about the definition of the dated event of the archaeological event of interest; a measurement on a skeletal element will be reasonably accurate for the date of death but this depends on the element dated and bone turn-over rates (see below). A measurement on a food crust should provide an accurate estimate for the use of the vessel but may not date the deposition of the sherd in an assemblage. A measurement on bark edge may provide an estimate for the felling date of a timber used for a coffin but this might not provide an estimate for the date of burial. In Chapter 3, we will see how the eminent American archaeologist Jeffery S. Dean developed a similar critical approach to the interpretation of dendrochonological data. We consider more broadly designing sampling strategies in Chapter 7.

Underlying principles

Radiocarbon (^{14}C) is one of three naturally occurring carbon isotopes. Radiocarbon is distinguished from the two main stable isotopes of carbon (^{12}C and ^{13}C) by its atomic mass. A radiocarbon isotope has eight neutrons in its nucleus, unlike ^{12}C (six neutrons) and ^{13}C (seven neutrons). This imbalance in the number of protons and neutrons means that ^{14}C is unstable and so subject to radioactive decay. This isotopic decay of radiocarbon occurs at a known rate, called the half-life, which is the measure of time over which half the radiocarbon in a sample will decay back to the parent isotope (^{14}N). Libby calculated the half-life of radiocarbon as 5568±30 years (Anderson and Libby 1951).

This is a relatively long half-life compared with many other radioactive isotopes and it this that means radiocarbon dating can be employed across the Holocene and into the Pleistocene. However, the time taken for all ^{14}C isotopes to decay back to ^{14}N is finite and it is this that determines the maximum upper age limit on the application of radiocarbon measurements. This upper limit is probably not more than ten half-lives, about 50–60,000 years ago.

Radioactive carbon is produced in the stratosphere by nuclear reactions between atmospheric nitrogen and thermal neutrons produced by cosmic rays (Fig. 2.1). Soon after production the radiocarbon isotope becomes oxidised to form $^{14}CO_2$ and enters the Earths biosphere by photosynthesis and atmospheric exchange with the ocean. The different masses of the carbon isotopes mean that they behave differently in physical and chemical processes and, as a result, different environments therefore had different proportions of carbon isotopes. The ratios of carbon isotopes available in different environments can be thought of as carbon 'reservoirs'.

From these reservoirs, carbon isotopes, including radiocarbon, are incorporated into the tissues of living organisms along the food chain (Fig. 2.1). As soon as an organism dies, this biogenic carbon exchange stops. The proportion of radiocarbon should now continuously decrease as radiocarbon decay occurs but the proportions of other stable carbon isotopes in an organism remain the same.

The radiocarbon age of a sample is a measure of how many radiocarbon isotopes are present in it and uses the known rate of decay to calculate the time interval since carbon exchange ceased. This calculation requires knowledge of the isotope proportions in the relevant reservoir and a clear understanding of the point at which carbon exchange should have ceased. Radiocarbon 'dates' are therefore an age calculation based on a measurement of the proportion of these isotopes in a sample.

To produce accurate age estimates, radiocarbon results also need to be calibrated. This calibration process accounts for the fluctuations in atmospheric carbon that have occurred over time and the various proportions of radiocarbon isotopes in different reservoirs. For example, the lower atmosphere has a different proportion of carbon

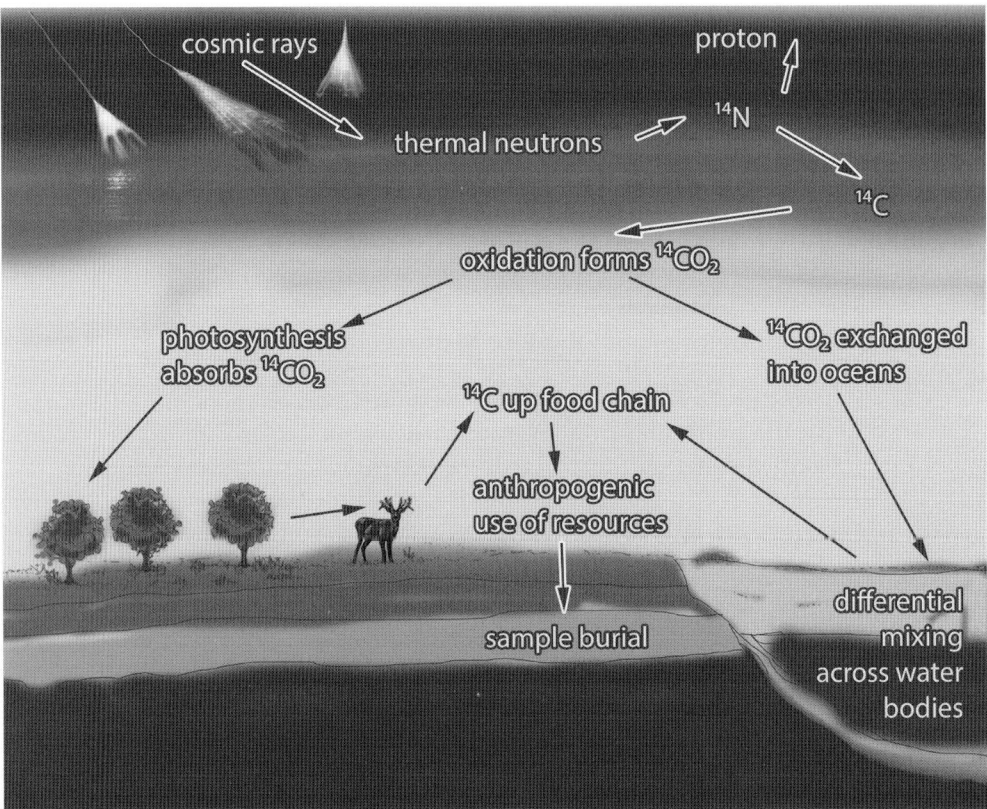

Figure 2.1. The carbon cycle which leads carbon isotopes to accumulate in different organisms. Copyright: Seren Griffiths.

isotopes to those in a marine reservoir. Samples that form at the same actual time in these different environments would have different proportions of radiocarbon and therefore appear to be of different radiocarbon ages if the appropriate calibration dataset is not used; the sample from the marine reservoir would have a lower proportion of radiocarbon and therefore appear older than the contemporary terrestrial sample. To produce accurate age ranges for measurements on these contemporary samples, we would need to calibrate the results using different calibration datasets (see discussion below). Internationally agreed calibration datasets (often called 'curves') exist and are updated regularly, for example there is a specific calibration dataset that is updated for terrestrial samples in the northern hemisphere (e.g. Reimer *et al.* 2009; 2013; 2020).

Samples for radiocarbon measurement may have been buried for long periods of time or have been conserved in museums. Both the burial environment and post-excavation and conservation processes can introduce exogenous carbon into samples. Samples may therefore require pretreatment to remove this exogenous carbon. The nature of the pretreatment depends on the material (see below).

Measurement

A variety of different radiocarbon measurement approaches have been developed. Older methods include Gas Proportional Counting and Liquid Scintillation Counting. Gas Proportional Counting uses high-purity carbon dioxide derived from the carbon samples to measure beta decay events. In Liquid Scintillation Counting, the carbon dioxide is converted to acetylene and then benzene (C_6H_6). The addition of a scintillant to the benzene enables beta decay events to be measured as photons using counters equipped with photo-multiplier tubes.

In beta counting systems, it is the radiation emitted as radiocarbon decay occurs that is measured. Beta counting systems require large sample sizes and, to satisfy the sample size required, archaeologists often submitted bulk samples of ecofacts. This had implications for the quality of chronologies, as such samples often mixed materials of different radiocarbon ages and with different archaeological associations. As a result of this mixing it is very difficult to establish what these samples mean in terms of any radiocarbon measurement. In these cases, definition of the dated event becomes very unclear and building meaningful chronologies from such samples is very difficult.

A significant change in archaeology and scientific dating occurred from the late 1970s when direct ion-counting measurement method was introduced – Accelerator Mass Spectrometry or AMS dating. In AMS measurement the carbon isotopes themselves are counted. The introduction of AMS dating resulted in a substantial reduction in the required sample sizes necessary to produce a radiocarbon measurement, with important implications for how archaeologists construct chronologies.

In AMS measurement a graphite target is produced from the prepared sample (see below for pretreatment of different sample types). This target is subject to ionisation, usually by sputtering with caesium ions. The ionisation step eliminates ^{14}N, the principal isobar (isotopes of different elements but with the same atomic weight), since nitrogen does not form a negative ion. The negatively-charged ions then enter a fast-moving energy beam, their trajectory tuned using electromagnets to select only mass 14 ions. In the accelerator part of the instrument, as the name suggests, the ions are accelerated at higher energy towards the terminal, where a stripper gas is used to break up the molecular ions and strip electrons from the particles changing them from negative to positively charged ions. The ions that pass through this step move extremely fast away from the terminal. Ions that fit with the velocity expected for ^{14}C are selected and those filtered then enter the detector where they are measured using a Faraday cup (a small metal cup that is used to catch charged particles in a vacuum). The stable isotopes, ^{12}C and ^{13}C, are usually also measured to assess the efficiency of the measurements. Ages are calculated based on the ratios of $^{14}C/^{13}C$ and $^{14}C/^{12}C$ with reference to measurements made on standards with known carbon isotope ratios.

Advances in accelerator physics have to led to precisions that are now equivalent to the highest levels previously seen in older systems. The advent of much smaller accelerators, such as the Mini Radiocarbon Dating System (MICADAS), and the imminent arrival of the Positive Ion Mass Spectrometry (PIMS) system, will further expand the range of samples that it is possible to measure and reduce the sizes required.

In all these measurement techniques, pretreatment of samples using physical and chemical means is essential. Pretreatment removes exogenous carbon from a sample. This step is essential in ensuring that we satisfy one of the basic principles of radiocarbon measurement outlined above – that we clearly understand the processes by which carbon entered a sample. Exogenous carbon is, in this sense, contamination; it could derive from carbon in the soil of the burial environment or carbon added to materials in the post-excavation or curation environment. If we do not remove this material, our radiocarbon measurement will include a contribution from the contaminant carbon. The result will be an accurate measurement of the carbon isotopes in the sample but it will not provide an accurate age estimate for the *archaeological* sample, for example, the date of death of an organism.

The proportional effect of contamination depends on the age of the sample to be measured. For very old samples that are approaching the background limit of measurement, a small proportion of modern carbon contaminant will have a much greater impact than on a younger sample. The modern material will swamp the very small remaining radiocarbon signal in the very old sample. Ten percent contamination with modern material in a sample approaching background will make the sample appear proportionally *much* younger than the same contamination of a Holocene sample, for example (see Fig. 2.2).

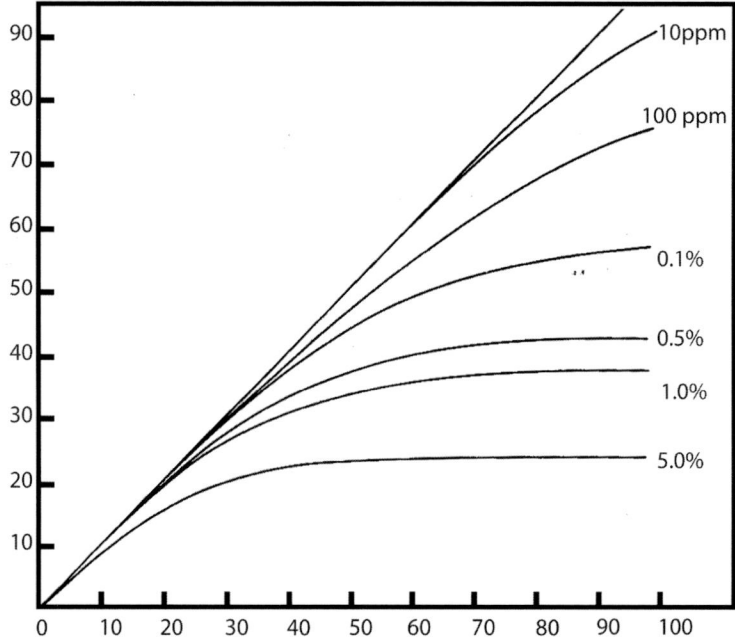

Figure 2.2. Graph showing the effect of contamination on samples of different ages. The effect of contamination on a sample depends in part on how old a sample is. The x axis shows age in thousands of years, the y axis shows measured age in thousands of years given the proportional impact of contamination. Redrawn from Taylor (1987, 117). Copyright: Seren Griffiths.

Pretreatment

Physical pretreatment involves the removal of exogenous material that is present on the surface or within a sample that has accumulated after the death of an organism. Typically, physical pretreatment may include the removal of the outer surface of bones, for example by abrasion. Roots and other adhering material will also be removed.

The exact nature of chemical pretreatment will depend on the sample type. Generally, the more complicated the sample type, the more involved the chemical pretreatment process. Well-established protocols have been developed or routinely measured sample types. In the case of plant remains, these make use of various acid and alkali washes to effectively remove carbon that has become chemically incorporated in a sample in the burial environment.

Bone samples can be more complicated to prepare. Unburnt bone samples contain both organic and inorganic carbon. The inorganic fraction, called hydroxyapatite, can be subject to exchange with groundwater carbon so is usually not targeted for dating. The organic collagen fraction is instead used in radiocarbon measurement.

Collagen is isolated using a series of chemical steps. First, the sample is decalcified using a dilute acid. This hydrolyses the hydroxyapatite and removes it. The remaining collagen is then purified and cleaned using a base solution, which removes contaminating humic compounds. The sample is then gelatinised, which removes further insoluble impurities. Many laboratories now apply an ultrafiltration protocol because it further purifies the collagen, removing low molecular-weight contaminants and degraded collagen (Higham *et al.* 2006). Studies have shown that, for bones, this can be an effective means of removing contaminating carbon. Several criteria are used as quality control indicators for samples, including indices for bone such as the carbon to nitrogen atomic ratio (C:N). Quality assurance indicators are discussed below.

Bone preservation varies greatly according to the burial environment. Soil pH, waterlogging and site temperature all play important roles in collagen preservation. When bone is well-preserved, chemical contaminants can be removed with the correct pretreatment process. However, when bone is poorly preserved and collagen content is low, caution is required. When contaminants are more difficult to remove, or of a higher molecular weight, additional rigorous methods are needed to date the bone reliably. This can be the case in very old Pleistocene samples, or samples that derive from burial environments that are not conducive to collagen preservation (for example extremely alkaline or acid burial conditions, or very warm environments). Recently, compound-specific approaches have been developed that can help produce accurate measurements on poorly preserved bone samples. In these techniques liquid chromatography is used to isolate a single amino acid for dating. Hydroxyproline is often targeted because this amino acid is produced in mammals' bodies as a major component of collagen, we can therefore be sure that radiocarbon measurements on this compound are contaminant-free and provide accurate age estimates (e.g. Devièse *et al.* 2018).

As well as plant remains and bone samples, archaeologists also often want to produce chronologies for palaeoenvironmental sequences. Making sure that there are robust associations between the dated events and the archaeological events of interest is very important in these cases. It can be tempting to use sediment samples for radiocarbon measurements, however, it can be very unclear how carbon accumulated in deposits (e.g. McGlone and Wilmshurst 1999; Brock *et al.* 2011; Griffiths *et al.* 2015). The construction of palaeoenvironmental chronologies is discussed more fully in Chapter 6.

Offsets

Offsets are systematic effects that shift the radiocarbon age of a sample for some reason (Bayliss *et al.* 2016, 56). Below we consider two of these types of offset: reservoir effects in bone samples and fuel-offsets in cremated bone samples. We also think about another example where radiocarbon ages are shifted – the 'old wood effect'. The old wood effect occurs when measurements are produced on samples that are already older in radiocarbon terms than the archaeological event of interest. In reality, old wood effects are not true age offsets because old wood samples are material that are already *physically* older than the archaeological event of interest (see discussion below). This contrasts with true offsets, in which samples will always be older in radiocarbon terms because they have formed with carbon from sources other than the atmospheric radiocarbon reservoir.

Marine or freshwater aquatic reservoir offsets

Terrestrial organisms are broadly in equilibrium with atmospheric levels of radiocarbon. This means that terrestrial plants and animals should be of broadly the same radiocarbon age as the atmosphere where they form. We can therefore use the appropriate terrestrial calibration dataset to convert radiocarbon measurements into age ranges. For northern hemisphere results the current dataset is IntCal20 (Reimer *et al.* 2020; Fig, 2.3) and for southern hemisphere results the dataset is SHCal20 (Hogg *et al.* 2020).

There is a significant difference, however, between the relative proportion of isotopes of carbon in the atmospheric and terrestrial ecosystems and those in freshwater aquatic and marine reservoirs. Freshwater and marine reservoirs are also globally more variable. Measurements on marine samples need to be calibrated using the global marine calibration curve (e.g., Heaton *et al.* 2020) but, in addition, because mixing of the marine reservoir is highly variable, it is important to apply a local marine reservoir correction. These local corrections reflect the different distributions of carbon isotope ratios across marine environments. Local marine offsets are calculated using terrestrial and marine samples that are known to be of the same age.

Freshwater aquatic reservoir offsets can exist in lakes or rivers due to carbonaceous inputs into the water-body (McGlone and Wilmshurst 1999). This tends to be more pronounced in larger bodies of water and, in some cases, can result in a freshwater reservoir offset of similar magnitude to a marine reservoir offset. In limestone environments, for example, water may erode geological sources of infinitely old carbon (radiocarbon-free) over the course of the river system. Any organisms living in isotopic equilibrium within this environment will form their tissues out of these

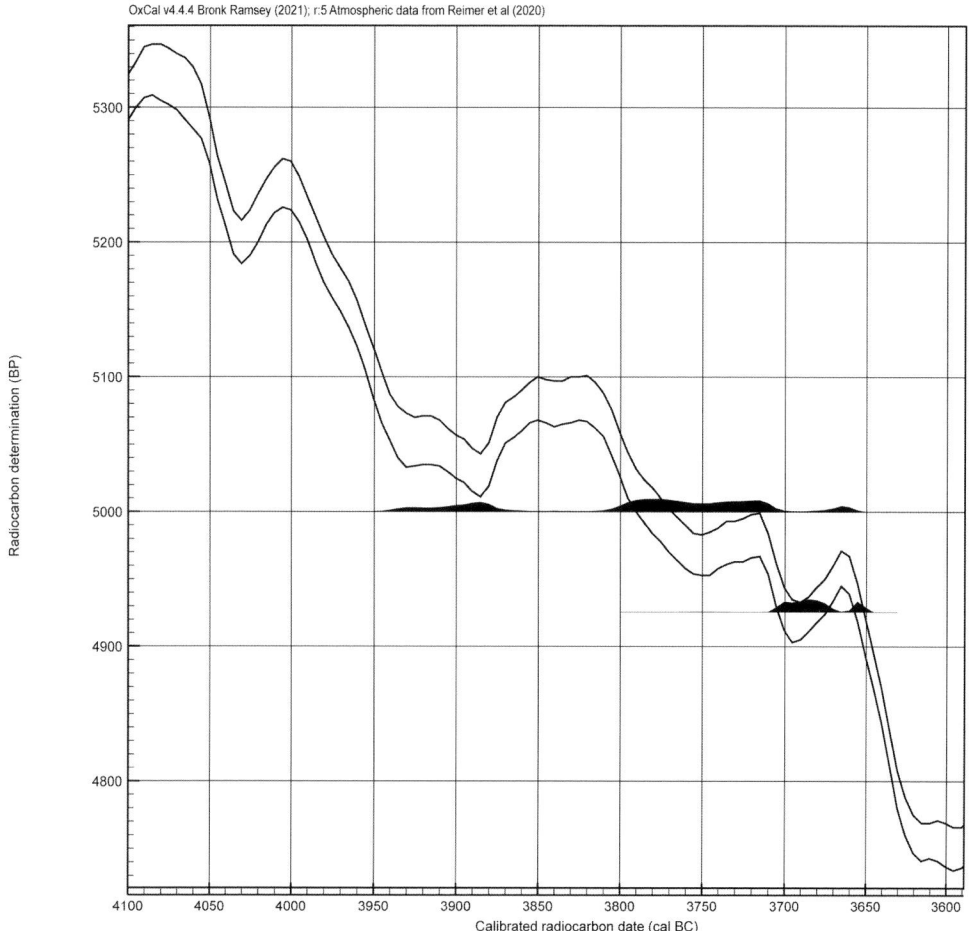

Figure 2.3. Part of the IntCal20 terrestrial calibration curve for the northern hemisphere (Reimer et al. 2020), with two radiocarbon results plotted on the curve. Copyright: Seren Griffiths.

carbon sources and will be consequentially proportionally older in radiocarbon terms than contemporary terrestrial animals. A very significant freshwater reservoir has been identified at the Mesolithic site of Lepenski Vir (Borić *et al.* 2018), at the Iron Gates gorge of the River Danube between Serbia and Romania (Fig. 2.4). Here the large volume of water and the underlying geology contributes to significant offsets. Bonsall *et al.* (2004) discuss the implications of these offsets on the chronology.

Both marine and freshwater offsets can affect the radiocarbon ages of any organism living in equilibrium with these reservoirs. While osteological samples from these environments are often identified as exhibiting a marine or freshwater offset, aquatic plants and mosses, or emergent species may also be affected depending on their carbon fixing processes.

Figure 2.4. The Iron Gates gorge of the Danube River. In a famous case study, results from the very important Mesolithic sites here had significant radiocarbon aquatic offsets. The huge volume of water that passes through the limestone geology meant that lots of infinitely old carbon isotopes were present in the water making fish that lived in the river and humans that fed off them seem older than they actually were, in radiocarbon terms. Details of the issues associated with these sites can be found in Cook et al. (2002). Copyright: Clive Bonsall.

Beyond organisms living in equilibrium with a marine or aquatic reservoir, offsets cycle up food chains. These are known as a diet-derived offsets. Isotopically, you are what you eat; organisms up the food web will appear older in radiocarbon terms if they consume marine food resources as part of their diet. The magnitude of any diet-derived offset depends on the local marine offset, the proportion of marine resources in an individual's diet, as well as the different types of carbohydrates and proteins in an individual's diet. When producing radiocarbon measurements on samples from humans or animals it is important to consider if they might have consumed marine or aquatic resources in order that an appropriate reservoir correction is applied and the appropriate calibration dataset used.

Evidence for marine or aquatic components may be identified in the ecofacts on a site. For example, oyster shells are frequently recovered from Romano-British sites in Britain, even those at relatively great distances from the sea. Consumption of non-terrestrial dietary resources can also be identified from direct stable isotope measurements of the bone samples themselves. Such measurements should be commissioned as a matter of course as part of the quality assurance (see discussion below).

Identifying the appropriate reservoir correction can be difficult. The appropriate correction depends on the diet of each individual. Secondly, there may not be very information about the most appropriate reservoir correction to apply. One way to mitigate against these issues might be to produce radiocarbon measurements on samples with both marine and terrestrial reservoirs, though this is not always possible.

Further discussion of some of the issues with freshwater case studies are given in Keaveney and Reimer (2012). Ascough *et al.* (2005) provide an introduction to marine reservoir calculations, while Petchey *et al.* (2013) detail some of the issues in producing accurate measurements on marine samples.

Fuel-derived offsets

Fuel-derived offsets can also shift radiocarbon ages of cremated bone so that they appear systematically older than the real age of sample formation. In the case of fuel-derived offsets, the shift occurs when bone is cremated during high temperature burning, rather than occurring as a result of *in vivo* metabolic processes.

Cremations use wood as fuel sources. Plants form woody tissues as they put on growth over time. The woody tissues have radiocarbon ages relating to the point in time when they were formed. In long-lived species such as oak or yew, the radiocarbon age of the oldest inner wood can be much older than the radiocarbon age of the bark, reflecting the lifespan of the tree. Fuel-offsets describe the systematic way in which old fuel sources can shift cremated bone samples to become older in radiocarbon terms.

As noted above, in bone samples that have not been affected by heat it is the collagen component that is used for radiocarbon measurements. This is because the mineral fraction of bone does not form a closed system and this fraction can still take up or lose carbon to the burial environment in a very unpredictable manner. However, during cremation at very high temperatures, the mineral fraction recrystallises forming structures that are much more resistant to carbon exchange. Here the point in time where the cremation took place is the dated event that the measurement defines. From the point in time when the cremation took place, the proportion of radiocarbon in the cremated bone should steadily decay, with no more carbon incorporated.

While the cremation acts as a zeroing event ending the potential for carbon exchange, carbon from a variety of sources can be recrystallised in the mineral fraction during the cremation process (Van Strydonck *et al.* 2010). This could include carbon from the atmosphere, from the organic bone collagen, *and* carbon from the fuel. If the fuel included very old wood there is the potential that carbon from this source may be transferred to cremated bone samples. The degree of any offset will vary in the case of each cremation, depending on the specific atmosphere in which the cremation takes place and the age profile of the wood fuel assemblage. In many cases, if no old wood was used in the cremation, there may not be a significant offset but these effects need to be considered in interpretations. Snoeck *et al.* (2014) and Rose *et al.* (2020) provide recent overviews of some of these issues in more detail.

Old wood effects

As we noted above, old wood effects are not strictly offsets. This effect does not change the proportions of carbon isotopes in a sample directly. Rather, it refers to the measurement of samples that are already older in radiocarbon terms than the archaeological event of interest. Radiocarbon scientists also refer to the old wood effect as the 'pre-sample age' or 'in-built sample age' (e.g. McFadgen 1982; Dee and Bronk Ramsey 2014).

Old wood effects have long been noted by archaeologists (e.g. Dean 1978). Patrick Ashmore's (1999) work explored the different results that were produced when samples of bulked charcoals with a range of radiocarbon ages were compared with measurements on individual charcoals. Ashmore demonstrated the importance of selecting single entity samples, individual elements of bone or items of plant material, in order to be really clear about the temporal definition of the dated event. The use of AMS technology means that it is now possible to produce chronologies on individual charcoal or wood fragments that have been identified to species level and for which the in-built age can be clearly identified. For example, a wood anatomist may be able to estimate the in-built age or identify the bark edge precisely. This means we can be sure that our measurements will not be affected by any old wood effect. Such samples are often referred to as short-lived samples. Individual leaves or nutshells represent plant tissues that have formed over a single season and offer other examples of clearly defined short-life samples. By using samples with the smallest possible in-built ages we can remove potential ambiguity from our chronologies by having a really clear temporal definition for the dated event. While it may not always be possible to produce measurements on samples with bark edge or only a very few years growth, we can still make useful comments about the in-built age. Sometimes even the curvature of tree rings in a potential sample will indicate that the tree survived to old age and might have significant in-built offset. In some hardwoods, specific cell structures, tyloses, form in mature trees as softwood is converted to hardwood. These structures can indicate samples which might have large in-built ages and are less useful for radiocarbon measurements.

Sample types

A wide range of organic materials can be radiocarbon dated. In addition, it is possible to produce measurements on very specialist sample types, such as lime mortar samples. As we saw with the discussion of old wood effects above, understanding how carbon enters a potential sample is key in building robust radiocarbon chronologies.

Generally, the best samples are single entities, which are short-life or do not have in-built age offsets, and which have clear associations with the archaeological events of interest (see below). Table 2.1 provides some indications of sample types it is possible to produce radiocarbon measurements on. Sample selection should evaluate the available sample types and their associations, and clearly articulate how potential samples relate to a project's research questions. On-site sampling strategies are discussed in more detail in Chapter 7.

Table 2.1: Potential radiocarbon sample types and some considerations in selecting sample types.

Radiocarbon sample type	Critical considerations in sample selection
Bone, teeth or antler	Collagen preservation can be variable, depending on the nature of burial conditions. For very valuable samples, it may be possible to pre-screen the level of preservation by testing the nitrogen content of a smaller sub-sample (Brock *et al.* 2011)
Cremated bone	Samples must be fully calcined, that is, burnt to whiteness, rather than simply black burnt bone. This is to ensure the sample has fully recrystalised at high enough temperatures. If in doubt, ask the laboratory or an appropriate specialist prior to sampling
Charcoal or charred plant remains	Individual seeds of some species such as, for example, domesticated cereal grains can sometimes be measured. These make excellent short-life, single entity samples if it can be can established that the samples have a good association with the archaeological event of interest. In some cases individual grains may not be sufficiently large for measurement. If only a single item of charcoal or charred plant remains is identified from a context it probably does not have a good association with any clearly defined archaeological event of interest. A critical consideration of the taphonomy and deposit formation is important in these cases
Waterlogged or dried plant remains (including wood), cotton, linen or paper	As with charred plant remains, single entity samples of waterlogged or dried seeds can be measured. Storage of waterlogged samples for radiocarbon measurement is important. Samples need to be kept cold to inhibit the growth of mould or bacteria, which could introduce contemporary carbon into a sample as a form of contamination
Charred food crusts on pottery	Measurements on charred food crusts should estimate the timing of the use of the pottery. Reservoir offsets have been known, presumably when pottery is used to cook fish or other marine or aquatic resources. Removing organic material without including the pottery surface can be delicate work and should take place in controlled conditions. Measurements on charred food crusts can add value by estimating the chronology of the use of diagnostic material culture, as well as providing information about the timing of stratigraphic archaeological events of interest on specific sites
Absorbed food residues in pottery	Measurements on absorbed residues should estimate the timing of the use of the pottery. Radiocarbon measurement on absorbed residues is a relatively new and important development requiring specialist extraction from pottery sherds (Evershed 2008). Archaeological lipid biomarkers in these residues can also indicate the nature of resources stored or cooked in pottery. This can add value by identifying the presence of specific food resources and directly dating their presence, as well as providing an estimate for the use of the pottery, and the timing of stratigraphic archaeological events of interest on specific sites. It is important not to contaminate sherds with contemporary lipids (from handling pottery for example), so sample recovery processes are critical. To assess whether sufficient lipids are present

(Continued)

Table 2.1: Potential radiocarbon sample types and some considerations in selecting sample types. (Continued)

Radiocarbon sample type	Critical considerations in sample selection
	a number of sherds may be destructively sampled. This could be in the order of 23–30 sherds per site phase. It is a good idea to contact the laboratory for specialist sampling and recovery advice prior to commencing fieldwork
Insect remains	This is a relatively specialised measurement technique (Panagiotakopulu *et al.* 2015), for which it is essential to contact the laboratory or an appropriate specialist prior to sampling. Thinking about the taphonomy of an assemblage is important. Storage in chemicals can compromise measurements. Sample size depends on the measurement methods used
Marine shells and marine skeletal material	Samples will be subject to marine offsets, so to ensure accurate age estimates it is vital that an appropriate local reservoir offset is applied. If possible, consider taking samples to calculate the local reservoir calculation (using paired measurements on terrestrial samples and marine samples from the same sealed contexts or which can otherwise be identified as of the same age). In working with marine samples it is a good idea to contact the laboratory or an appropriate specialist during the project design stage and prior to sampling
Peat and sediment	Direct measurements on peat require consideration of how carbon has entered the deposit. Different chemical fractions can be used for measurements or plant macrofossils extracted. Chronologies on different peat carbon fractions can be inconsistent and difficult to interpret. Short-life, single entity, horizontally bedded plant macrofossils with a terrestrial reservoir may produce clearer dated events than chemical fractions. Samples on chemical fractions from less carbonaceous sediment are even more problematic than peat in terms of the carbon origins. Measurements on sediment should not be made

Prior to any form of destructive sampling it is a good idea to contact the laboratory for current sample sizes, turn-around times, and to get advice on the proposed sample type

Quality indicators: being a critical consumer

Laboratory quality assurance

In order that laboratories know that they are getting the right answer when they produce radiocarbon measurements a number of quality assurance exercises take place. These include regular laboratory inter-comparison exercises (e.g. Scott *et al.* 2010), where lots of laboratories all measure the same samples blind and check they get the correct answer, in the case of known-age standards, or the consensus value in other cases. Use of known age standards, including synthetic standards, and standards approaching background ensure that error terms on radiocarbon results are realistic and that the results (including the standard deviations) capture the measurement reproducibility.

Reporting results

Conventions for reporting radiocarbon results have recently been summarised by Millard (2014) and Bayliss (2015), following those initially outlined by Stuiver and Polach (1977). These publications detail how any radiocarbon measurement should be reported by the archaeologist who commissions the result, using details of the measurements produced by the laboratory *and* important archaeological information. Both the laboratory details and the archaeological information are essential for re-use of radiocarbon data by other researchers, not least because the calibration curve is updated. It is vital that the original measurements and their associated archaeological details are presented in any publication produced by the archaeologist who commissioned the results, as verifying these details represents one of the most significant challenges in working with legacy data.

For every measurement, details of the pretreatment and measurement methods, the result and any associated measurements should be detailed in publication reporting. It is most important that the laboratory measurement should be reported as a Conventional Radiocarbon Age (i.e. BP). Conventional Radiocarbon Ages (Stuiver and Polach 1977) make use of the Libby half-life and include:

- the use of a known age, internationally approved standard (e.g., Oxalic Acid I or II),
- measurements reported at ±1 standard deviation (e.g. 4560±32 BP),
- a correction made to the radiocarbon measurement to account for the isotopic fractionation that occurs in biochemical pathways (the ^{13}C measurement taken during the measurement process),
- and a requirement to quote the result as being Before Present (BP), where present is AD/CE 1950 (Stuiver and Polach 1977, see also Millard 2014 for a recent summary).

All this information will be supplied by the laboratory to the archaeologist, along with a radiocarbon certificate which should be retained in the site archive in paper or digital form as appropriate.

The nature of the sample needs to be reported in any publication produced by the archaeologist who commissioned the result. This should include identification to species or genus level for organisms, or to demonstrate the short-life status of the sample. For bone samples the percentage collagen yield, C:N ratio, and stable isotope measurements ($\delta^{13}C$ and $\delta^{15}N$) taken separately from those used to calculate fractionation should also be reported.

Details that identify where the sample came from should also be published. This could include, for example site code, context number, site sample number, or museum accession number. Increasingly, there are moves towards digital archiving and improving data discoverability, which is a challenging aspect in terms of chronology building (Griffiths 2022).

The dataset that was used for calibration needs to be quoted with the results, including any reservoir correction for marine or aquatic freshwater samples that was employed. Computer software used for calibration should be cited. When the calibrated result is quoted, the associated range (e.g., 95% or 68% confidence) should also be cited, along with the form of timescale used (e.g., cal. BCE/cal. CE/; cal. BC/cal. AD/cal. BP). So for example,

Radiocarbon measurements include laboratory calculated standard deviations; because of laboratory inter-comparisons we know that these measurements should be accurate. Any attempt to summarise these distributions, for example by quoting the mid-point in a calibrated date range, should be avoided as a potentially misleading over-simplification. Presenting results both as calibrated date ranges and as probability distribution graphs illustrates important different ways of thinking about individual measurements and groups of data. If any analysis of individual measurements or groups of data is undertaken, archaeologists must be very clear about the methods applied (Chapter 8).

Case studies

Case study: Coneybury 'Anomaly' pit, Wiltshire, UK

The so-called Coneybury 'Anomaly' (Richards 1990; 51.173484 N, 1.809418 W (WGS84) was a large pit located close to the Coneybury henge monument, which lies just south-east of Stonehenge, Wiltshire. The feature was about 2 m across and 1.25 m deep. The pit contained a large assemblage of material culture diagnostic of the British 'Neolithic package'. This included early Neolithic pottery, flint tools, domesticated animal bones and charred cereal grains. Material culture was also recovered from the feature that was more in keeping with the regional Mesolithic package. This included wild animal resources represented by roe deer, red deer and beaver bones. The feature may have been open or been conspicuous in the landscape for some time as Bronze Age-type pottery was also recovered from the upper layers. The status of the anomaly has been much debated (Gron *et al.* 2018), especially with regard to how the use of wild and domesticated resources contributes to our understanding of the local Mesolithic and Neolithic groups. Did this range of materials represent the coming together of various traditions, and possibly people, to produce this mixed deposit? The fauna and early Neolithic assemblage may represent a dump of material that all entered the features at the same time. However, we also know that people using Neolithic material culture in Britain curated things prior to deposition in pits (Garrow 2006). Before starting to think about building a chronology, it is important to recognise that several possible processes could have resulted in the formation of this assemblage.

Radiocarbon results
Twelve radiocarbon results were produced for two phases of research on the assemblage (Richards 1990; Barclay *et al.* 2018; Fig. 2.5). Details of the results are available in the open

access report published by Barclay *et al.* (2018). The results were produced at the Scottish Universities Environmental Research Centre (SUERC) Radiocarbon Laboratory, and at the Oxford Radiocarbon Accelerator Unit (ORAU). Measurements were produced on bone samples and charred food crust residues adhering to the pottery sherds recovered from the feature. The Bayesian chronological modelling of these results is discussed further in Chapter 8.

Sample selection
Radiocarbon measurements were selected from domesticated cattle (OxA-1402, OxA-24988, OxA-24989, SUERC-35964), wild animals represented by deer (OxA-24986, OxA-24987, SUERC-35960) and beaver (OxA-25766, SUERC-35959) and from charred food crusts adhering to ceramic vessels (OxA-25086, OxA-25087, SUERC-35958). These measurements provide an indication of the radiocarbon ages of various different

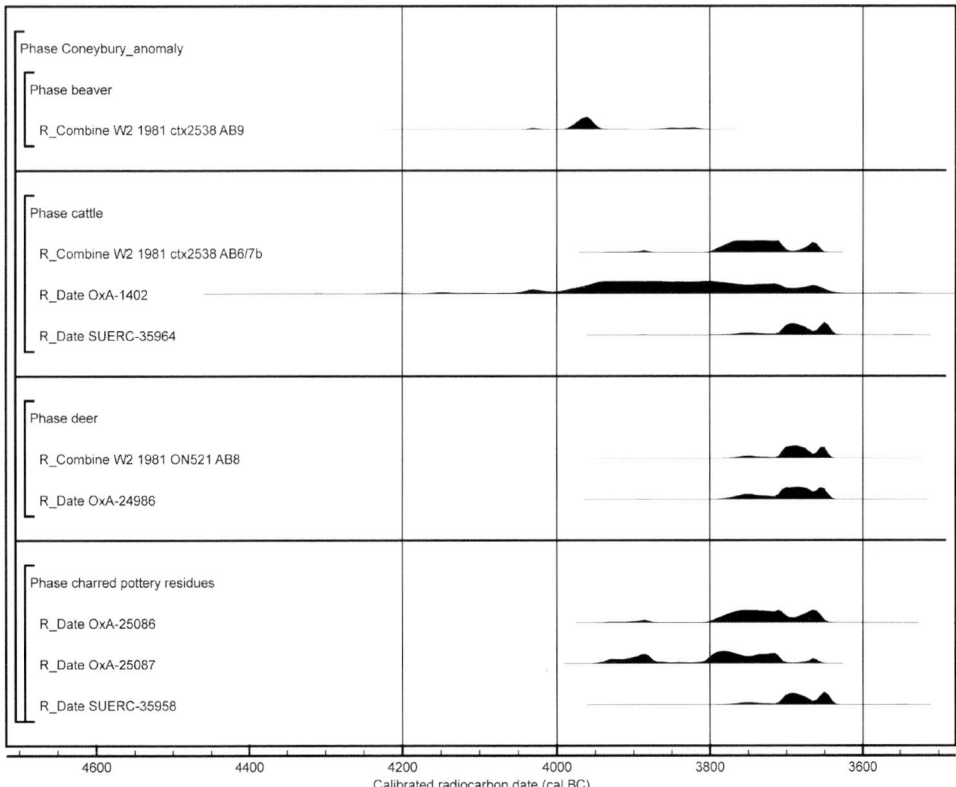

Figure 2.5. Calibrated radiocarbon results from the Coneybury 'Anomaly', an important feature which produced early Neolithic material culture. The modelling of these data is discussed in Chapter 8. Copyright: Seren Griffiths.

elements from the assemblage. Do the age ranges of the different materials indicate a relatively short-lived pattern of use, or would they reveal a time-depth indicative of more complex histories?

Discussion of the scientific dating considerations

Repeat measurements were taken on some of the bone samples. The results were meaned and their statistical fit assessed using a Chi-squared test (see Table 2.2; Chi-squared tests are discussed further in Chapter 8). In Figure 2.5 these error-weighted mean values are shown as calibrated ages. We can now start to think about these results as a group.

As we can see from Figure 2.5, the calibrated weighted mean of the beaver bone measurements is older than the other results from the deposit. The beaver bone measurements pass a Chi Squared test, and are statistically consistent at the 5% significance level (T'=0.1; T'5%= 3.8; ν=1; Ward and Wilson 1978). Moreover, these two results were produced at different radiocarbon laboratories with slightly different pretreatment and measurement methods. We therefore believe that these measurements accurately reflect the radiocarbon content of this sample. What reasons are there that this element could be older in radiocarbon terms than the rest of the material from this assemblage?

Table 2.2: Radiocarbon results from the Coneybury Anomaly.

Lab. no/	Sample material and context	Radiocarbon age (BP)	$\delta^{13}C$	$\delta^{15}N$	C:N ratio
OxA-1402	W2 1981, IL, 2538, 420 Animal bone. Cattle from primary pit fil	5050±100	−21.0*		
OxA-24986	W2 1981 ON169 AB5 Antler. Red deer from primary pit fill. Frag. from beam modified as a pick	4925±30	−21.4±0.2	3.7±0.3	3.2
OxA-24987	W2 1981 ON521 AB8 (1) Animal bone. Roe deer, articulating 1st & 2nd phalanges from primary pit fill	4941±32	−23.4±0.2	4.7±0.3	3.2
SUERC-35960	Replicate of OxA-24987	4900±30	−23.7±0.2	4.8±0.3	3.2

Weighted mean of repeat measurements 521 roe deer AB8521 roe deer AB8
^{14}C: 4919±22 BP T'=0.9
$\delta^{13}C$: −23.55±0.14, T'=1.1
$\delta^{15}N$ 4.75±0.21; T'=0.1

(Continued)

Table 2.2: (Continued)

Lab. no/	Sample material and context	Radiocarbon age (BP)	$\delta^{13}C$	$\delta^{15}N$	C:N ratio
OxA-24988	W2 1981 ctx2538 AB6/7b Animal bone. Cattle from primary pit fill. 2 × 1st phalanges with fitting unfused epiphyses articulating with distal metatarsal shaft from neonate	4952±32	−22.0±0.2	4.0±0.3	3.2
OxA-24989	Replicate of OxA-24988	4997±31	−22.0±0.2	3.7±0.3	3.2
Weighted mean of repeat measurements of Cattle AB6/7b ^{14}C: 4975±23 BP; T'=1.0 δ^{13}C: −22.0±0.14, T'=0.0 δ^{15}N 3.9±0.21; T'=2.8					
OxA-25086	W2 1981 ctx2247 ON365 Carbonised residue adhering to interior of pottery sherd, from primary pit fill	4997±31	−26.1±0.2		
OxA-25087	W2 1981 ctx2247 ON475 Carbonised residue adhering to interior of pottery sherd, from primary pit fill	5003±30	−25.9±0.2		
SUERC-35958	W2 1981 ctx 2538 ON1213 a+b Carbonised residue adhering to interior of pottery sherd, from primary pit fill. 2 refitting sherds (a+b) with internal charred residue	4905±30	−25.8±0.2		
SUERC-35959	W2 1981 ctx2538 AB9 Animal bone. Beaver, immature. Rib & radius shaft, from primary pit fill	5135±30	−23.5±0.2	5.8±0.3	3.2
OxA-25766	Replicate of SUERC-35959	5149±32	−23.2±0.2	6.1±0.3	3.1
Weighted mean of repeat measurements of beaver bone ^{14}C; 5142±22 BP, T'=0.1 δ^{13}C: −23.35±0.14, T'=1.1 δ^{15}N 5.95±0.21; T'=1.1					
SUERC-35964	W2 1981 ctx2538 AB6/7a Animal bone. Mature adult cattle phalanx articulating with other phalanges, from primary pit fill	4905±30	−22.3±0.2	4.6±0.3	3.3

See Barclay *et al.* (2018) for full details. * denotes an assumed value (see text). Approaches to the Bayesian analysis of these results are discussed in Chapter 8 with the code we have applied presented in the Appendix

There are a number of options. Firstly, the element could represent material that really was older than the rest of the assemblage. The beaver bone could have been residual, and accidentally incorporated with the rest of the material. Or the beaver bone and the other material could have become amalgamated in a midden deposit over a long period of time prior to being redeposited in the feature. Or the beaver bone could also have been deliberately curated by people and incorporated into the assemblage.

Another option which relates to radiocarbon reservoirs could also exist. Here we need to think about the beaver bone, and the ways in which carbon entered the sample during the life of the animal. It may be that the beaver lifecycle includes a contribution from an aquatic foodchain. The measurements may therefore be accurate in terms of the radiocarbon content of the sample, but they may not be accurate estimate of when the animal died if calibrated using a terrestrial dataset. An aquatic offset may make these measurements too old in radiocarbon terms for the date of death of the animal. Without understanding exactly the isotopic signatures of the carbon reservoirs that this animal was exploiting we cannot be sure. In this case, because of the difficulties accurately estimating the aquatic offset, Barclay *et al.* (2018) suggested that these two results on the beaver element were best understood as *terminui post quos*, or dates after which the animal died.

Excepting the beaver results, all the other measurements on terrestrial fauna and pottery residues from this feature are statistically consistent at the 5% significance level, meaning that they might of the same actual age (T'=14.5; T'5%=16.9; v=9; Ward and Wilson 1978). Given that these results were produced on several different species and on different pottery residues we might suggest that the activity that produced this assemblage occurred over a relatively short period of time. We estimate how long and when this activity occurred in Chapter 8.

Case study conclusions
Producing **repeat measurements** on the same sample in different laboratories helps us to establish that radiocarbon measurements are **accurate**. Producing measurements on **multiple types of sample** help us explore the formation of this assemblage. Excluding the beaver results, all the other result could be of the same actual age.

However, there is still potential for different interpretations of these results. These measurements on terrestrial animal bones estimate their formation or remodelling (see Chapter 8), and the estimates on the food crusts date the use of the pottery. These measurements do not directly provide estimates for the date of deposition in the pit, and so even though the group might represent an assemblage that formed over a relatively short period of time, they do not resolve the potential that these things were curated in some way before being deposited. Critical consideration of the **association** between the measurements and the archaeological events of interest is always important in building interpretations.

Case study: Vaynor henge, Carmarthenshire, UK

Vaynor henge (51.798896 N, 4.543661 W (WGS84)) was excavated in advance of the South Wales high pressure gas pipeline between Milford Haven and Aberdulais, and Felindre and Brecon (Barber and Hart 2015; Darvill *et al.* 2020; Fig. 2.6). The site was unknown prior to commencements of the infrastructure scheme. The henge monument had two opposing entrances and comprised rock-cut ditches 8 m wide, which survived up to 3.4 m deep. Within the area demarcated by the ditches was a series of post-holes that could have contained timber posts or standing stones. Higher up the ditch fill sequence a series of un-urned later cremation deposits was recovered. Henge monuments are classically thought of as a British late Neolithic culture historic site. However, they are also the focus for other activity (e.g. Gibson *et al.* 2019) including practices associated with Bronze Age and Iron Age material culture, in the post-Roman period, as well as being the focus of early medieval activity.

Radiocarbon results

Radiocarbon sample details are given in Table 2.3 and Figure 2.7. Full details of the results and modelling can be found in Darvill *et al.* (2020) and the unpublished report by Barber and Hart (2014). The modelling is discussed further in Chapter 8.

Figure 2.6. Aerial photograph showing Vaynor henge under excavation. Copyright: Cotswold Archaeology.

Sample selection

Producing a chronology for the henge presented a problem which is quite common in archaeology; how to try and create accurate chronologies for the creation and use of a site when the associations between samples and the events of interest were not always clear.

The underlying geology in this part of the world means that bone is not preserved unless it has been cremated. While cremated bone was recovered from upper deposits in the henge ditch fills and measurements on these samples give good indications of the timing of the cremation events, the rest of the ecofacts available for radiocarbon

Table 2.3: *Radiocarbon results from Vaynor henge (Barber and Hart 2015;* Darvill *et al. 2020).*

Lab. no.	Sample material & context information	Radiocarbon age (BP)	$\delta^{13}C$
SUERC-51702	Charred plant remains: *Corylus* sp. charcoal Context 503153, sample 503072B. Lower henge ditch fill	4057±33	−26.0‰
SUERC-52100	Charred plant remains: Maloideae charcoal Context 503153, sample 503072A. Lower henge ditch fill	3928±30	−26.6‰
GU33241	Charred plant remains: Maloideae charcoal Context 503153, sample 503072A. Lower henge ditch fill	Failed on AMS	–
SUERC-51704	Charred plant remains: *Quercus* sp. roundwood Context 503051, sample 503068B. Henge ditch fill, later than 503153. Earlier than samples <503007> and <503065>	3815±33	−24.8‰
SUERC-51705	Charred plant remains: *Corylus* sp. roundwood charcoal Context 503051, sample 503068A. Henge ditch fill, later than 503153. Earlier than samples <503007> and <503065>	3777±33	−27.9‰
SUERC-51706	Charred plant remains: *Corylus avellana* nutshell Context 503153, sample 503067B. Lower henge ditch fill	8429±33	−26.7‰
SUERC-51707	Charred plant remains: *Corylus* sp. charcoal Context 503153, sample 503067A. Lower henge ditch fill	3939±33	−25.8‰
SUERC-51708	Charred plant remains: *Corylus* sp. charcoal Context 503050, sample 503066B. Upper henge ditch fill. Earlier than (50319)	2820±33	−25.3‰
SUERC-51712	Charred plant remains: barley seeds Context 503050, sample 503066A. Upper henge ditch fill. Earlier than (50319)	2742±33	−23.6‰
SUERC-51713	Charred plant remains: Maloideae charcoal Context 503051, sample 503065B. Henge ditch fill, later than sample <503068>	3589±33	−27.3‰
SUERC-51714	Charred plant remains: *Corylus* sp. charcoal Context 503051, sample 503065A. Henge ditch fill, later than sample <503068>	3464±33	−28.7‰

(Continued)

Table 2.3: (Continued)

Lab. no.	Sample material & context information	Radiocarbon age (BP)	$\delta^{13}C$
SUERC-51715	Charred plant remains: *Betula* sp. charcoal. Context 503019, sample 503063B. Upper henge ditch fill. Earlier than later cremation 50314	1947±33	−24.1‰
SUERC-51716	Charred plant remains: *Corylus* sp. charcoal. Context 503019, sample 503063A. Upper henge ditch fill. Earlier than later cremation 50314	1947±33	−24.1‰
SUERC-51717	Charred plant remains: barley seeds. Context 503053, sample 503056B. Fill of henge ditch. Poor agreement with position in fill sequence (see text)	2845±33	−22.2‰
SUERC-51718	Charred plant remains: *Corylus* sp. charcoal. Context 503053, sample 503056A. Fill of henge ditch. Poor agreement with position in fill sequence (see text)	2789±33	−26.2‰
SUERC-51722	Charred plant remains: Maloideae charcoal. Context 503150, sample 503034B. Fill of henge post-hole	3906±33	−26.5‰
SUERC-51723	Charred plant remains: *Corylus* sp. charcoal. Context 503150, sample 503034A. Fill of henge post-hole	3851±33	−25.3‰
SUERC-51724	Charred plant remains: spelt wheat seeds. Context 503141, sample 503015C. Late cremation in ditch fill	1851±33	−22.1‰
SUERC-52365	Charred plant remains: oat seeds. Context 503141, sample 503015B. Late cremation in ditch fill	1877±26	−22.5
SUERC-51726	Charred plant remains: *Quercus* sp. roundwood charcoal. Context 503141, sample 503015A. Late cremation in ditch fill	1805±33	−26.4‰
SUERC-51727	Charred plant remains: *Corylus* sp. charcoal. Context 503090, sample 503008B. Fill of henge post-hole	3904±33	−25.2‰
SUERC-51728	Charred plant remains: *Corylus avellana* roundwood, with pith & bark. Context 503051, sample 503007B. Henge ditch fill, later than sample <503068>	3836±33	−28.6‰
SUERC-51732	Charred plant remains: *Corylus* sp. charcoal. Context 503051, sample 503007A. Henge ditch fill, later than sample <503068>	3754±35	−26.0‰
SUERC-51733	Charred plant remains: *Corylus avellana* nutshell. Context 503097, sample 503006B, Fill of post-hole	4650±33	−26.9‰
SUERC-51734	Charred plant remains: *Corylus* sp. charcoal. Context 503097, sample 503006A. Fill of pos-thole	3923±33	−26.1‰
SUERC-51735	Charred plant remains: *Corylus* sp. charcoal. Context 503067, sample 503002. Fill of henge pos-thole	3972±33	−26.6‰

The Bayesian analysis of these results is discussed in Chapter 8 and the code we have applied is provided in the Appendix measurement comprised charred plant remains including charcoal. A bulk sampling strategy had been developed to recover these from the henge ditch fills and from the post-holes within the henge. Some of the deposits were so rich that they appeared to be dumped or placed in the henge fill sequence but others were sparser. Charred plant remains including charcoal had also been recovered from the fills of post-holes within the henge. How best to select charred plant remains for measurement? And what associations would these samples have with any archaeological events of interest?

Experimental archaeology (Reynolds 1995) has shown that artefacts and ecofacts in post-holes often derive from the use of a structure, with material becoming incorporated into voids in the fill of the post-hole as the structure settles or the post degrades. The charred plant remains in the post-holes could therefore represent estimates for the *use* of the henge monument. Similarly, material in the henge ditches may be associated with activity with the use of the site. However, these samples may not be associated with the very first excavation and creation of the henge monument. We also cannot exclude the possibility that this charred material was residual, representing older activity in the vicinity. We equally cannot exclude the possibility that the ecofacts represent later activity, only incorporated into the ditch fills as the monument went out of use after some unknown interval of time. To further complicate matters, the size and sorting of the fill sequence also suggested that there might have been several phases of infilling within the henge ditches.

To take account of this potential for residual or intrusive ecofacts duplicate radiocarbon measurements from many deposits were produced. To make sure that these were not simply two measurements on different parts of the same organism (which should produce consistent radiocarbon measurements), samples of different genus or species were preferentially submitted from the same deposits. This approach starts to explore the taphonomy of samples in a deposit; if samples of two different genera or species return consistent radiocarbon ages then we may have greater confidence that they represent *in situ* anthropogenic activity.

Samples were also selected from different types of features and archaeological phases of activity at the henge. This was aimed at understanding the history of the use of the site across the sequence, rather than simply targeting the very earliest activity, or a selective part of the site's history. The site phases that produced radiocarbon samples included the earlier henge ditch fill sequence, the later henge ditch fill sequence, the post-hole fills and the later cremations.

Discussion of the scientific dating considerations

The repeat measurements from different contexts were statistically not significantly different at the 5% significance level in many cases. In these cases, the consistency of the measurements on different types of samples gives us greater confidence that these results represent anthropogenic activity associated with the use of the henge.

In the cases where repeat measurements were produced from the same context and were not consistent the results are telling us something about the site. Figure 2.7 shows the results from Vaynor henge grouped by the contexts from which they were recovered. Some of the results from this site are what Bayliss *et al.* (2016) term 'misfits'.

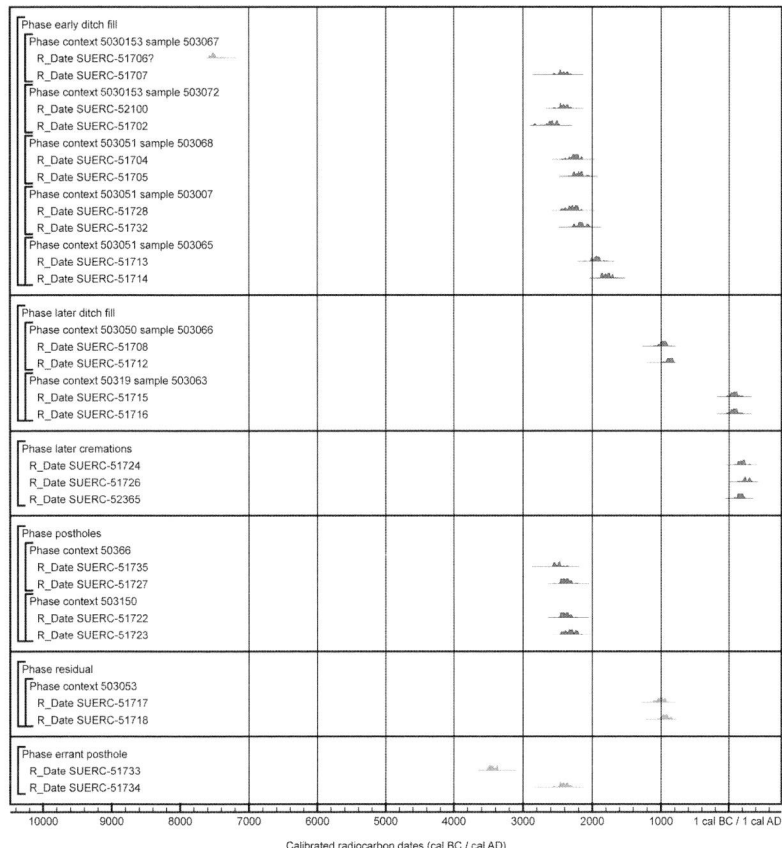

Figure 2.7. Calibrated radiocarbon results from Vaynor henge. A Bayesian statistical model for these results is provided in Chapter 8. Copyright: Seren Griffiths.

We can see that SUERC-51706 is much earlier than any of the other activity associated with use of the henge site. This measurement probably represents residual material.

The radiocarbon results also revealed aspects of the site's history of which we were not aware. SUERC-51717 and SUERC-51718 are statistically consistent and pass a Chi Squared test at the 5% significance level (T'=1.4; T'5%=3.8; ν=1; Ward and Wilson 1978). However, they were recovered from high up in the fill sequence and were immediately below a deposit which produced a post-Roman result. These results are too late for their stratigraphic position. The results suggest this deposit included redeposited material.

Finally, two measurements – SUERC-51733 and SUERC-51734 – were statistically inconsistent at the 5% significance level (T'=241.8; T'5%=3.8; ν=1; Ward and Wilson 1978). Both these results could be consistent with what we know about the timing of activity at the site. We cannot therefore identify if one of these results is residual or the other intrusive or if both have a poor association with the deposit from which they were recovered. These misfits needed to be considered critically before we could think about the site chronology. In Chapter 8 we use a site-specific stratigraphic Bayesian model to analysis these results further.

Case study conclusions
This case study demonstrates the importance of **repeat measurements** when thinking about **complex stratigraphy**. We can use repeat measurements to think about sample **taphonomy** and **deposit formation**. Sampling across archaeological phases of activity can help identify changes in activity and use at a site that are not apparent without independent scientific dating. The duration of activity represented by some of the contexts at Vaynor henge was not apparent in the field. It may therefore be important to build chronologies that represent the **range of activity** at a site not just to target the earliest or latest activity.

Case study: Tipping Street, Stafford, UK

Excavations were carried out at Tipping Street, Stafford (52.807909 N, 2.19970 W (WGS84)) where evidence was uncovered for the production of Saxon Stafford Ware pottery in 2009 and 2010 (Dodd *et al.* 2014). Stafford was of key importance in the 9th and 10th centuries AD. The *Anglo-Saxon Chronicle* identified it as a burh or a defended settlement which was founded in AD 913 by Æthelflæd, daughter of the West Saxon king Alfred the Great. According to the *Chronicle* the burh at Stafford was one of a series of these defended settlements constructed in response to the Viking threat, when the Vikings controlled the area known as the Danelaw to the east of Britain. The exact nature of the early Saxon settlement at Stafford has been obscured by subsequent urban development which resulted in truncation and deep and complicated stratigraphic sequences. A number of archaeomagnetic and radiocarbon results existed from Tipping Street and other sites in Stafford when recent work (Dodd *et al.* 2014) began on this site and subsequent radiocarbon results were produced by the Oxford University FeedSax project led by Helena Hamerow (Hamerow *et al.* 2020; Fig. 2.8; Table 2.4). The FeedSax project was interested in the chronology of domesticated resources in Saxon England, including the increase in cereal surpluses as a means to create wealth, and the growth in urban centres.

Radiocarbon results
The recent excavations identified three kilns which produced Saxon Stafford Ware at the Tipping Street site. From these, 11 radiocarbon results and one archaeomagnetic age estimate were produced. We discuss the archaeomagnetic results in Chapter 5 and the Bayesian modelling in Chapter 8.

Sample selection
Results from the 2009–2010 work were designed to sample the fuel deposits from the three kilns (3408, 3401 and 4287). This sampling strategy was designed to produce a

chronology for the production of Stafford Ware. Two initial radiocarbon measurements were produced from fuel deposits from each kiln. Subsequently the FeedSax project produced measurements on charred cereal grains from these deposits. In addition, an archaeomagnetic result was produced from kiln 3401. The archaeomagnetic measurement should provide an age estimate for the last firing of the kiln (see Chapter 5).

Discussion of the scientific dating considerations
The radiocarbon results from kiln 3401 are not statistically significantly different at the 5% significance level and could be of the same actual age (SUERC-38778, SUERC-38779, OxA-37627; T'=0.4; T'5%=6.0; ν=2; Ward and Wilson 1978). The radiocarbon results from kiln 4287 also could be of the same actual age (SUERC-38997, SUERC-38780, OxA-37628; T'=2.4; T'5%=6.0; ν=2; Ward and Wilson 1978). However, the radiocarbon results from kiln 3408 *are* statistically significantly different at the 5% significance level

Table 2.4. Selected radiocarbon results from the Saxon Stafford Ware kilns at Tipping Street (Dodd et al. 2014; Hamerow et al. 2020).

<Sample no.> (context no.)	Dated material	Context description	Lab. no.	Radiocarbon result (BP)	$\delta^{13}C$
		Kiln 3408			
<205>, (3203)	*Triticum* sp. seed		SUERC-38774	1160±30	−22.3‰
	Alnus glutinosa charcoal frag.	Fill of stoke pit	SUERC-38773	1230±30	−26.2‰
	3 × *Triticum* free-threshing grains		OxA-37625	1082±25	?
<204>, (3205)	3 × *Triticum* free-threshing grains	?	OxA-37626	1159±26	?
		Kiln 3401			
<203> (3201)	*Triticum* sp. seed		SUERC-38778	1105±30	−25.0‰ assumed
	Corylus avellana charcoal fragment	Fine grey charcoal & material on kiln floor	SUERC-38779	1130±30	−25.9‰
	3 × *Triticum* free-threshing grains		OxA-37627	1121 ± 26	?
		Kiln 4287			
<407> (4338)	*Triticum* sp. seed	Ashy, charcoal-rich base of kiln	SUERC-38997	1160±30	−23.2‰
<403> (4304)	*Triticum* sp. seed		SUERC-38780	1100±30	−20.1‰
<406> (4319)	3 × *Triticum* free-threshing grains	?	OxA-37628	1109±26	?

The archaeomagnetic results are discussed in Chapter 5 and the modelling in Chapter 8

(SUERC-38773, SUERC-38774, OxA-37625, OxA-37626; T'=14.7; T'5%=7.8; ν =3; Ward and Wilson 1978). These results derive from different contexts within the feature but even looking at these contexts separately suggests several possible interpretations of the chronological data.

Figure 2.8 shows the radiocarbon and the archaeomagnetic results. Radiocarbon results on short-life charcoal samples are SUERC-38773 and SUERC-38779 and the archaeomagnetic result is shown as the distribution GRP3408_2020. The other radiocarbon results were produced on charred cereal remains. The older three radiocarbon measurements from this kiln are statistically consistent (SUERC-38773, SUERC-38774, OxA-37626; T'=3.9; T'5%=6.0; ν=2; Ward and Wilson 1978). However, one of the grain samples from this feature (OxA-37625) is not consistent with the other results at the 5% significance level.

Resolving this part of the site chronology requires us to consider all the evidence. In this case we have an additional important independent scientific measurement, an archaeomagnetic measurement which should date the last firing of the kiln. The radiocarbon results measure different dated events from the archaeomagnetic result;

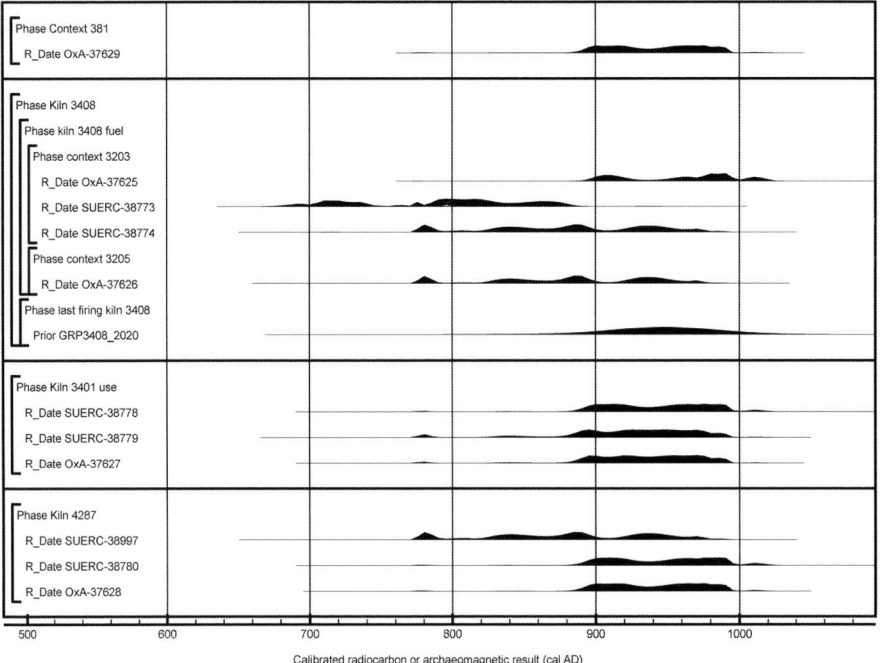

Figure 2.8. Calibrated radiocarbon and archaeomagnetic results from Tipping Street, Stafford. The archaeomagnetic result is identified as 'Prior GRP3408_2020' while the radiocarbon results are identified using the prefix 'R_Date'. Different features or contexts are indicated by the horizontal lines and the brackets along the left of the image. The archaeomagnetic result from this site are discussed in Chapter 5 and the Bayesian statistical modelling of these data in Chapter 8. Copyright: Seren Griffiths.

they should estimate the end of carbon exchange in the different plants when they are harvested, and these may not all represent the same point in time, nor does any of these date events have the same definition as the archaeomagnetic result. Thinking about the association between these different dated events is important, and we discuss the radiocarbon results with the archaeomagnetic evidence from this site in Chapter 5.

Case study conclusions
Thinking critically about sample **association** is important in building robust chronologies. It is important to **consider inconsistencies** in measurements and the range of possible interpretations in terms using the archaeological evidence and in terms of what any dated events actually represent. In urban sites, or sites with **complex stratigraphy**, there may be several reasons for tensions in site chronological data. Using different scientific dating techniques can provide different information about site histories.

Chapter conclusions

Radiocarbon measurements provide the sequential **backbone** for archaeology. The application of the method led to a **revolution** in the history of archaeological thought. The suitability of a wide range of commonly found archaeological samples for radiocarbon measurements means this method can be applied at sites across the world and across many periods of archaeological research. Critical consideration needs to be given to all potential radiocarbon samples to think about the **association** between the dated event and the archaeological event of interest. A radiocarbon measurement is just a number, it is important to think about how the **dated event** is temporarily defined, and how this relates to the timing of the **archaeological events of interest** that are being investigated.

Bibliography

Anderson, E. and Libby, W. 1951. World-wide distribution of natural radiocarbon. *Physical Review* 81(1), 64–9

Arnold, J. and Libby, W. 1949. Age determinations by radiocarbon content: checks with samples of known age. *Science* 110, 678–80

Ascough, P., Cook, G. and Dugmore, A. 2005. Methodological approaches to determining the marine radiocarbon reservoir effect. *Progress in Physical Geography: earth and environment* 29(4), 532–47

Ashmore, P. 1999. Radiocarbon dating: avoiding errors by avoiding mixed samples. *Antiquity* 73, 75–86

Barber, A. and Hart, J. 2015. South Wales Gas Pipeline Project. Site 503. Archaeological excavation. Kemble: unpublished report, Cotswold Archaeology Project 9150/13328/Dyfed Archaeological Trust Event Number 102846

Barclay, A., Bayliss, A. Bronk Ramsey, C., Cleal, R., Cook, G., Healy, F., Higbee, L., Marshall, P., Pelling, R. and Stevens, C. 2018. *Dating the earliest Neolithic Ceramics of Wessex*. Historic. Portsmouth: England Research Report Series no. 63–2018

Bayliss, A. 2009. Rolling out revolution: using radiocarbon dating in archaeology. *Radiocarbon* 51(1), 123–47

Bayliss, A. 2015. Quality in Bayesian chronological models in archaeology. *World Archaeology* 47, 677–700

Bayliss, A., Beavan, N., Hamilton, D., Köhler, K., Nyerges, É., Bronk Ramsey, C., Dunbar, E., Fecher, M., Goslar, T., Kromer, B., Reimer, P., Bánffy, E., Marton, T., Oross, K., Osztás, A., Zalai-Gaál, I. and Whittle, A. 2016. Peopling the past: creating a site biography in the Hungarian Neolithic. *Bericht der Römisch-Germanischen Kommission* 94, 23–91

Bonsall, C., Cook, G., Hedges, R., Higham, T., Pickard, C. and Radovanović, I. 2004. Radiocarbon and stable isotope evidence of dietary change from the Mesolithic to the Middle Ages in the Iron Gates: new results from Lepenski Vir. *Radiocarbon* 46(1), 293–300

Borić, D., Higham, T., Cristiani, E., Dimitrijević, V., Nehlich, O., Griffiths, S., Alexander, C., Mihailović, B., Filipović, D., Allué, E and Buckley, M. 2018. High-resolution AMS dating of architecture, boulder artworks and the transition to farming at Lepenski Vir. *Scientific Reports* 8, 14221 [https://doi.org/10.1038/s41598-018-31884-7]

Brock, F., Lee, S., Housley, R. and Bronk Ramsey, C. 2011. Variation in the radiocarbon age of different fractions of peat: a case study from Ahrenshöft, northern Germany. *Quaternary Geochronology* 6, 505–55

Bronk Ramsey, C. 2008. Radiocarbon dating: revolutions in understanding. *Archaeometry* 50, 249–75

Buck, C., Kenworthy, J., Litton, C. and Smith, A. 1991. Combining archaeological and radiocarbon information: a Bayesian approach to calibration. *Antiquity* 65, 808–21

Cook, G., Bonsall, C., Hedges, R., McSweeney, K., Boroneant, V., Bartosiewicz, L. and Pettitt, P. 2002. Problems of dating human bones from the Iron Gates. *Antiquity* 76, 77–85.

Darvill, T., David, A., Griffiths, S., Hart, J., James, H. and Rackham, J. 2020. *Timeline. The Archaeology of the South Wales Gas Pipeline: Excavations between Milford Haven, Pembrokeshire and Tirley, Gloucestershire*. Kemble: Cotswold Archaeology Monograph 13

Dean, J. 1978. Independent dating in archaeological analysis. *Advances in Archaeological Method and Theory* 1, 223–55

Dee, M. and Bronk Ramsey, C. 2014. High-precision Bayesian modeling of samples susceptible to inbuilt age. *Radiocarbon*. 56(1), 83–94 [doi:10.2458/56.16685]

Devièse, T., Comeskey, D., McCullagh, J., Bronk Ramsey, C. and Higham, T. 2018. New protocol for compound-specific radiocarbon analysis of archaeological bones. *Rapid Communications in Mass Spectrometry* 32, 373–79.

Dodd, A., Goodwin, J., Griffiths, S., Norton, A., Poole, C. and Teague, S. 2014. Excavations at Tipping Street, Stafford, 2009–10: Possible Iron Age roundhouses, three Stafford-type Ware kilns, and medieval and post-medieval urban remains. *Staffordshire Archaeological and Historical Society Transactions* 47, 1–114

Evershed, R. 2008. Organic residue analysis in archaeology: the archaeological biomarker revolution. *Archaeometry* 50, 895–924

Garrow, D. 2006. *Pits, Settlement and Deposition during the Neolithic and Early Bronze Age in East Anglia*. Oxford, British Archaeological Report 414

Gibson, A., Neubauer, W., Flöry, S., Schneidhofer, P., Allen, M., Allison, E., Carruthers, W., Challinor, D., French, C., Rushworth, G. and Sheridan, A. 2019. Survey and sampling at the Castle Dykes Iron Age 'henge', Wensleydale, North Yorkshire. *Antiquaries Journal* 99, 1–31

Griffiths, S. 2022. Radiocarbon: big data and cross-border histories. *British Archaeology* 184, 10–11

Griffiths, S., Sturt, F., Dix, J., Gearey, B. and Grant, M. 2015. Chronology and palaeoenvironmental reconstruction in the sub-tidal zone: a case study from Hinkley Point. *Journal of Archaeological Science* 54, 237–53

Gron, K., Rowley-Conwy, P., Fernandez-Dominguez, E., Gröcke, D., Montgomery, J., Nowell, G. and Patterson, W. 2018. A meeting in the forest: hunters and farmers at the Coneybury 'Anomaly', Wiltshire. *Proceedings of the Prehistoric Society*. 84, 111–44 [doi:10.1017/ppr.2018.15]

Hamerow, H., Bogaard, A., Charles, M., Forster, E., Holmes, M., McKerracher, M., Neil, S., Bronk Ramsey, C., Stroud, E. and Thomas, R. 2020. An integrated bioarchaeological approach to the medieval 'Agricultural Revolution': a case study from Stafford, England, *c.* AD 800–1200. *European Journal of Archaeology* 23(4), 585–609

Heaton, T., Köhler, P., Butzin, M., Bard, E., Reimer, R., Austin, W., Bronk Ramsey, C. Grootes, P., Hughen, K., Kromer, B., Reimer, P., Adkins, J., Burke, A., Cook, M., Olsen, J. and Skinner, L. (2020). Marine20 – the marine radiocarbon age calibration curve (0–55,000 cal. BP). *Radiocarbon* 62(4), 779–820 [doi:10.1017/RDC.2020.68]

Higham, T., Jacobi, R. and Ramsey, C. (2006). AMS radiocarbon dating of ancient bone using ultrafiltration. *Radiocarbon* 48(2), 179–95

Hogg, A., Heaton, T., Hua, Q., Palmer, J., Turney, C., Southon, J., Bayliss, A., Blackwell, P., Boswijk, G., Bronk Ramsey, C., Pearson, C., Petchey, F., Reimer, P., Reimer, R. and Wacker, L. 2020. SHCal20 southern hemisphere calibration, 0–55,000 years cal. BP. *Radiocarbon* 62(4), 759–78 [doi:10.1017/RDC.2020.59]

Keaveney, E. and Reimer, P. 2012. Understanding the variability in freshwater radiocarbon reservoir offsets: a cautionary tale. *Journal of Archaeological Science* 39(5), 1306–16

McFadgen, B. 1982. Dating New Zealand archaeology by radiocarbon. *New Zealand Journal of Science* 25, 379–92

McGlone, M. and Wilmshurst, J. 1999. Dating initial Maori environmental impact in New Zealand. *Quaternary International* 59, 5–16

Millard, A. 2014. Conventions for reporting radiocarbon determinations. *Radiocarbon* 56(2), 555–9

Panagiotakopulu, E., Higham, T., Buckland, P., Tripp, J. and Hedges, R. 2015. AMS dating of insect chitin–A discussion of new dates, problems and potential. *Quaternary Geochronology* 27, 22–32

Petchey, F., Ulm, S., David, B., McNivern, I., Asmussen, B., Tomkins, H., Dolby, N., Aplin, K., Richards, T., Rowe, C., Leavesley, M. and Mandui, H. 2013. High-resolution radiocarbon dating of marine materials in archaeological contexts: radiocarbon marine reservoir variability between *Anadara, Gafrarium, Batissa, Polymesoda* spp. and Echinoidea at Caution Bay, southern coastal Papua New Guinea. *Archaeological and Anthropological Sciences* 5, 69–80

Reimer, P., Baillie, M., Bard, E., Bayliss, A., Beck, J., Blackwell, P., Bronk Ramsey, C., Buck, C., Burr, G., Edwards, R., Friedrich, M., Grootes, P., Guilderson, T., Hajdas, I., Heaton, T., Hogg, A., Hughen, K., Kaiser, K., Kromer, B., McCormac, F., Manning, S., Reimer, R., Richards, D., Southon, J., Talamo, S., Turney, C., van der Plicht, J. and Weyhenmeyer, C. 2009. IntCal09 and Marine09 radiocarbon age calibration curves, 0–50,000 years cal. BP. *Radiocarbon* 51(4), 1111–50

Reimer, P., Bard, E., Bayliss, A., Beck, J., Blackwell, P., Bronk Ramsey, C. Grootes, P., Guilderson, T., Haflidason, H., Hajdas, I., Hatté, C., Heaton, T., Hoffmann, D., Hogg, A., Hughen, K., Kaiser, K., Kromer, B., Manning, S., Niu, M., Reimer, R., Richards, D., Scott, E., Southon, J., Staff, R., Turney, C. and van der Plicht, J. 2013. IntCal13 and Marine13 radiocarbon age calibration curves 0–50,000 years cal. BP. *Radiocarbon* 55(4), 1869–87

Reimer, P., Austin, W., Bard, E., Bayliss, A., Blackwell, P., Bronk Ramsey, C., Butzin, M, Cheng, H., Edwards, R., Friedrich, M., Grootes, P., Guilderson, T., Hajadas, I., Heaton, T., Hogg, A., Hughen, K., Kromer, B., Manning, S., Muscheler, R., Palmer, J., Pearson, C., van der Plicht, J., Reimer, R., Richards, D., Scott, E., Southon, J., Turney, C., Wacker, L., Adolphi, F., Büntgen, U., Capano, M., Fahrni, S., Fogtmann-Schultz, A., Friedrich, R., Köhler, P., Kudsk, S., Miyake, F., Olsen, J., Reinig, F., Sakamoto, M., Sookdeo, A. and Talamo, S. 2020. The IntCal20 northern hemisphere radiocarbon age calibration curve (0–55 cal. kBP). *Radiocarbon* 62(4), 725–57

Renfrew, C. 1976. *Before Civilisation: the radiocarbon revolution and prehistoric Europe*. Harmondsworth: Penguin

Reynolds, P. 1995. The life and death of a post hole. In E. Shepherd (ed.), *Interpreting Stratigraphy* 5, 21–5. Norwich; Norfolk Archaeological Unit.

Richards, J. 1990. *The Stonehenge Environs Project*. Swindon, English Heritage Monograph 10

Rose, H., Meadows, J. and Henriksen, M. (2020). Bayesian modeling of wood-age offsets in cremated bone. *Radiocarbon*. 62(2), 379–401 [doi:10.1017/RDC.2020.3]

Scott, E., Cook, G. and Naysmith, P. 2010. The fifth international radiocarbon intercomparison (VIRI): an assessment of laboratory performance in stage 3. *Radiocarbon* 52(3), 859–65

Snoeck, C., Brock, F. and Schulting, R. 2014. Carbon exchanges between bone apatite and fuels during cremation: impact on radiocarbon dates. *Radiocarbon* 56(2), 591–602

Stuiver, M. and Polach, H. 1977. Discussion, reporting of ^{14}C data. *Radiocarbon* 19(3), 355–63

Taylor, R. 1978. Radiocarbon dating: an archaeological perspective. In G. Carter (ed.), *Advances in Chemistry Series* 171, 33–69. Washington DC: American Chemical Society

Taylor, R. 1987. *Radiocarbon Dating: an archaeological perspective*. London: Academic Press

Van Strydonck, M., Boudin, M. and Mulder, G. 2010. The carbon origin of structural carbonate in bone apatite of cremated bones. *Radiocarbon* 52(2), 578–86

Ward, G. and Wilson, S. 1978. Procedures for comparing and combining radiocarbon age determinations: a critique. *Archaeometr.* 20, 19–31

Waterbolk, H. 1971. Working with radiocarbon dates. *Actes du VIIIe congrès international des sciences préhistoriques et protohistoriques* 1, 11–25

3. Dendrochronology

Martin Bridge and Seren Griffiths

Trees put on hard woody tissue as they get older. The rate of growth can vary seasonally and, over the longer term, the rate of annual growth may vary in response to changes in climate. In certain parts of the world some species form clearly identifiable annual rings. It is these rings that form the basis of dendrochronology with different responses to changes in growing conditions at the heart of tree-ring studies. The ring-width of individual annual rings can be limited either by the available moisture or the ambient temperature. These responses depend on the tolerances of different species of trees and the environments in which they are growing. In Britain, generally the main limiting factor is rainfall whereas, in other locations, for example at higher altitudes, temperature may be the primary factor affecting growth patterns. The evidence for annual growth rings is generally much less marked in the tropics than it is in temperate regions, which have much more noticeable winter and summer seasons.

Chronologies are built by measuring the annual growth rings in trees (Fig. 3.1). While, at its most simple, dendrochronology can be used to estimate the age of living trees or trees that are recently felled, developments in cross-dating – or the identification of the same responses in ring width in different trees – has allowed the creation of very long chronological sequences. This key development means that dendrochronology can be used to date the death of samples from trees or timber recovered from the archaeological record. Dendrochronology is unique in terms of scientific dating techniques because of the precision that the technique can provide. Dendrochronology can produce exact felling dates for a tree when the bark edge is present. In some species it is possible to identify the season in which a tree was felled. In other cases, where the bark edge is not present, a *terminus post quem* for a felling date can be produced.

'Wiggle matching' combines radiocarbon measurements and dendrochronology on individual timbers. This approach has allowed more timbers to successfully 'date' than was previously the case. It has also allowed shorter ring sequences to be dated and has sometimes resulted in exceptional precision, for example in recent years for some standing buildings (see below). Dendrochronological dating is only one aspect of the study of tree-rings however. Study of annual growth cycles preserved in wood can give indications of abrupt palaeoenvironmental events (Chapter 6) and longer-term changes in climate.

Figure 3.1. The annual growth rings on a dendrochronological sample. The scale is in cm. Copyright: Martin Bridge.

History of methodological development

Despite following a relatively simple premise – that trees in temperate regions have an annual pattern of growth reflecting local conditions – tree-ring measurement was not applied for scientific dating purposes until the start of the 20th century. Dendrochronology was the first independent dating technique available to archaeologists. However, its impact has been less significant internationally than that of radiocarbon dating because the nature of the samples required for dendrochronology limits the application of the method.

It was the work of A.E. Douglass (1919; 1938; Fig. 3.2) that provided the first systematic observations of annual tree-ring responses. Douglass's work as an astronomer led him to research solar cycles and the ways that these were registered in tree-ring records. Douglass identified 11-year cycles in the patterns of tree-ring growth in samples from across very arid areas of Arizona. This established the technique as a form of scientific dating.

Dendrochronology was an innovative approach in early studies of the archaeology of the south-western USA. For the first time it allowed comparisons between archaeological sites from across regions and between different individual site sequences. In another methodological advance, Douglass developed the first examples of dendrochronological cross-dating, where the same climatic trends are identified in the growth responses in different timbers over several years. By working with living trees and thus knowing the age of the outer ring, Douglass was able to build a master curve of climatic responses back to AD 1382 using the long-living yellow pine (*Pinus ponderosa*) species from around Flagstaff, Arizona (Douglass 1919; Baillie 1982), followed by the longer-lived Californian sequoia trees with their *c.* 2000–3000 year lifecycles.

By using living trees, Douglass was able to relate the resultant tree-ring chronologies, and the climate signals they indicated, to the present. This provided an annual chronology working backwards. However, archaeological samples, of course, are no longer living and therefore cannot be as easily anchored to a known age. In this sense, they represent floating chronologies where, despite similar responses showing in the climate responses in annual tree-rings, these chronologies cannot be related to any calendar year.

During the 1920s, Douglass received funding from the National Geographical Society to undertake a series of expeditions. These aimed to recover archaeological samples to bridge the gap between the tied chronologies derived from living trees and the floating chronologies that existed from archaeological samples. These were referred to as the Beam Expeditions because they sought out timbers – most

Figure 3.2. A.E. Douglass the American astronomer who pioneered the archaeological applications of dendrochronology and gave the world the first scientific dating technique. Copyright: University of Arizona.

often beams – preserved on sites in the dry conditions of the south-west USA. The expeditions targeted the important sites of Aztec, New Mexico and Pueblo Bonito, at Chaco Canyon, also in New Mexico (Nash 1997, 32). In his advice to the archaeologists charged with sampling these sites, Douglass had already developed the central tenets of subsequent dendrochronology. These included the advice to sample a long-lived species (in this case pine *Pinus ponderosa*), to recover individual samples of 50 or more growth rings, to recover multiple samples from different timbers from different structures, and to target structures that could be related in a relative chronology (Nash 1997).

By 1920, Douglass had cross-dated timbers to produce a floating chronology from Aztec and Pueblo Bonito. This allowed him to have a relative chronology for the use of the two sites. It took another nine years and 30 sites to establish a 585-year floating chronology. Then, on 22 June 1929, timber HH-39 was sampled at Whipple Ruin, Show Low, Arizona on the Third Beam Expedition. This timber 'bridged the gap' that allowed these 'floating' chronologies to be related to the known-age chronology which worked back from living trees. This sample turned relative 'prehistory' into calendar years and allowed the precise and accurate dating of archaeological sites in the south-west USA back to AD 701 (Baillie 1999, 18).

The initial impact of the dendrochronological method was huge. Dendrochronology was '… without equivocation … the greatest contribution ever made to American archaeology …' (Haury 1935, 98). In the early 20th century there were competing 'long' and 'short' chronologies for the remains excavated at sites such as Chaco Canyon and Mesa Verde in Colorado. These chronologies were linked to models of social evolutionary change developed from 19th century anthropology (e.g. Morgan 1878). Some archaeologists of European descent favoured a long, gradualist model of social change (Nash 1997, 50), in part because they felt that the complexity that was identified at these sites could not be attributed to the ancestral people of the region over a relatively short time frame. Dendrochronology provided an anchored sequence for the sites of the south-west that challenged such gradualist models. Dendrochronology also has huge significance in archaeology as it is key to the production of radiocarbon calibration datasets, allowing the production of accurate radiocarbon age estimates.

Underlying principles

The basis of dendrochronology is that trees of the same species, growing at the same time in similar habitats, produce similar ring-width sequences. These patterns of varying ring-widths are unique to the period of growth. Each tree naturally has its own response superimposed on the basic climate signal. These differences can result from the individual tree's genetic variations in the response to external stimuli, the changing competitive regime between trees or damage, disease, management and so on.

The development of dendrochronological dating in the south-west USA demonstrated that in order for accurate chronologies anchored in time to be developed for periods without written records, a continuous sequence of samples from climate-responsive, long-lived trees need to be available from a single region. This is essential to ensure that the same climatic responses can be cross-dated across different timbers.

Dendrochronological sequences are essentially therefore both *regionally* and *species* specific. Sample preservation is a very important limiting factor in the ability to build a regional dendrochronology sequence. Preservation of large timbers or trees of course can vary greatly given the nature of previous human activity and the nature of the burial environment. The environment of the south-west USA meant that timbers suitable for cross-dating were preserved in very dry conditions and allowed Douglass to develop the technique. In much of north-western Europe, in contrast, there are two common ways in which large timbers of the type that may be suitable for dendrochronological dating are preserved. The first is by waterlogging. This often occurs in peat bogs or riparian alluvial deposits, like the famous bog oaks (*Quercus* sp.) of Germany and Ireland. Preservation by waterlogging means that dendrochronology (and other tree-ring studies) is often applied to shipwreck sites. The other major preservation mechanism is in standing buildings and structures, or art-historical artefacts. In Europe oaks were often used for structural or ship-building purposes and are suitable for dendrochronology; they are long-lived, have clear growth rings and respond to seasonal variation in weather conditions.

Measurement

In temperate climates like north-west Europe ring width measurements are taken initially from timber samples. These measurements may form a site chronology which is then compared to the master or regional chronology by a trained dendrochronologist, visually and using a computer program. This comparison is essentially a statistical process and therefore requires sufficiently long sequences for one to be confident in matches between the site chronology and the master chronology (see sampling considerations below).

Measurements are increasingly carried out using a moving stage with a linear transducer and a binocular microscope, with dedicated software, or even direct from scans or digital photographs. This measurement technique allows additional subsequent analysis, for example DENDRO for Windows (Tyers 2004) which is used widely in the UK and nearby areas of the European continent.

Following measurement, ring sequences will be plotted to allow visual comparisons between different samples (or photographs, for example in some art-historical contexts). This visual inspection provides additional quality control in identifying any errors in the measurements when samples cross-match. Long master chronologies can be developed by cross-matching the innermost rings of modern timbers with the outermost rings of older timbers moving successively back in time, adding data from numerous sites. These master chronologies are necessary for regions with distinct climates or species with different responses, though especially significant climate events may feature across different regions and species.

Statistical comparison is undertaken using, for example, the Student's t-test (Baillie and Pilcher 1973; Munro 1984), an established technique for looking at the significance of matching between two datasets. The t-test compares the actual difference between the two means from the site chronology and the master chronology. This provides an objective measure of the similarity between the two chronologies and whether the site chronology matches or 'dates'. When a series of ring-widths gives strong statistical matches in the same position against a number of independent chronologies the series becomes dated with an extremely high level of confidence.

Given that tree-ring responses are individual to specific trees – with all the variability in growing conditions, health and so on – it follows that the chances of matching a single sequence are not as great as for matching a tree-ring width series derived from a group of measurements made on many individual trees. This is because the process of aggregating measurements from groups of samples will remove variation unique to an individual tree and reinforce the common signal resulting from widespread influences, such as significant climate events. However, a single sequence may be dated successfully, particularly if it has a long ring sequence.

Growth characteristics vary over space and time, for example, trees in south-eastern Britain generally grow comparatively quickly and with less year-to-year variation than in many other regions of Britain (Bridge 1988). This means that even comparatively large timbers in this region often exhibit few annual rings and are less useful for dating by this technique.

As with any chronometric measurement, dendrochronological results need to be interpreted. Matching a site chronology to a master chronology may not provide the felling date of a timber. Here, the presence or absence of the bark edge, sapwood and, in oak species, the heartwood–sapwood transition, is critical in establishing what the last dated ring means in terms of a site narrative.

In oak, in north-west Europe, if the bark edge is present, the year and even the season of the year of felling can be determined. This is because oak species in this part of the world respond very closely to annual temperate cycles and water availability by forming different cell structures. It is therefore possible to differentiate a spring or summer felling date, depending on the presence of large spring vessels and the subsequent summer growth (Fig. 3.3). In north west Europe, for example, oaks felled in the early spring will only show the initial beginnings of the spring vessels, and generally this occurs in March or April. The presence of the large spring vessels will indicate that a tree survived to between May and September. After October or November, oaks are dormant and do not laydown additional growth.

If the bark edge is not present, a reasonably accurate estimate for the felling date may still be possible providing some of the sapwood is present. The sapwood represents the outer margins of a tree, a living annulus of cells. Moving into the centre of the tree, the inner rings become converted to more durable heartwood. Reasonably good estimates for the time duration that sapwood takes to form hardwood are available for many species. Sapwood ring number estimates vary between workers and the area from which the timber or tree originates. For example, in the UK oaks appear to have more rings than areas further to the east, such as Estonia and Poland (cf. Wazny 1990; Miles 1997; Tyers 1998). Based on the number of surviving sapwood rings on oak it may therefore be possible to estimate the greatest possible interval between the last ring of timber as it is preserved and the felling date.

Where no sapwood is present it is not possible to determine how much wood has been removed. In these cases, regardless of any match to a master chronology, the last dated ring in a timber can only provide a *terminus post quem* or date after which the timber must have been felled. Such a *terminus post quem* may still provide archaeologically important evidence, depending on the research aims of the scientific dating exercise. In

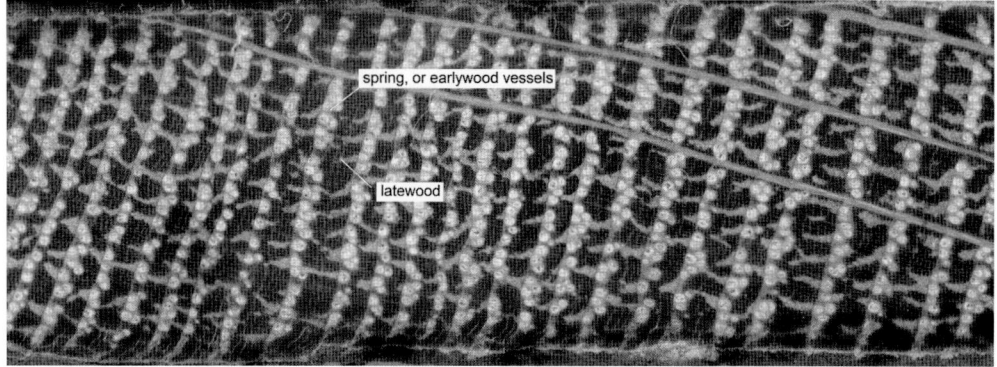

Figure 3.3. Cell structures in a dendrochronological sample including spring growth. Copyright: Martin Bridge.

species other than oak, it may not be possible to differentiate heartwood and sapwood; in these cases, without the bark edge, the last dated ring simply only provides a *terminus post quem*.

One of the advantages of dendrochronology above nearly any other forms of scientific dating technique is that, with precise felling date estimates from bark edges, it is possible to distinguish phases of archaeological activity that may only be separated by a very few years.

Issues effecting sample measurement
Sufficient sequence
There is no definite minimum length of a tree-ring series that can be confidently cross-matched but as a working hypothesis most dendrochronologists use series of at least 50 years growth. Of course, the survival of an appropriate sequence on a site or in a structure depends to some extent on cultural choices in the past and the potential for preservation. Use of species that are not especially responsive to changes in climate, that are not especially long-lived or that do not put on clear annual growth rings will limit the application of dendrochronology on a site. Further aesthetic or cultural choices may limit the utility of a sequence in answering specific scientific dating questions, for example by the processing of wood into timbers and the removal of the bark edge and sapwood (see below).

Bog oaks
As noted above, very local growing conditions can lead to atypical responses in different trees, if all available timbers on site display atypical responses – for example because they were all grown close to each other – then it may not be possible to date or match a floating site chronology to a master one. An example of both atypical growing conditions and the significance of local preservation conditions can be seen in the importance of bog oaks in constructing north-west European dendrochronologies (see below). Bog oaks are oak trees that grew on areas of wetland. They can provide many samples for master dendrochronologies as well as for the radiocarbon calibration curve (Chapter 2). However, because of the atypical growing conditions on bogs – with high degrees of wetness and the effects of freezing in winter – some individual trees can prove difficult to cross-match because of their highly atypical responses.

Use of non-local wood resources
Being able to match a site chronology with a master chronology and translate annual growth rings into calendar years depends on understanding which master chronology is most appropriate. Generally, the master chronology local to the archaeological site or find spot may be appropriate. However, some timbers may have travelled considerable distances prior to their use in a structure or deposition on site. In these cases the origin of timbers may be unclear. This can also be the case in trying to apply dendrochronology to shipwreck sites, where vessels may had sunk many kilometres from the location where the timber was grown. This was the case in the Newport ship (Nayling and

Susperregi 2014), a medieval vessel that was recovered in Newport, south Wales but which the tree-ring studies demonstrated was constructed from timbers grown in the Basque Country of Spain and France.

From the medieval period onwards, Europe saw increasing long-distance trade, including in timber. The presence of imported timbers on terrestrial sites has led to issues with establishing the correct master chronology in some instances and subsequent difficulties in getting the dendrochronological measurements to cross-match or to 'date'. This was the case, for example, in the amendments to the nave roof in Ripon Cathedral, Yorkshire, UK. Here it was difficult to match timbers from repairs that occurred in the second half of the 19th century (Bayliss *et al.* 2014). In this example, the dendrochronology revealed a complex history of construction and trade. The structure had been modified with timbers that had apparently been stockpiled prior to use and the dendrochronological measurements also revealed that some of the timbers appeared to have been imported, probably from the Baltic region of northern Europe. This all meant dendrochronological measurements from some parts of the structure did not 'date' by matching any reference chronologies from the UK.

Sample selection

The most important consideration in producing dendrochronological measurements may be safe access to the site; dendrochronology can require lone working at height or in the intertidal zone. In any project sample selection will need coordination between the project director and the dendrochronologist as well as other specialists who might include buildings archaeologists and waterlogged wood curators. Timbers will require assessment by a dendrochronologist, who will consider variables including: species identification, the number of rings that may be present, how a timber has been converted from the parent tree and what event the last ring preserved in the sequence corresponds to – is there sapwood or bark present? This will help maximise the chances of matching samples.

The relationships between timbers on a site is important in building a site chronology. This requires consideration of the different site phases or the history of construction and modification of the building prior to sampling. These relationships provide important primary information about the expected relative felling dates of a group of timbers. However, the potential for timber storage prior to use, timber re-use, or the mis-phasing of structures or sites mean these observations always need to be evaluated critically as part of the analysis.

Samples can be removed by coring, using a chain saw or whole timbers can be extracted. These samples need to be kept in consistent conditions as closely mirroring the on-site preservation conditions as possible. So, if timbers have been preserved in anaerobic, waterlogged conditions, they should be kept wet; liaison with specialist wood curators is key here. Sampling needs to be undertaken in a controlled manner by the dendrochronologist to minimise damage and distortion to the timbers or cores (see Chapter 7 for further on-site considerations).

Quality indicators: being a critical consumer

Commissioning a successful dendrochronological 'date' on a timber is only part of the process. The association between the dendrochronological measurement and the archaeological event of interest is very important. Even if a felling date has been established, the date needs to be considered in terms of the site history. Building timbers may be stockpiled or reused. Structures may be repaired or modified. In some cases, for example, the use of green unseasoned wood in medieval building in north west Europe, we can rule out significant storage. However, in particularly large or grand construction projects, the stockpiling of timbers from wide regions over a considerable period may occur. It may therefore be necessary to undertake several phases of sampling, after producing initial dendrochronological measurements, in order to build the most comprehensive chronology of a structure or a site.

As in any chronological research, thinking about how measurements relate to the sequence being investigated is really important. As Waterbolk (1971) was critical in discussing the interpretation of radiocarbon results (Chapter 2), Jeffery Dean (1978, 227) made an important contribution in the critical examination of dendrochronological measurements. In Figure 3.4 we can see Dean (1978) discriminating between different degrees of association between the dated event and the archaeological event of interest or, in Dean's terms, the 'target event'. This attempt at rigorously defining types of events owes much to Processual Archaeology approaches at the time Dean was working. Dean's language is also indebted to the history of dendrochronology research in the south-west USA. His use of the term 'bridging event' recalls Douglass's search for timbers to 'bridge' his floating chronologies. Dean's concepts may be difficult to apply in research contexts outside the use of dendrochronology in the south-west USA – in contrast to Waterbolk's (1971) focus on association. However, Dean eloquently emphasisees the importance of thinking critically about how scientific measurements are used to build chronological sequences. This kind of formal expression of what a dated event represents is a useful exercise in building any chronology.

Reporting results

We can think about the reporting of dendrochronological measurements as comprising four areas:

- identifying the location of the different measured sequences on site (using plans, photographs, and the written record using unique identifiers for each sampled sequence);
- describing the method of sample recovery and ring counting;
- analysing the sequence and validating this analysis (in terms of cross-matching sequences from the same site, cross-matching from master chronologies; *and* detailing the *t*-test counting statistics);
- interpreting the results (in terms of chronology: age estimates from different timbers for an individual site or structure history; non-chronological dendrochronological information such as the number of timbers, and their potential origins).

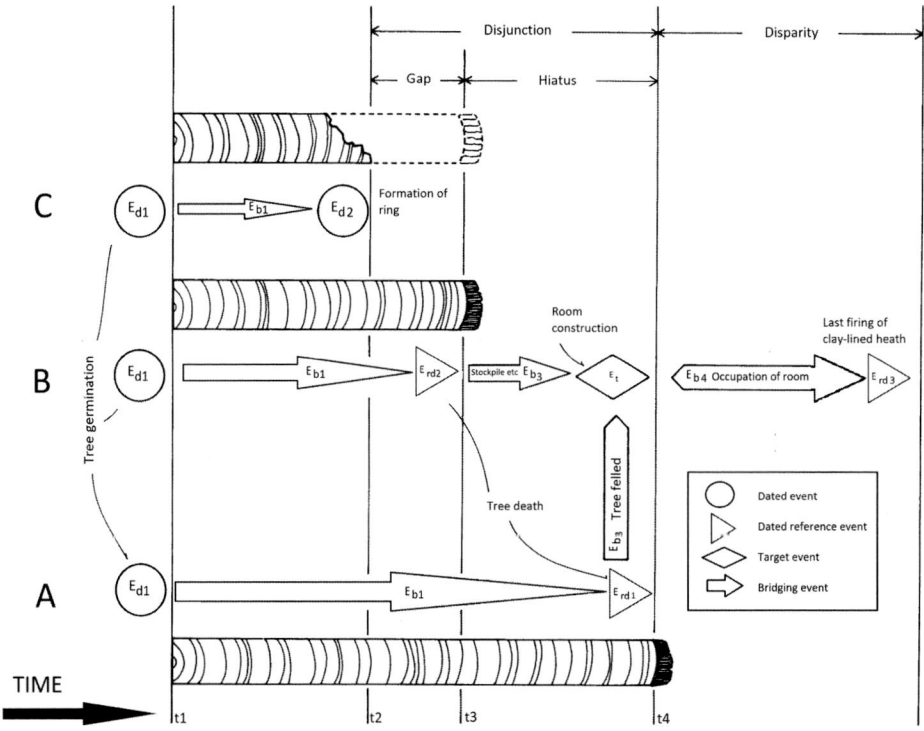

Figure 3.4. Jeffery S. Dean's (1978) visualisation of different types of event and how these related to the production of archaeological chronologies and narratives. In this image: 'E_{d1} represents tree germinations at t_1, that are related to the trees' deaths (E_{rd1} and E_{rd2} at t_4 and t3) and to the formation of a particular ring (E_{d2} at t_2) by the sequence of years recorded in the trees' ring chronologies (E_{b1}) E_{rd3} is the firing of a clay hearth at t_5, and E_t is the construction at t_4 of a room in which the wood and hearth are found. The simplest dating situation is represented by A, in which the relationship between E_{rd1} and E_t is specified by events (E_{b2}) that establish contemporaneity at t_4. B indicates a situation in which a hiatus exists between E_{rd2} at t_3 and E_t at t_4, with the two events joined by other bridging events (E_{b3}). C illustrates a situation with both a gap between E_{d2} at t_2 and E_r at t_3, and a hiatus between E_r at t_3 and E_t at t_4 exist. A disparity between E_t at t_4 and E_{rd3} at t_5, is spanned by another series of events (E_{b4}) related to the occupation and use of the room' (Dean 1978, 227). This way of visualising events is indebted to the language of the time, however, it is notable as one of the relatively few examples where archaeologists attempted to think formally about events and chronology building. Copyright: Seren Griffiths.

Publication reporting should therefore include details of the origins of the samples, for example which timbers were sampled and their locations on sites or standing buildings; identification of sample points and sequences on drawn plans and sections, in the photographic record, and in the written record using unique identifiers. The archaeologist who commissioned the measurements should also publish full details of the dendrochronological sample recovery process and the measurement and age estimation methods, as well as the dendrochronological results. This should include details of the construction of the site chronology and cross-dating process (including which reference chronologies were employed and the cross-dating statistics).

Dendrochronological age estimates (e.g. the last measured heartwood ring) may be quite distinct from any archaeological event of interest (e.g. the construction of a structure). It is therefore very important that all the details of the measurement are published, *as well as* the dendrochronological interpretation of these measurements. For example, the last measured heartwood ring can only provide a *terminus post quem* for the construction of any structure because there will have been some interval between the formation of that ring and the felling date of the timber (in addition to potential issues of storage and re-use). Where incomplete sapwood rings are present details of the process for estimating the felling date should be included in the publication.

Reporting of chronological results may be achieved through the use of bar charts illustrating the number and nature of rings preserved from timbers from a site (e.g. the last dated ring preserved in different sequences, the presence of heartwood and sapwood, the heartwood–sapwood transition, the present of bark edge) and text describing any age estimate. The text should detail the number of rings preserved in a sequence, the *t*-test results across a site and the *t*-test results for cross-matching across any reference chronology. In addition, other non-chronological aspects of the study of the tree-rings from any site should also be reported. This should include population details of the parent trees (age; size; number of trees represented; number of woodlands exploited; whether timbers were imported from different regions or internationally etc).

The dendrochronological interpretation of these measurements provides vital information about the measurements and should be included in their publication (together with the interpretations of standing buildings specialist and/or the excavator). Details of the sample archive locations (i.e. with individual laboratories or in museum archives) should be given.

Wiggle matching

'Wiggle matching' is a relatively specialist approach to scientific dating that combines dendrochronological and radiocarbon measurements. As we saw in Chapter 2, the production of radiocarbon has not been constant over time. The radiocarbon calibration dataset includes measurements on samples that have been independently dated by dendrochronology. The calibration dataset or 'curve' therefore has shape in it that reflects the variation in production in radiocarbon over time. The resultant wiggles in the calibration dataset can in turn be used by archaeologists as the basis for wiggle matching. Wiggle matching can provide dates for timbers that cannot be matched by dendrochronology alone and can provide chronologies with precision that may not be possible to achieve when using radiocarbon measurements alone. Wiggle matching can be undertaken by visually matching groups of results from the same timber with the calibration curve. However, statistical analysis techniques now exist (Christen and Litton 1995) that allow these approaches to be applied using computer programs (Galimberti *et al.* 2004; Chapter 8).

In wiggle matching a series of radiocarbon measurements is produced from a dendrochronological sequence that does not 'date' on its own. These radiocarbon measurements can be closely related, using the age intervals between radiocarbon dated samples as established by dendrochronological ring counts. In wiggle matching timbers, AMS measurements can be taken from an individual tree-ring or a block of tree-rings representing a relatively short period of time (for example 5 years). It is then possible to use the radiocarbon measurements and the known intervals between them to match the radiocarbon results to the wiggles in the calibration dataset.

Case studies

Case study: Holme-next-the-Sea, Norfolk, UK

Two timber circles were identified at Holme-next-the-Sea (52.977155N, 0.548830E; 52.977395N 0.547280E (WGS84)), Norfolk, UK (Groves 2002; Tyers 2014; Fig. 3.5). The timber circles had been preserved by waterlogging in intertidal locations off the north coast, about 0.1 km apart.

Figure 3.5. One of the timber circles at Holme-next-the-Sea under excavation. Copyright: Norfolk County Council.

The first monument – 'Seahenge' or Holme I – was identified in 1998. It comprised an inverted oak tree-bole (the tree root system), which was surrounded by a circle of 55 oak timbers, so closely-set as to form a continuous ring. Many timbers had been produced by splitting tree trunks in half. The research aims of the scientific dating project were to establish if the timber circle and the tree-bole were contemporaneous and to try and date the construction of these elements. Full details of the sampling and measurement approaches for the first circle are detailed in Groves (2002).

The second circle – Holme II – comprised three elements: an outer circle of close-set, split oak tree trunks; an inner arc of oak posts set at intervals; and two central horizontal timbers surrounded by stakes. The research aims of the scientific dating project were to establish the chronological development of this monument and its relationship with the first timber circle. Full details of the sampling and measurement approaches for the first circle are detailed in Tyers (2014).

Dendrochronology results

The sample recovery in both cases was challenging because of the intertidal location. Samples from Holme I were recovered by excavation and from Holme II by test-pitting. From Holme I, 55 timbers were dendrochronologically analysed in two phases of work (Brennand *et al.* 2003). The preservation at the site meant that many of the timbers assessed for dendrochronological measurement were complete with bark edges and in some cases had the intact bark surface. As a whole, the timbers cross-dated to produce a 181-year relative or 'floating' site chronology. During the initial dendrochronological analysis of work the relative site chronology could not be matched to any master chronology. Radiocarbon measurements were produced and analysed with the dendrochronological measurements in a Bayesian wiggle match (see Chapter 8; Brennand *et al.* 2003; Tyers 2014). The similarity in growth patterns shown by some of the timbers suggested that the same tree was represented by different timbers on the site. In this case study, the same-tree samples were aggregated; this was important to ensure that these samples were not over-represented in matching the site chronology to the regional chronology. By comparing the site chronology with chronologies from Britain and other parts of Europe it was possible to identify a match, with the site chronology of annual rings represented dating to 2229–2049 BC. The preservation of bark edge and intact bark surface meant that it was possible to identify that the majority of timbers had been felled in 2049 BC

Some of the timbers had spring vessels, while others had grown slightly longer with the start of summer wood just forming. This suggested that many of the timbers might have been felled in the first half of 2049 BC. The consistency of these results suggested that stored timbers were not likely to have been used for the structure and that the felling date was accurate for the construction of the circle in the early summer of 2049 BC.

The consistency of results also suggested that the monument was built as a planned single-phase construction, with both the inverted tree-bole and the timber circle built at the same time. The similarity in some of the timbers suggests that they were harvested from a single common source and, taking into account the similarities in timbers, it seems that only 15–20 trees were felled for the monument, with the tree used for the central tree-bole also represented by several of the posts. These would have been relatively tall oak trees, each with 5–6 m of trunk employed in the monument construction, with additional height afforded by the tree canopies (Brennand *et al.* 2003, 35).

Six timbers were sub-sampled for dendrochronological analysis from Holme II; these included one timber from the inner arc and five from the outer circle. Storm action had damaged the site in 2004 and two timbers were rescued from the central setting and made available for analysis. Five samples cross-matched against each other and produced a site chronology that represented growth over 328 years. Comparison of this with British and northern European reference chronologies demonstrated that the sequence dated to 2376–2049 BC. Both the outer circle and the central setting produced samples with bark edge and an incomplete ring indicating timbers that were felled in the spring or summer of 2049 BC. The inner arc could not be dated by dendrochronology as there were too few rings present and no sapwood.

This demonstrates that the features on Holme II were contemporaneous and probably built as a single planned construction. The same pattern of using a limited number of trees for multiple timbers was suggested as had also been observed at Holme I. Both timber circles were therefore probably constructed in the same year, most likely at the same general time in the spring or summer. Similarities in the timbers suggest that a restricted group of trees was felled, possibly from the same source woodland.

Discussion of the scientific dating considerations
Multiple timbers with the bark edge complete were preserved at both these monuments. This allowed precise felling dates to be generated for each. The consistency of the felling dates is critical to the interpretation. Here, the dendrochronological measurements indicate that there is no offset between the measurements and the construction of the sites. High similarities between the ring growth suggest that the same trees were used for multiple timbers taken from a restricted woodland source. These were planned, contemporaneous monuments. They may have been in use for a relatively short duration of time because there is no evidence of repair or modification.

Case study conclusions
Wiggle matching combines the precision of dendrochronology and the wide-ranging applicability of radiocarbon. As such it is a powerful tool in scientific dating. This case study demonstrates the importance of thinking critically about groups of dated events and the **relationships** with the archaeological event of interest. Here the group of measurements need to be considered together. The range of measurements from this site allows us to think more broadly about the history of activity here; this would not be possible with a smaller group of measurements.

Case study: the Mary Rose, *English Channel*

The *Mary Rose* wreck site (50.76391460 N 1.10424481 W (WGS84)) is internationally famous because of the spectacular nature of the recovery exercise, the level of preservation, and the historical importance of the vessel. The *Mary Rose* (AD 1510–45) was King Henry VIII's flagship and sank off Portsmouth Harbour in July 1545. In this

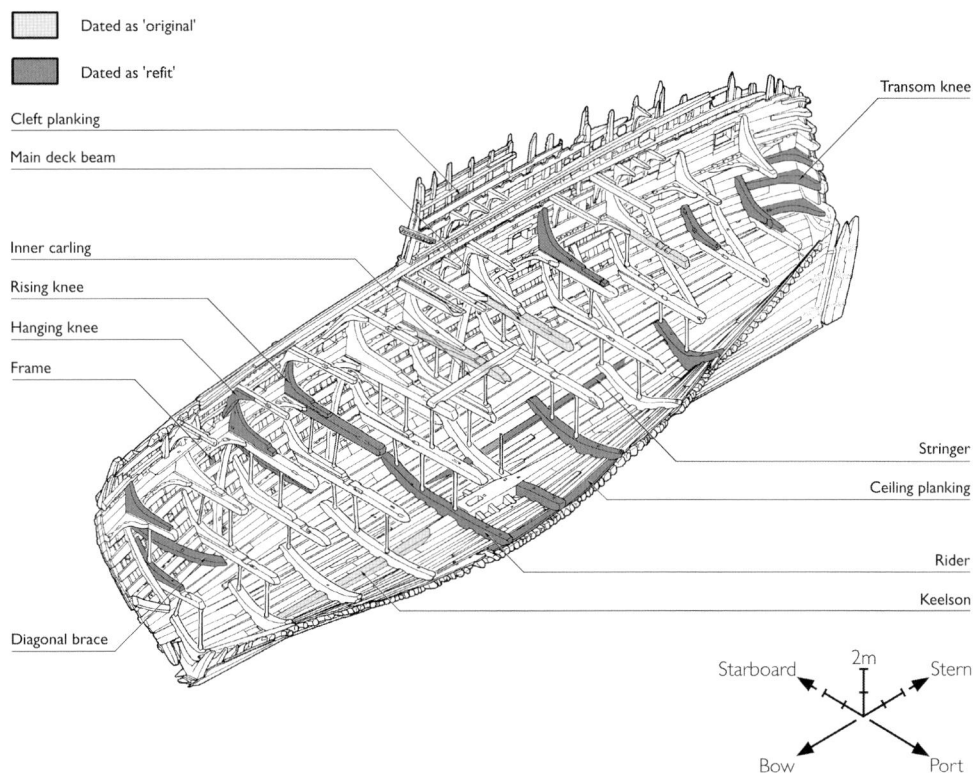

Figure 3.6. Timbers from the Mary Rose *and their archaeological interpretation. Copyright: Mary Rose Trust.*

case, as well as with other wreck sites and standing buildings, dendrochronology can tell us about the history of construction and the economy that existed at the time. The wreck was the focus of significant dendrochronological analysis to explore the history of construction and repair and the sources of timber used for the vessel.

Dendrochronology results

The large number of oak timbers preserved on the wreck allowed a detailed exploration of its construction history (Fig. 3.6; Dobbs and Bridge 2000; 2008). Timbers were selected for analysis to represent those that, on archaeological grounds, appeared to represent original timbers and timbers included as a result of a known refit, perhaps as part of a reconfiguration to hold more and/or bigger guns (Fig. 3.6).

When the original dendrochronological work was undertaken a few of the timbers cross-matched with others from the vessel. However, this research demonstrated that timbers had been added in several phases of construction and modification. Chronologically, original timbers could be attributed to construction in Portsmouth in AD 1510/11, as well

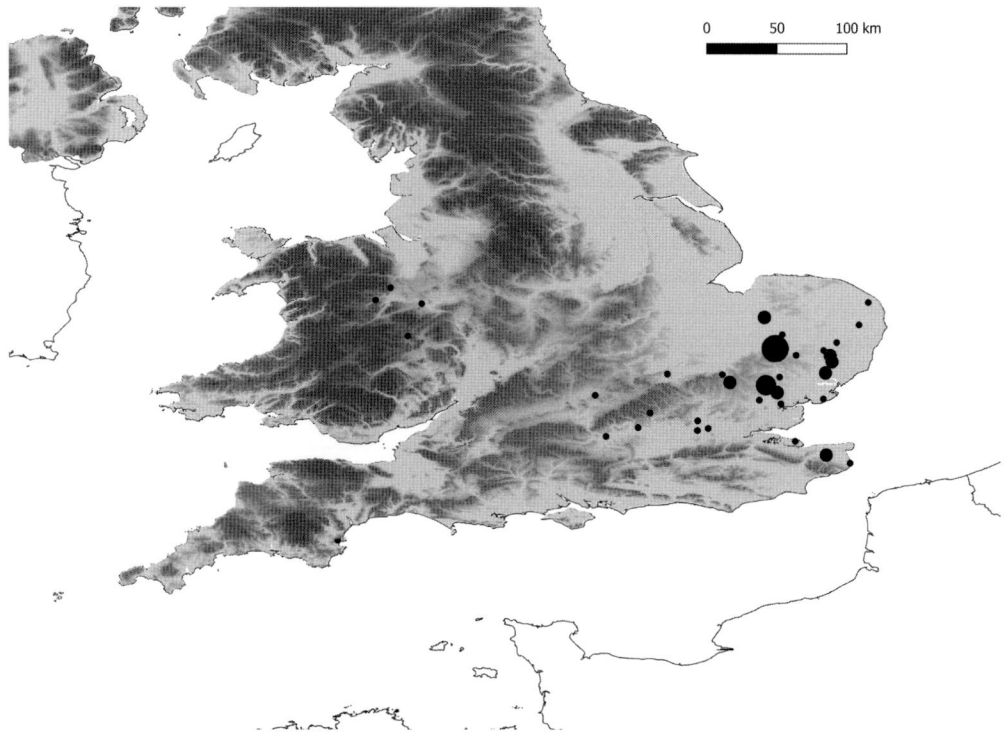

Figure 3.7. An illustration of the t*-values for one of the timbers from the* Mary *Rose. The higher the* t*-value, the larger the circle, and the more similar the timber is to reference chronologies from different regions. Copyright: Martin Bridge.*

as several subsequent refits of the vessel, including an historically attested refit in 1536 on the River Medway and a tree that was used to produce one frame which was still growing in 1540 (Dobbs and Bridge 1996; Bridge and Dobbs 2000). However, when the original research was undertaken, the timbers did not easily form a master chronology as there was very limited cross-matching between the different timbers.

As subsequent research has produced more regional chronologies from across Britain it has been possible to revisit the *Mary Rose* timbers with these new reference chronologies (Bridge 2011; Fig. 3.7). The distinctions between the ring sequences suggested that the timbers resulted from different habitats and demonstrated that the refits utilised timbers with quite distinct geographical signatures from across England and Wales.

Discussion of the scientific dating considerations

The *Mary Rose* case study demonstrates the underlying fundamental principles of dendrochronology – the importance of trees' responses to *local* environmental growing conditions. In looking for cross-matches from wreck sites it may be important to consider a geographically wide-ranging series of master chronologies. The dendrochronology from this wreck was able to inform on the construction history of the vessel. Sampling a wide range of timbers provided significant research outcomes even though limited numbers cross-matched at the time of the initial reporting. The nature of the tree-ring sequences from the *Mary Rose* tells us much more than simply the construction history, by giving an indication of the provenance of timbers used in repairs and different structures of the ship, the sequences provide invaluable information on the economy and wider society of 16th century England and Wales (Bridge 2011).

Case study conclusions
This case study demonstrates the importance of a **wide-ranging sampling strategy** that includes evidence for archaeological phases of activity, construction or modification. In dendrochronological analysis it is important to consider both spatial and temporal factors affecting **tree-ring development** and which may be the most relevant master chronology. Finally, it may be useful to **revisit dendrochronological sequences** which have initially failed to match. As more master and species chronologies are developed, it may be possible to match legacy measurements.

Case study: Church of St Peter, West Liss, Hampshire, UK

The Church of St Peter, West Liss (51.052298 N, 0.902090 W (WGS84)) is a protected with Grade II* Listed Building status, meaning that it has statutory protection. The listing entry details the complicated series of historically attested modifications that occurred to the structure since the 13th century AD, and which includes a porch dating from the 17th century. The foundations of the church are believed to date to sometime after AD 900. The church comprises a nave, south aisle and porch with timber roofs. To better understand the sequence of construction and modification, and to inform conservation and management plans, dendrochronological and wiggle matching analyses were carried out on timbers from the structure (Arnold and Howard 2012; Arnold *et al.* 2020; Fig. 3.8). In total 49 samples were taken by coring for dendrochronological analysis.

Dendrochronological results
The nave roof was thought, on architectural grounds, to date to the early 13th century and the south aisle roof to the late 13th century. However, several timbers could not be 'dated' by dendrochronology alone. To resolve these chronologies samples were also submitted for radiocarbon measurements (Fig 3.9) and a programme of wiggle matching was undertaken. One of these sequences (LSSASQ02, sample LSS-A37) is used as our Bayesian wiggle matching case study in Chapter 8. This sample had the heartwood/sapwood transition preserved but some of the sapwood rings had been removed. In this case, the last ring measured by dendrochronology provides a *terminus post quem* for the felling date. In Chapter 8 we estimate the felling date using radiocarbon measurements and the local estimate for the number of sapwood rings oak trees produce on average in this part of the world.

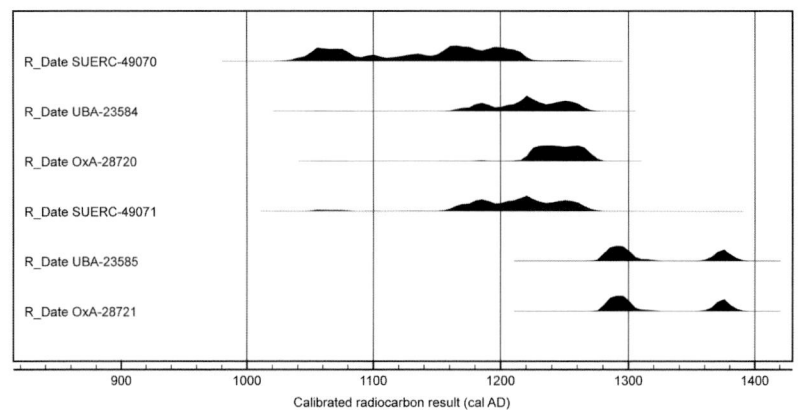

Figure 3.8. Inside the Church of St Peter, West Liss, Hampshire. Copyright: Alison Arnold.

Figure 3.9. Radiocarbon measurements on timber sequence LSS-A37 from St Peter, West Liss, Hampshire. Copyright: Seren Griffiths.

Discussion of the scientific dating considerations
Using dendrochronology to analyse lots of sequences provided new information about the history of this building. Combining dendrochronology measurements and radiocarbon measurements in a Bayesian wiggle matching analysis may be required to 'date' sequences. We return to this example in Chapter 8.

Case study conclusions
For long lived species such as oak trees it is important to think about what the last ring preserved in a sequence means in a site chronology. In this example, unlike the Holme-next-the-Sea sequences, the last ring does *not* represent the **felling date** of the timber (we describe a means to estimate this in Chapter 8). To further complicate interpretation here, the **multi-phase** nature of the structure means there is potential for **modification** and **re-use** which we need to consider in our analysis of the site.

Chapter conclusions

The application of dendrochronological work in the south-west USA had some significant implications for the history of archaeological thought in the early- and mid-20th century. Dendrochronology produces chronologies of a **precision** not matched by other scientific dating techniques. This has meant that it can produce histories for periods without written records, or chronologies for events, objects or structures that were not recorded in historical sources. To produce **accurate** age estimates for archaeological events of interest we need to consider what the last dated ring means in terms of a site chronology. We can do this formally following the work of Jeffery Dean (1978). The number of rings in a specific sequence was previously a limiting factor in the ability to produce chronologies. However, recent **combination with radiocarbon** measurements has increased the circumstances where precise chronologies can be produced.

Bibliography

Arnold, A. and Howard, R. 2012. Church of St Peter, West Liss, Hampshire: Tree-Ring Dating of Timbers. Portsmouth: English Heritage Research Report Series 40–2012 (online) [https://historicengland.org.uk/research/results/reports/6084/ChurchofStPeterWestLissHampshire_Tree-RingDatingofTimbers]

Arnold, A., Bronk Ramsey, C., Cook, G., Griffiths, S., Reimer, P. and Marshall, P. 2020. Church of St Peter, West Liss, Hampshire. Tree-ring analysis and radiocarbon wiggle-matching of the nave, south aisle and porch roof. Portsmouth: Historic England Research Report Series (online) [https://historicengland.org.uk/research/results/reports/69-2015]

Baillie, M. 1999. *Exodus to Arthur: catastrophic encounters with comets*. London: Batsford

Baillie, M. 1982. *Tree-ring Dating and Archaeology*. London: Croom Helm.

Baillie, M. and Pilcher, J. 1973. A simple cross-dating program for tree-ring research. *Tree-ring Bulletin* 33, 7–14

Bayliss, A., Bronk Ramsey, C., Cook, G., Freeman, S., Hamilton, W., van der Plicht, J. and Tyers, C. 2014. Cathedral Church of St Peter and St Wilfred, Ripon, North Yorkshire, nave roof and ceiling, wiggle match radiocarbon dating of timbers. Portsmouth, Historic England Research Report Series 73–2014 (online) [https://historicengland.org.uk/research/results/reports/73-2014]

Brennand, M., Taylor, M., Ashwin, T., Bayliss, A., Canti, M., Chamberlain, C., Fryer, V., Gale, R., Green, F., Groves, C., Hall, A., Linford, N., Murphy, P., Robinson, M., Wells, J. and Williams, D. 2003. The survey and excavation of a Bronze Age timber circle at Holme-next-the-Sea, Norfolk, 1998–9. *Proceedings of the Prehistoric Society* 69, 1–84

Bridge, M. 1988. The dendrochronological dating of buildings in southern England. *Medieval Archaeology* 32, 166–74

Bridge, M. 2011. Resource exploitation and wood mobility in northern European oak: dendroprovenancing of individual timbers from the Mary Rose (1510/11–1545). *International Journal of Nautical Archaeology* 40(2), 417–23

Bridge, M. and Dobbs, C. 1996. Tree-ring studies on the Tudor warship Mary Rose. In J. Dean, D. Meko and T. Swetnam (eds), *Tree-rings, Environment, and Humanity: proceedings of the International Conference, Tucson, Arizona, 17–21 May 1994*, 491–6. Tucson AZ: University of Arizona Press

Christen, J. and Litton, C. 1995. A Bayesian approach to wiggle-matching. *Journal of Archaeological Science* 22, 719–25

Dean, J. 1978. Independent dating in archaeological analysis. *Advances in Archaeological Method and Theory* 1, 223–55

Dobbs, C. and Bridge, M. 2000. Preliminary results from dendrochronological studies on the *Mary Rose*. In J. Litwin (ed.), *Down the River to the Sea, Proceedings of the Eighth International Symposium on Boat and Ship Archaeology, Gdansk, 1997*, 257–62. Gdansk: Polish Maritime Museum

Dobbs, C. and Bridge, M. 2008. Construction and refits: tree-ring dating the Mary Rose. In P. Marsden (ed.), *Your Noblest shippe. Mary Rose: anatomy of a Tudor warship*. Portsmouth: Mary Rose Trust, 361–7

Douglass, A. 1919. *Climatic Cycles and Tree Growth I*. Washington DC: Carnegie Institute

Douglass, A. 1938. Estimated tree-ring chronology: 450–600 AD. *Tree-ring Bulletin* 4, 8

Galimberti, M., Bronk Ramsey, C. and Manning, S. 2004. Wiggle-match dating of tree-ring sequences. *Radiocarbon* 46, 917–24

Groves, C. 2002. Dendrochronological analysis of a timber circle at Holme-next-the-Sea, Norfolk. Portsmouth: unpublished report, Centre for Archaeology Report 6/2002

Haury, E. 1935. Tree-rings; the archaeologist's time piece. *American Antiquity* 1(2), 98–108

Miles, D. 1997. The interpretation, presentation, and use of tree-ring dates. *Vernacular Architecture* 28, 40–56

Morgan, L. 1878. *Ancient Society*. New York: Henry Holt

Munro, M. 1984. An improved algorithm for crossdating tree-ring series. *Tree-ring Bulletin* 44, 17–27

Nash, S. 1997. A History of Archaeological Tree-Ring Dating: 1914–1945. Unpublished PhD Thesis, University of Arizona, Tucson

Nayling, N. and Susperregi, J. 2014. Iberian dendrochronology and the Newport medieval ship. *International Journal of Nautical Archaeology* 43(2), 279–91

Tyers, I. 1998. Tree-ring analysis and wood identification on timbers excavated on the Magistrates Court Site. Kingston upon Hull: unpublished report, ARCUS Report 410

Tyers, I. 2004. Dendro for Windows Programme Guide. London: unpublished report, ARCUS

Tyers, I. 2014. Timber circle II, Holm-Next-The-Sea, Norfolk. Dendrochronological analysis of oak timbers. Portsmouth: Historic England Research Report Series 26–2014 https://historicengland.org.uk/research/results/reports/26-2014

Waterbolk, H. 1971. Working with radiocarbon dates. *Actes du VIIIe congrès international des sciences préhistoriques et protohistoriques* 1, 11–25

Wazny, T. 1990. Aufbau and Andwendung der Dendrochronologie für Eichenholz Polen. Unpublished dissertation. University of Hamburg

4. Luminescence: Optically Simulated Luminescence and Thermoluminescence

Seren Griffiths and Abi Stone

Crystalline minerals such as quartz and feldspar can build up trapped charge in their structures. The trapped charge builds up because of exposure to naturally occurring ionising radiation. Luminescence measurements use this built up charge as a proxy for the passage of time. The trapped charge can be emptied by exposure to heat and/or light; this emptying is known as a 'zeroing' or resetting event. In the case of Thermoluminescence (TL) dating the zeroing of the signal occurs during exposure to high temperatures. In the case of Optically Stimulated Luminescence (OSL is used as shorthand for both quartz and feldspar dating, thereby incorporating IRSL, infra-red stimulated luminescence, which is used for feldspar) dating, the zeroing occurs during exposure to light and is also known as 'bleaching'. The build-up of trapped charge after the zeroing event is time dependent so we can use this to calculate for the time elapsed since the zeroing event. To estimate the proportion of charge that has built up, samples are exposed to heat or light in the laboratory. This exposure resets the sample. As a sample is exposed, the charged particles are emptied from their traps and light is released. This light is the 'signal' or 'luminescence' that is measured and provides the basis for the age calculation.

Unlike radiocarbon dating or dendrochronology, luminescence does not require the presence of organic materials which may be selectively preserved in different burial environments. Thus, luminescence offers the potential to measure samples and produce age estimates for sites with low levels of preserved ecofacts and for archaeological deposits which have incorporated sand or loess or deposits like hearths which have been heated (Table 4.1). Grains of quartz and feldspar can become incorporated into archaeological deposits in the sedimentary environment and these minerals are also found within material culture – such as ceramics – as well as within fired clay deposits that have been exposed to high temperature processes.

OSL is especially important for archaeologists, as it allows age estimates to be produced for the formation of a wide range of deposits and palaeo-environmental sequences that have been exposed to light during their formation. However, calculating accurate age estimates involves a number of specialised sampling requirements and measurement techniques. It is also necessary to undertake a detailed consideration of the sedimentary sequence, both in terms of the transport and depositional process and any evidence for post-depositional disturbance. Both TL and OSL require specialist radiation measurements in the field as

Table 4.1: Comparison of OSL and TL techniques in the production of archaeological chronologies.

Considerations	Optically Stimulated Luminescence (OSL)	Thermoluminescence (TL)
'Zeroing' event	Exposure to light prior to burial, important to ensure complete 'bleaching'	High temperature burning
Materials	Grains of quartz or feldspar transported by aeolian action (fluvial, colluvial or marine transportation can lead to incomplete bleaching)	Ceramic building materials, burnt clay (heaths etc), pottery or burnt flints
Burial conditions	Ideally windblown sequences, such as dunes, or perhaps ditch fill deposits (provided complete bleaching has occurred!), ceramic building materials that include quartz grains	Anthropogenic materials that have been heat effected and preserved on site
Types of anthropogenic activity	Depending on the completeness of bleaching, infilling of ditches or other negative feature fills, storm events, or other wind-blown deposits. Production of ceramic building materials	Manufacture of ceramic building materials or pottery, or modification of portable material culture (burnt flints)
Issues with association to archaeological event of interest	Formation of a deposit may provide a *terminus post* or *ante quem* for an archaeological event of interest rather than estimate the timing of that event directly. Direct age estimates for the creation of ceramic building materials.	The timing of the firing of deposits or formation of materials can be directly estimated

well as samples that are recovered for laboratory measurements. The samples taken to the laboratory are not only used to measure the signal from the release of the trapped charge population but also to assess the composition and particle size distribution of the sample and to estimate the sample moisture content. The burial conditions, including the background radiation, influence the annual dose rate that a sample will experience and therefore the build up of charge over the burial history. An accurate assessment of the annual dose rate is essential for age calculation.

It is also very important that samples are fully zeroed. Incomplete zeroing has important implications for the calculation of age estimates. Incomplete zeroing occurs in the case of OSL when samples are not fully exposed to light or, in the case of TL, when samples did not pass through sufficiently high temperatures. Incomplete zeroing will result in an over-estimation of the burial dose and so can therefore only be used as an estimate of maximum age of the sample unless suitable measures are applied to deal with incomplete bleaching.

Both OSL and TL can provide chronologies over very long timescales, from the very recent past into the Pleistocene. Luminescence measurements, using routinely applied protocols for quartz, can be applied to samples up to *c.* 200,000 years old (Duller and Wintle 2012). There are also many protocol developments that aim to extend the age range to *c.* 5,000,000 years old and even further (see Stone and Fenn 2020 for a recent overview). These techniques are also applicable in many different parts of the world. There is no need for a regional master chronology (as with dendrochronology; Chapter 3) or calibration curve (as with archaeomagnetic dating; Chapter 5).

Compared to radiocarbon dating, age estimates are relatively imprecise, with 10% precision at one standard deviation, though it may be possible to achieve more precise measurements depending on the behaviour of individual samples. The application of Bayesian statistical techniques to samples within a stratigraphic section can also make it possible to improve precision (e.g. Wood *et al.* 2016).

Rigorous quality control measures are put in place as part of luminescence protocols to ensure internal consistency of measurements and accurate age estimates. An assessment of the accuracy of ages can also be made with comparison to independent dating methods.

Principles and methodological developments

Underlying principles

Radiation is naturally present due to the occurrence of uranium (U), thorium (Th) and potassium (K) in the burial environment and cosmic radiation from the Sun and outside the solar system. As radioactive decay occurs, the energy that is released into the environment interacts with minerals such as quartz and feldspar, creating ionising electrons. These electrons become captured at trapping sites in the minerals' structure. As time elapses, the quartz or feldspar is exposed to more radiation, which ionises more electrons, meaning that proportionally more electrons become captured at trapping sites. This accumulation will continue until the sample is exposed to another zeroing event, when light (of wavelengths with sufficient energy) or heat (100–300°C) evict these electrons from their traps. The zeroing event resets the luminescence clock.

As the electrons are evicted, they recombine back into the mineral structure. During this recombination, some of the electrons emit photons of light as they return to their ground-state energy level. It is this light signal (or luminescence) that is measured in luminescence laboratories. The signal is proportional in strength to the number of electrons evicted and, in turn, is proportional to the radiation dose a sample received over its burial history, which reflects the time elapsed since the previous zeroing event (Aitken 1990, 144).

Figure 4.1A is an energy level diagram within quartz which underpins the fundamental principles of luminescence dating techniques (a model for feldspar is given by Jain and Ankærgaard 2011). During exposure of a mineral to radiation (or 'irradiation') in the burial environment electrons are ionised from the valence band to higher energy levels. Some of these electrons become trapped at sites in the crystal structure of the minerals, shown by the positions T1 and T2 in Figure 4.1A2. This process of electron eviction continues for as long as the sediment is exposed to radiation, with the electrons remaining in the traps (Fig. 4.1A3). Re-exposure to light or heat will evict these electrons and they will recombine with ions, producing light which is measured in the luminescence laboratory (Fig. 4.1A4)

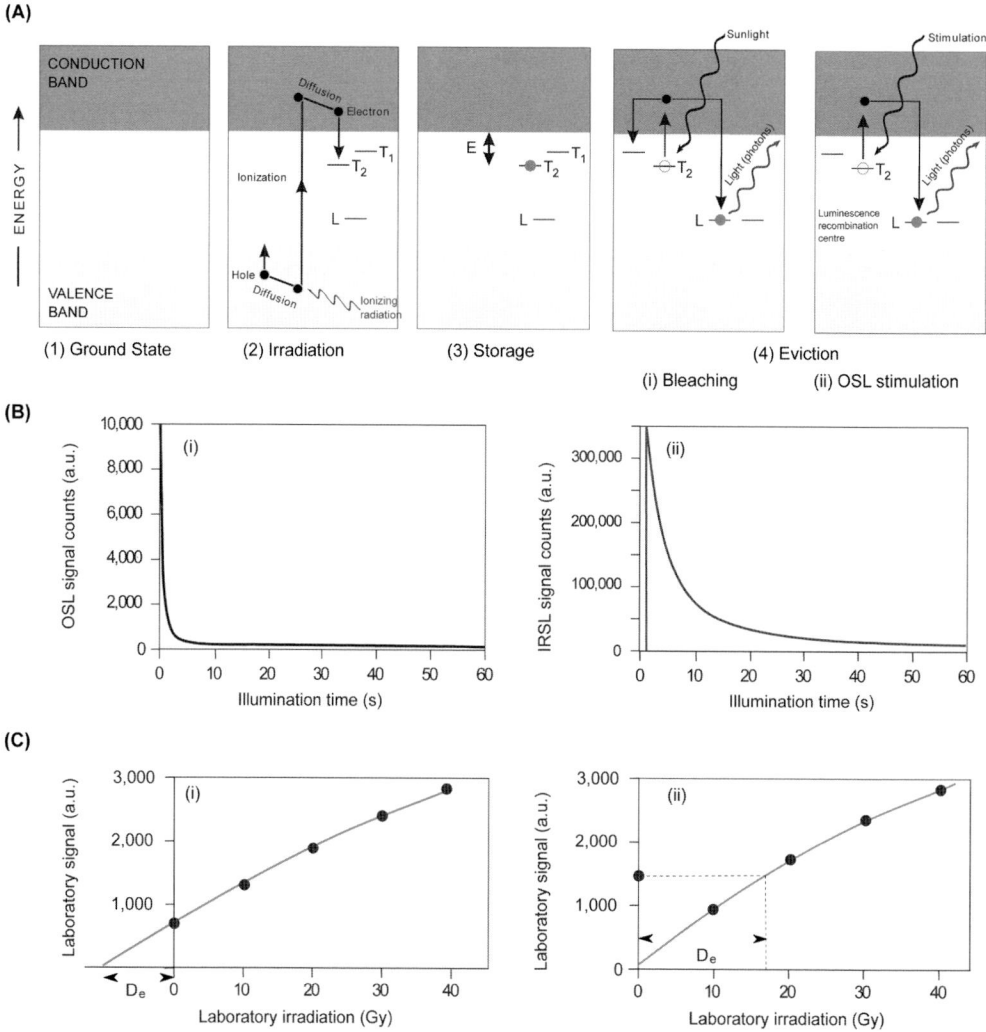

Figure 4.1. A: schematic diagram showing the movement of electrons while a sample is in the burial environment and in the laboratory, 1A2 shows the eviction of electrons to traps during ionizing radiation damage in the burial environment, 1A4 shows recombination and luminescence during measurement in the laboratory; B: the shine down curves or the luminescence emission that is measured over time in the laboratory for (i) quartz and (ii) feldspar; C: the dose-response curves for samples measured in the laboratory in order to calculate the luminescence response of a sample, using an additive method (i) or a regenerative method (ii). Copyright: Abi Stone.

The luminescence age of a sample is equivalent to the total energy accumulated by the sample from the environment (the burial dose), divided by the annual rate of exposure to energy from radiation during sample burial since the zeroing event (the dose rate). To calculate an age (Equation 1), the total radiation to which the sample was exposed has to be ascertained in a laboratory and an estimate for the annual rate at which the sample was exposed to this radiation needs to be made. The units of radiation exposure are measured in grays (notation Gy; the Dose Rate).

Age (years) = Equivalent Dose (mGy)/Dose Rate (mGy a^{-1})   (Equation 1)

In order to estimate the age of a sample, the light signal that is released from that sample (representing the burial dose) needs to be compared to signals released from it after exposure to known laboratory doses of radiation. This is effectively a 'calibration' of the light signal. For this reason, the burial dose (sometimes called palaeodose, or 'P') is known as Equivalent Dose (D_e). This is the equivalent amount of laboratory radiation dose required to cause the sample to emit the same light signal as that which had built up from exposure to natural radiation during its burial history. All samples behave differently and this calibration process allows an accurate estimate of the Equivalent Dose based on the behaviour of an individual sample in the laboratory.

The Dose Rate is derived from two broad sources (Fig. 4.2), which must be calculated:

- the radiation that the sample received from the burial environment and the surrounding sediment, and
- the energetic particles that bombard the Earth, known as cosmic rays. The cosmic ray flux received by a sample is mediated by sample location and burial depth.

Prescott and Hutton (1988; 1994) developed a protocol for calculating the cosmic dose rate for a sample using geomagnetic latitude, altitude and overburden density. The dose rate varies geographically with sites toward the poles receiving lower cosmic doses than sites towards the equator because areas near the poles are relatively shielded from cosmic rays by the magnetic field of the Sun and the Earth. Sample depth is also important because cosmic rays attenuate substantially with depth, roughly halving over ~0.5 m. In the majority of settings, the cosmic dose constitutes a small proportion of total dose rate.

The specific background radiation at every individual sample location should be measured directly however to calculate the dose rate because this background radiation varies between locations. Three types of radiation are present within the burial environment: alpha (α) and beta (β) particles and gamma (γ) rays. These forms of radiation have different penetration distances. Gamma radiation penetrates to the greatest depth (c. 30 cm). It is therefore very important to consider the surrounding deposits around a sample location and how heterogeneous these might be. Ideally sample locations should be surrounded by homogeneous material which should therefore have had a homogeneous irradiating effect on the sample over the burial history. Moisture within a sediment sample attenuates the exposure to radioactive energy. Accurate calculations of the environmental dose therefore require additional samples to measure moisture content, and composition in the sample and surrounding matrix (for example presence of calcium carbonate, sediment density and particle size distribution; see below).

Disequilibrium can occur within the radioactive decay chains of U, Th and K resulting in isotopes with different physical properties. For example, some isotopes in these decay chains are soluble in water, others are not; U can be removed selectively relative to Th during water percolation because U is soluble and Th is not. Changes in the water table, or other changes in the moisture content of a deposit, could therefore result in changes in the background radiation that a sample is exposed to over time. To better understand this total dose, and the annual rate of exposure, samples for hydrology need to be taken.

Archaeological understandings of deposit formation and site history are important in selecting potential samples that have consistent and well-understood hydrological histories and have homogeneous burial environments. So, for example, samples should be located away from interfaces between contexts that might result in heterogeneous exposure to radiocarbon over the burial history (see discussion below). Durcan *et al.* (2015) provide a comprehensive review of how the dose rate can be calculated in luminescence measurements.

Sample types

OSL samples: quartz, feldspar, ceramic materials

OSL dating is ideal for producing accurate chronologies for sandy deposits and for silts (loess) transported and deposited by the wind because signal bleaching occurs within seconds to minutes of exposure to bright sunlight. It is also possible to provide chronologies for the deposition of sediments within fluvial environments, although there is a risk of incomplete bleaching where the sample is not fully zeroed, with subsequent implications for age overestimation.

OSL age estimates can be produced on samples of sand or silt-sized quartz grains, or feldspar grains. Quartz and feldspar are suitable OSL dosimeters (materials that respond, and store, a response to ionising radiation) because they are common within sedimentary deposits and their luminescence properties can be measured reliably and replicated in the laboratory. These minerals are widespread in soils formed on many geologies but are especially useful for producing chronologies of dryland environments with lots of sand.

Quartz has the advantage over feldspar in that it does not exhibit the anomalous fading (loss of luminescence signal during sediment burial) that feldspar signals experience (e.g. Spooner 1994; Huntley and Lamothe 2001). However, feldspar has a higher saturation dose (the dose response curve grows to higher levels) than quartz which means it has the potential for a higher upper age limit for dating. In addition, there has been a great deal of work over the past decade or so developing protocols that appear to access a potentially non-fading signal in feldspars, known as post-infrared IRSL (pIRIR) protocols (Thomsen *et al.* 2008) including protocols

4. Luminescence: Optically Simulated Luminescence and Thermoluminescence

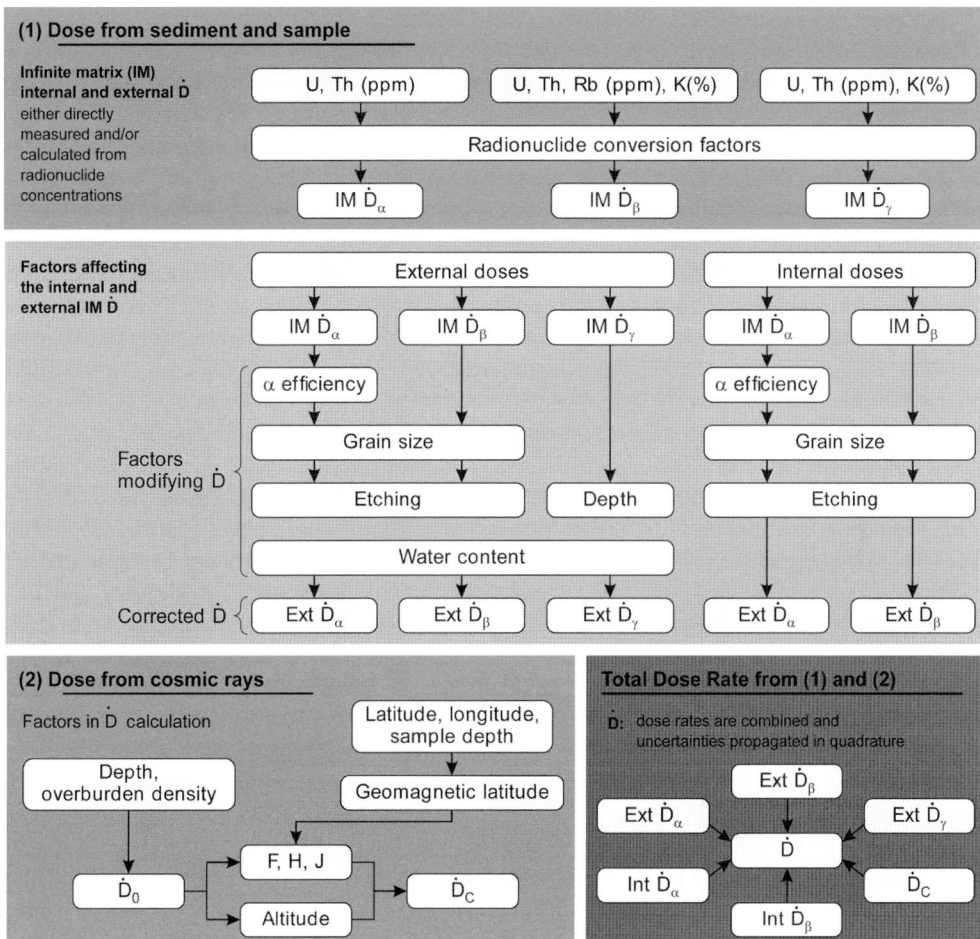

Figure 4.2. Schematic overview of the calculation of dose rate for luminescence dating (modified from Durcan et al. 2015) where α is alpha radiation, β is beta radiation and γ is gamma radiation; Dc is used to depict the Equivalent Dose from cosmic rays; F, H and J are values in a look-up table. Copyright: Abi Stone.

that employ multiple measurements at elevated temperatures (MET pIRIR) (e.g. Li and Li 2011).

The chosen mineral is isolated during laboratory sample preparation, with both quartz and feldspar grains requiring selective extraction. Chemical protocols apply acids to remove carbonates, hydrogen peroxide to degrade organic matter and a density separation to remove heavy minerals. Grains are selected by size and isolated via sieving. Both sand-sized grains (>63 μm and up to 250 μm) and fine-grains (typically 4–11 μm) can be measured depending on the nature of the sediment. For coarse grain quartz, preparation also involves etching the grains with hydrofluoric acid to remove the

c. 20 μm exterior of the grain which will be affected by alpha irradiation. This etching has the added advantage of making dose rate calculation much simpler (Fig. 4.2). Fine grain sediment is treated with hexafluorosilicic acid to dissolve feldspar when using quartz for dating.

There is a growing body of research that applies OSL dating to ceramic materials (e.g. Cano *et al.* 2014; and see case studies below). As with sediment dating, the outer surface of the ceramic material that has been exposed to light during the archaeological recovery process has to be removed. This requires a sample size prior to processing of at least 10 mm thickness and 30 mm across and it also means that ceramic building material samples need to have a homogeneous fabric without voids evident on the surface through which light might penetrate.

Thermoluminescence samples (TL): brick, pottery, heat affected stone
TL measurements can be made on any heat modified material that contains crystalline minerals. These can either be added to a mixture, for example as inclusions in ceramic building materials or pottery, or can be part of crystalline/cryptocrystalline materials that have been heated, as with burnt flint. Datable lithic and ceramic samples need to have sufficient volume that the outer surface (light-exposed) can be removed in the laboratory prior to measurement of the luminescence response.

Flint is a silica-rich cryptocrystalline mineral. This means that it can act as the luminescence dosimeter (Richter 2015). In samples of burnt flint, the sample must have been heated to *c.* 300–400°C to be fully zeroed. For burnt stones, ceramic building material or pottery the duration of heating required to zero a sample is generally proportional to the size of the artefact. In general, the process of zeroing takes longer during heating for TL than it does for light exposure for OSL, and TL samples may therefore contain a residual unbleachable component. For both OSL and TL samples, a subsample of the burial matrix from which the artefact was recovered is needed for accurate measurement of dose rate (see sampling requirements discussed below; Bailiff 2019).

Measurement

Equivalent Dose (D_e) or Palaeodose (P) measurements
Estimating the Equivalent Dose (Fig. 4.2) requires a form of internal sample calibration using something called a dose-response curve. This process explores the responses of samples to different laboratory radiation doses. Samples from different areas, with different luminescence properties, will produce a different luminescence response to the same burial dose. Each sample will also therefore produce different responses following exposure to radiation sources in the laboratory (Fig. 4.3). It is therefore necessary to characterise each sample (in terms of its luminescence behaviour) when exposed to different doses of radiation. This means each sample needs *both* a measurement of its initial luminescence response (the sample's natural signal that results from burial dose) and a measurement of the responses to a range of laboratory-applied doses. Different responses occur between quartz and feldspar with different provenances (including the geological source and weathering histories; e.g. Wang and

Miao 2006; Chithambo *et al.* 2007) and responses may also be influenced by the sample burial history (including variations in temperature and the number of burial cycles the material has been through).

Two broad approaches to deriving the Equivalent Dose have been developed. The first takes aliquots (subsamples) and adds laboratory doses to samples that still contain the luminescence signals acquired from the burial environment. This is known as the additive method. The Equivalent Dose is then inferred by extrapolating the dose-response curve. We can see this in Fig. 4.1Ci, where the curve is extrapolated to give the Equivalent Dose value.

The second approach is known as the regenerative method. In this method, the luminescence signal derived from the burial environment is measured first. The same aliquots are then subject to a series of laboratory doses of known radiation. After each laboratory dose the luminescence signal is measured. The aliquot is then subject to the next laboratory radiation dose, which increases in magnitude from that which went before. At some point, the sample will respond with a luminescence signal that is *greater* than the initial luminescence signal that represented the dose from the burial environment. When this occurs, the Equivalent Dose can be interpolated (Fig. 4.1Cii), where the natural luminescence signal is plotted along the x axis at 0 (no laboratory irradiation). Regenerative methods are more commonly applied than additive methods.

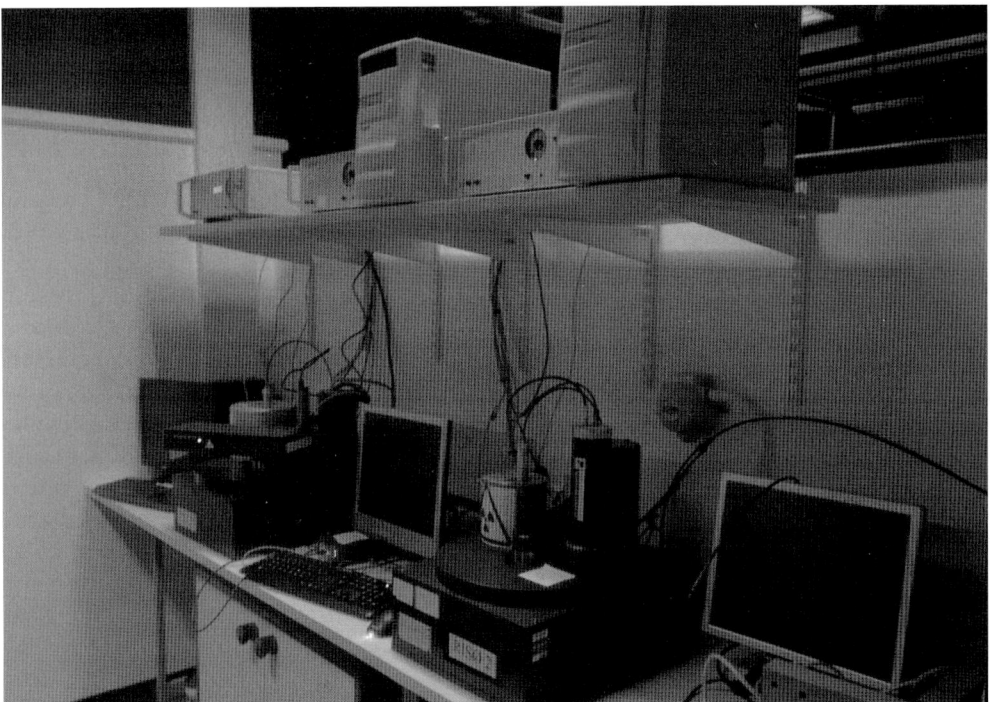

Figure 4.3. The interior of a luminescence dating laboratory showing instrumentation for luminescence measurements. Preparation work is undertaken in red light conditions in order that the samples are not partially bleached during these processes. Copyright: Ian Bailiff.

Single Aliquot Regenerative (SAR) dose protocol

The Single Aliquot Regenerative-dose (SAR) protocol (Murray and Wintle 2000; 2003; Wintle and Murray 2006) was a significant development in estimating the Equivalent Dose and is now very commonly applied in luminescence dating. A series of measurements is made on the same aliquot of a sample and a number of aliquots (often 18 or more) are measured from the same sample to derive a representative estimate of Equivalent Dose. The SAR protocols test for the reproducibility of signals and consistent behaviour of multiple dosimeters from a single sample. Different protocols are applied to quartz and feldspar. The multiple aliquots from a sample could comprise individual grains of quartz or feldspar (see below). These tests establish how internally consistent the estimate for Equivalent Dose might be across a sample.

Single grain measurements

Luminescence signals can be measured on individual grains of quartz or feldspar using purpose-built luminescence readers (see Bøtter-Jensen *et al.* 2003). These approaches allow separate measurements of Equivalent Dose for each grain (Murray and Roberts 1998; Reimann *et al.* 2012). The single grain approach therefore allows a comparison of the behaviour of many grains from an individual sample. This allows an assessment of whether grains have been completely bleached, subject to heterogeneous irradiation over their burial history or exhibit any other erroneous luminescence behaviour. However, it can still be challenging to account for the difference causes of high dispersion in Equivalent Dose values.

Other measurement protocols

For feldspar dating, infrared stimulation (IRSL) is used in a SAR protocol to isolate a non-fading feldspar signal (Duller 2003; Thomsen *et al.* 2008; 2012; Li and Li 2011). A range of approaches is being developed in order to extend the age range for quartz measurements (see Stone and Fenn 2020 for an overview).

Applied sampling considerations

Identifying good sampling locations for luminescence measurements is very important (Fig. 4.4) and will require close liaison between the luminescence specialist and the archaeologist. Samples should be located where there is a homogeneous contribution from background radiation. This avoids the need for detailed work to establish a representative dose rate from the surrounding sediment matrix, particularly for the beta and gamma radiation component, and will result in a more accurate estimate of both dose rate and sample age. Samples should therefore be located away from interfaces, the soil surface, from ancient soil surfaces or the 0.5 m of the edge of cut features. Deposits that might have experienced bioturbation or disturbance over the burial history should be avoided.

4. Luminescence: Optically Simulated Luminescence and Thermoluminescence

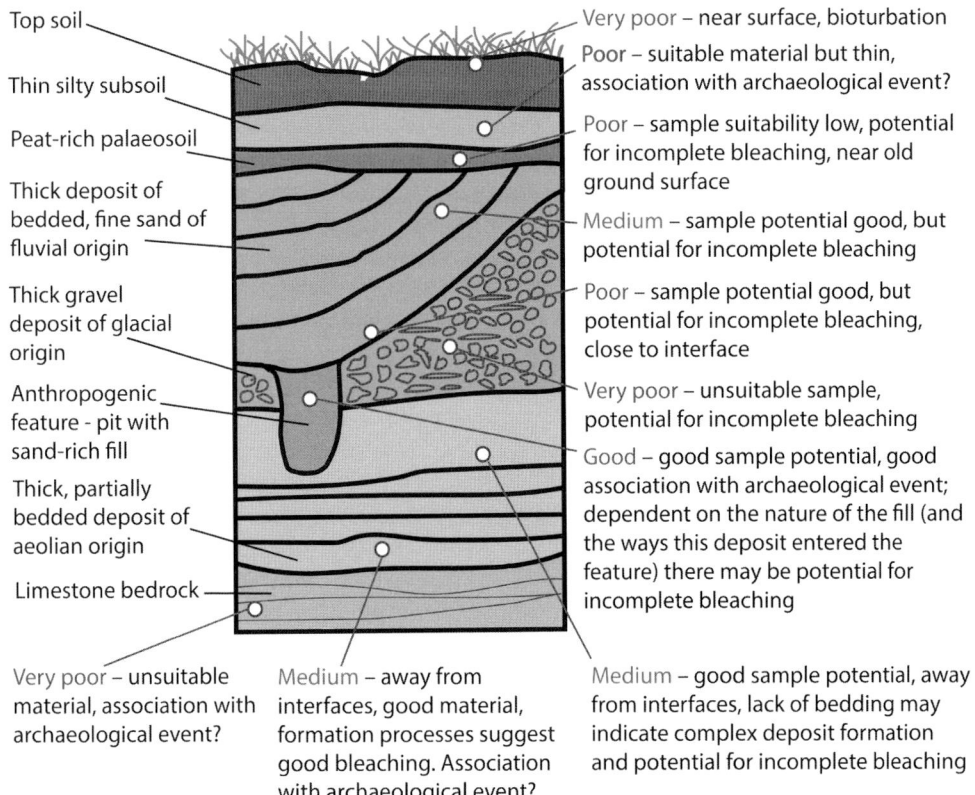

Figure 4.4. Diagram showing considerations that might be made in the assessment of different potential sample locations for OSL measurements. Trying to select samples from locations where there will have been homogeneous and consistent background radiation is key to achieving accurate measurements. Adapted from Aitken (1998, 189). Copyright: Seren Griffiths.

Sample collection for luminescence requires care that material is not exposed to light during the recovery process. This can be done either by sampling in low-light conditions (cleaning back the profile and sheltering it with opaque sheets) and/or taking a large enough sample, so that the outer edge of (light-exposed) material can be removed in the laboratory. The easiest way to undertake this is to sample from an exposed archaeological section after it has been recorded on the section drawing and photographed and after any loose material has been cleaned from the section.

In most cases, sample tubes are hammered into the profile (Fig. 4.5A). Samples should be photographed *in situ*. After the sample is recovered the exposed ends need to be capped and the samples should be stored in light-proof conditions. Back in the laboratory, any field-exposed material can be removed prior to sample preparation.

The voids from which the samples have been recovered are then used as the locations for measurements of dose rate (e.g. Fig. 4.5, 3). Gamma rays can penetrate between 300 and 400 mm of sediment, which means that it is important to consider

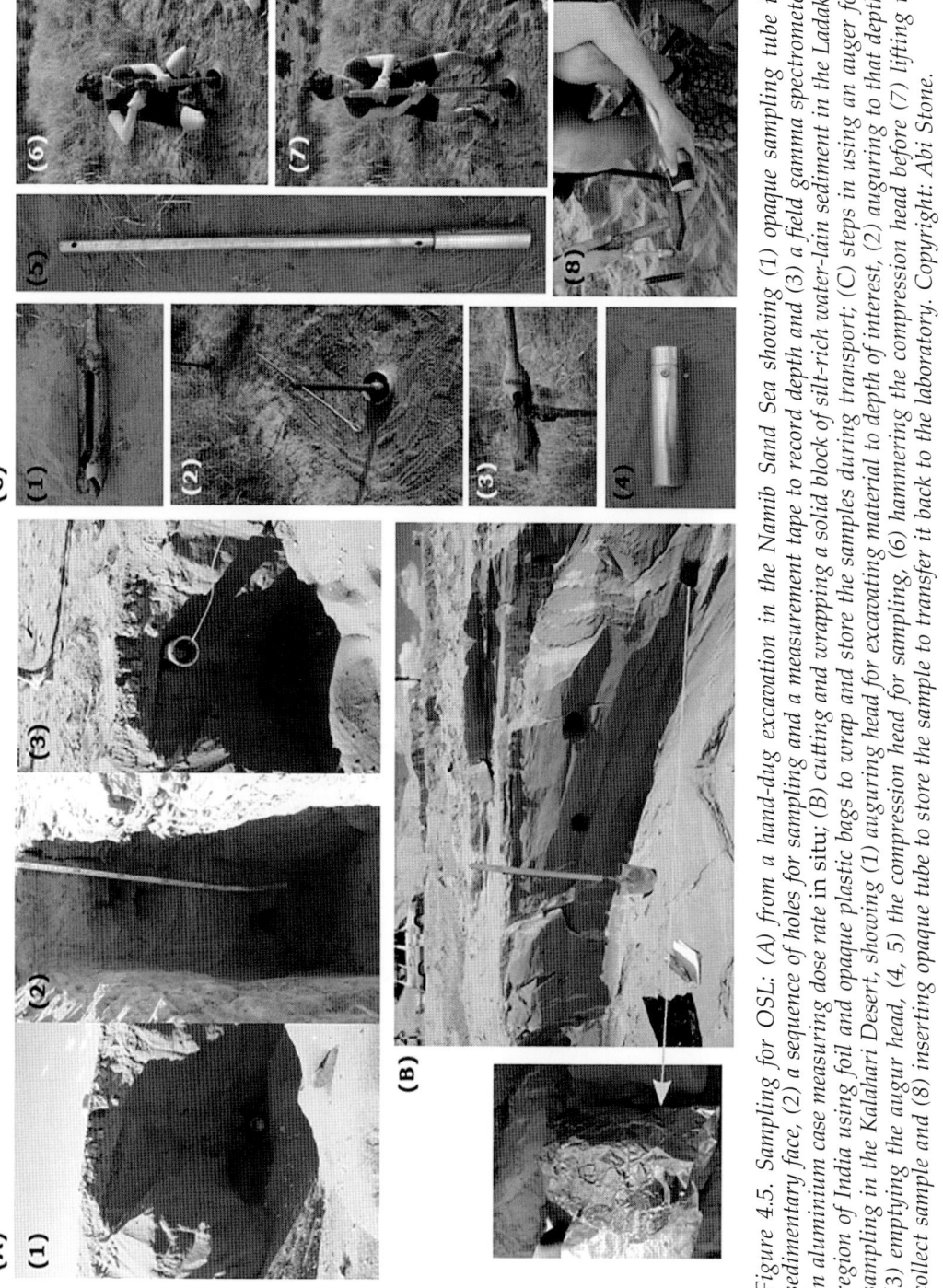

Figure 4.5. Sampling for OSL: (A) from a hand-dug excavation in the Namib Sand Sea showing (1) opaque sampling tube in sedimentary face, (2) a sequence of holes for sampling and a measurement tape to record depth and (3) a field gamma spectrometer in aluminium case measuring dose rate in situ; (B) cutting and wrapping a solid block of silt-rich water-lain sediment in the Ladakh region of India using foil and opaque plastic bags to wrap and store the samples during transport; (C) steps in using an auger for sampling in the Kalahari Desert, showing (1) auguring head for excavating material to depth of interest, (2) auguring to that depth, (3) emptying the augur head, (4, 5) the compression head for sampling, (6) hammering the compression head before (7) lifting to collect sample and (8) inserting opaque tube to store the sample to transfer it back to the laboratory. Copyright: Abi Stone.

the contribution from gamma radiation from this radius around the sample. Ideally, therefore luminescence sample locations should be identified at points with *c.* 300 mm of homogeneous surrounding matrix. It is worth remembering that samples for dating may be recovered from different locations, or different contexts on an archaeological site, which means that a series of gamma radiation measurements may need to be made during any excavation. This has practical implications for sampling, as these measurements need to be collected by a luminescence specialist, and each gamma radiation measurement can take up to an hour. There are other methods for calculating the dose rate including beta counting in the laboratory (Thomsen 2015). However, *in situ* gamma radiation measurements represent best practice.

Sample moisture content is also important in calculating the dose rate. This can be derived from samples (*c.* 20 g) collected in the field. Sediment samples to estimate the water content need to be stored in sealed bags to ensure no moisture is lost. It is also necessary to estimate the average water content of the sample throughout its burial history. This requires an understanding of the site setting, the likelihood of changes in the water table and any potential for saturation of the sample during its burial history. The presence of water within a sample reduces the exposure to radiation and the effect is not trivial, with a 1% increase of water content leading to *c.* 1% increase in calculated sample age (Duller 2015). It is therefore useful to try and identify samples that have not been subject to large changes in wetness over their burial history, for less complicated and more reliable, dose rate calculation. Identifying consistent sample wetness over burial history is challenging but sampling away from context interfaces and avoiding deposits which have obviously been subject to changing hydrological regimes is advisable.

Palaeo-environmental studies

Any sample site in which quartz (or feldspar) is present in the soil from the underlying geology can be suitable for luminescence measurements. There are, however, geological provinces of quartz that have inherently dim luminescence signals (e.g. glacial outwash sediment on the Swiss plateau in front of the Rhone-Aare glacier; Trauerstein *et al.* (2017) and in volcanic terrains in Indonesia, where the *Homo floresiensis* skeletal material has been recovered; Westaway *et al.* 2009).

Other than geological controls on luminescence behaviour, there are two significant considerations in palaeo-environmental luminescence studies. First, there is the possibility that a sample was not fully bleached prior to deposition (which results in an over-estimation of sample Equivalent Dose and therefore age). Secondly, there may be issues estimating a representative water content over the burial history of the sample (which results in an under-estimation of dose rate and an over-estimation in sample age). In some cases therefore, luminescence results for paleoenvironmental reconstruction may be challenging. This includes the application of the technique in fluvial or alluvial contexts and makes the application for sediment in peat sequences extremely challenging (e.g. Preusser and Degering 2007).

The possibility of incomplete bleaching is also more likely in deposits that form in many temperate climates and for sediment transport mechanisms that do not involve aeolian transport. Wind-blown sand deposits, such as dunes, are an ideal setting for OSL and this is not restricted to dryland environments, with excellent applicability at coastal dune sites (see below). However, the nature of soil formation in many parts of the world provides challenges for accurate and precise OSL dating.

In these cases, considerations need to be made of the modes of sediment transport and deposition and the nature of the soil formation processes that have occurred, including the potential for post-depositional mixing or disturbance. The use of single grain analyses (see above) may help to explore the distribution of Equivalent Doses for a deposit and then the application of statistical analysis to obtain a value that best represents the primary burial age of the sample (Roberts and Jacobs 2015).

Questions of the association between the sample and the archaeological event of interest may also be important in palaeo-environmental chronology building. For example, the timing of the infilling of a ditch or negative feature is often an event that archaeologists would wish to estimate. However, the rapidly formed primary deposits in ditches may include material that is not fully bleached (see below). Similar concerns exist with the formation of many archaeological deposits, including those formed by water-lain processes, or in tertiary soils deriving from agricultural practices. These considerations mean that the selection of deposits for OSL measurements for robust palaeo-environmental chronologies will require close cooperation between archaeologists, palaeo-environmental specialists and luminescence specialists.

Historic buildings

Using TL or OSL measurements on ceramic building materials opens up huge potential to contribute new data about the construction of historic buildings beyond documentary sources (Bailiff 2007). TL has been used on brick-built structures since the 1970s (e.g. Cramp *et al.* 1977; Goedicke *et al.* 1981), and measurements can be produced on ceramic building materials with both fine-grained non-quartz crystals and larger quartz inclusions (e.g. Hütt *et al.* 2001). More recent work has developed OSL measurements of ceramic building materials, most successfully on bricks (Fig. 4.6). This technique rests on the full bleaching of quartz grains in the clay matrix prior to firing. Work comparing TL dating of bricks with the OSL dating of quartz grains extracted from bricks has suggested that the OSL measurements may be more robust (Bailiff and Holland 2000). Using ceramic building materials as samples means the OSL measurements can be applied in Europe as far back as the Roman period and many applications of luminescence measurements on ceramic building materials in Europe have been on relatively high status buildings (Bailiff 2007).

For measurements by either TL or OSL, samples need to be of sufficient size to remove the outer, light-exposed layers. For OSL, samples can be taken from standing buildings using a diamond-tipped drill. Sample cores of *c.* 50 mm diameter and 100 mm long are suggested (Bailiff 2007). Alternatively, where building footings or buried structures are encountered, whole bricks could be removed for subsampling at the laboratory. As with palaeo-environmental sampling though, the background environmental radiation and water content of the surrounding material need to be measured and so sampling by a luminescence specialist is essential.

4. Luminescence: Optically Simulated Luminescence and Thermoluminescence 77

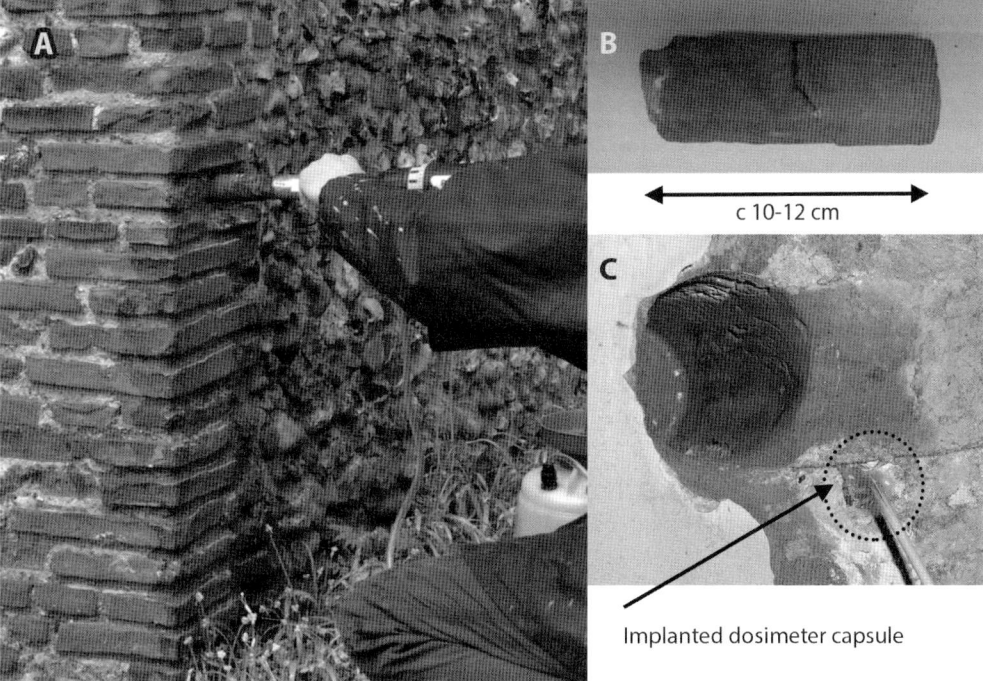

Figure 4.6. Sampling ceramic building material for OSL samples. Here a solid core is recovered from the in situ structure using a drill. The sample is then packed in light-safe material for transport to the laboratory. The resultant void in the structure is used for the in situ radiation measurements. Copyright: Ian Bailiff.

Understanding the relationships between the ceramic building material and the archaeological event of interest is also important when attempting to develop chronologies for structures with complex histories. The chance that bricks or tiles were re-used, or that structures were repaired, is often high. The selection of samples from buildings will therefore require close cooperation between archaeologists, buildings archaeologists and luminescence specialists.

Quality indicators: being a critical consumer

Luminescence age estimates require complex measurements and calculations. There are many areas where samples might have been subject to processes that compromise some of the key principles that underpin the process of age calculation. Challenges in producing luminescence chronologies include incomplete zeroing, changes to the burial environment and so on. For example, variation in the moisture content of a sample location can have important effects on a sample dose rate and therefore resultant age estimates. Increasingly, portable luminescence readers are being used to assess sample suitability in the field (see the Cava Petrilli case study below).

The complexity of these considerations, together with an involved process of luminescence sample pretreatment and measurement in the laboratory, mean that there are a number of variables that need to be considered when working with luminescence results.

Laboratory quality assurance and result reporting

Unlike radiocarbon measurements, there are no international inter-comparisons, in part because measurement of the initial dose cannot be repeated. However, it is possible to send subsets of a sample to different laboratories for comparative measurements. Each laboratory measurement should be reported to the archaeologist who commissioned the measurements with detailed methods and should include all details relevant to the sample and the age calculation. These include:

- sample, deposit and site identifier codes which correlate with the site archive;
- sample latitude, longitude and altitude, and its recovery process (noting orientation of sample on the packaging);
- how the components of dose rate were measured and calculated, including how measurements (and estimates) of sample moisture content across the sample burial history were made;
- the laboratory preparation process for the sample measured for the Equivalent Dose (including which mineral was isolated, in what grain size range);
- how the laboratory Equivalent Dose measurements were made, including the instruments (and radiation source, noting any calibration of the source), whether the measured sample was a single aliquot, or used a single grain method, and details of protocol used, how many replicates were measured;
- shine-down curves showing the luminescence signals used to calculate the Equivalent Dose can be presented, to give a sense of signal-to-noise and the decay rate of luminescence signals;
- dose-response curves to illustrate how close the Equivalent Dose is to luminescence signal saturation;
- details of the statistical approach/models used for calculating a representative Equivalent Dose from the multiple measurements (aliquots or single grains) for each sample, for which the inclusion of graphs of the Equivalent Dose distribution are useful;
- the error terms on the Equivalent Dose and dose rate (including components of the dose rate), and the sample age and error terms.

Luminescence ages are unique to the burial history of specific samples; they are not verifiable by the independent measurement of known age samples in the same way that radiocarbon or dendrochronological measurements are. It is therefore essential that the archaeologist who commissioned the luminescence measurements publishes both the laboratory details listed about them and the archaeological information that is essential for re-use of the data by other researchers.

Case studies

Case study: Base Court, Hampton Court Royal Palace, UK

Situated on the north bank of the River Thames at East Molesey in the south-western outskirts of London, Hampton Court Royal Place (51.403333 N, 0.3375 W (WGS84)) is a complex, multi-phase structure that is most famous for the brick-built Tudor buildings begun by Cardinal Thomas Wolsey in AD 1515. The complex was later acquired by King Henry VIII. Base Court (Fig. 4.7) was the first courtyard in Wolsey's design and also contained lodgings.

Hampton Court also has a longer history with royal associations back to the 14th century when King Edward III visited the site. From the 13th century the site was occupied by the Knights Hospitaller of Saint John. In 1494, the lease was held by Giles Daubney, King Henry VII's Lord Chamberlain. The Palace continued to be a favoured royal residence from the 16th century and was modified accordingly.

Figure 4.7. Excavations at Base Court at Hampton Court Palace. Much of the Palace structure in Base Court was constructed from ceramic building material suitable for OSL measurements. The complex stratigraphy and historical records made this a particularly interesting application of the technique. Copyright: Ben M. Ford, Oxford Archaeology.

Excavation in advance of refurbishment of Base Court in 2009 recovered a series of OSL samples (Bailiff 2009; 2012; Ford *et al.* 2009). The excavations produced 14th and 16th century pottery and structures apparently representing post-16th century water features within the courtyard. The modifications to the courtyard meant that the stratigraphic sequence was very complex with a high degree of truncation.

The scientific dating aimed to unpick this complicated history and provide a chronology for the modifications. In many cases the archaeological events of interest were the construction of different structures within the courtyard. In addition, because good documentary evidence existed for some activity it was possible to compare the archaeological evidence with the historic sources. This posed a challenge to the available precision of the OSL methods.

Sample selection
The brick-built structures offered the ideal opportunity to produce OSL measurements on ceramic building materials, especially because suitable radiocarbon samples with robust associations with archaeological events of interest were relatively rare from the site. Eighteen OSL measurements were produced on ceramic building material recovered from the various phases of modification to the courtyard, along with 14 radiocarbon measurements on samples from deposits associated with these structures. The results from the radiocarbon measurements and the OSL measurements were analysed together in a Bayesian model (full details of the results are given in Ford *et al.* 2009). Here we discuss only the OSL measurements (Fig. 4.8).

Samples of ceramic building materials (brick and tile) were selected for OSL measurements from three types of features. Nine OSL measurements were produced on tile and brick samples from the barn which was later modified to serve as a mason's lodge used in the construction of the Tudor Palace by Wolsey (Dur09OSLQi372-1–3; Dur12OSLQi372-5, -11, -12, -18, and -19). This represented the earliest phase investigated by scientific dating.

In the north-west of the courtyard two workshops were constructed which were also thought to relate to Wolsey's work. The southern structure was dated by Dur09OSLQi 372-6 and Dur09OSLQi 372-7, while the northern structure was dated by Dur12OSLQi372-15, -16, and -17.

Later than both the workshops and the barn/mason's lodge was a series of water features and an associated drainage system. These features related to the remodelling of the courtyard to serve a more ornamental role. Measurements were made on the octagonal structure of one water feature (Dur09OSLQi372-8), and from parts of the soakaway and tank (Dur12OSLQi372-13 and Dur09OSLQi372-9). In another part of the courtyard another soakaway associated with these water features was dated by Dur09OSLQi372-10.

Samples for OSL and radiocarbon measurements were selected in tandem as part of a multi-technique scientific dating programme (Chapter 7). The sample selection strategy made use of the underlying principles of the two techniques. This meant that age estimates could be produced on different types of sample with different associations between the dated events and the archaeological events of interest. OSL measurements could produce age estimates for the formation of the ceramic building materials but with relatively imprecise estimates. The radiocarbon samples, in most cases, had much less robust

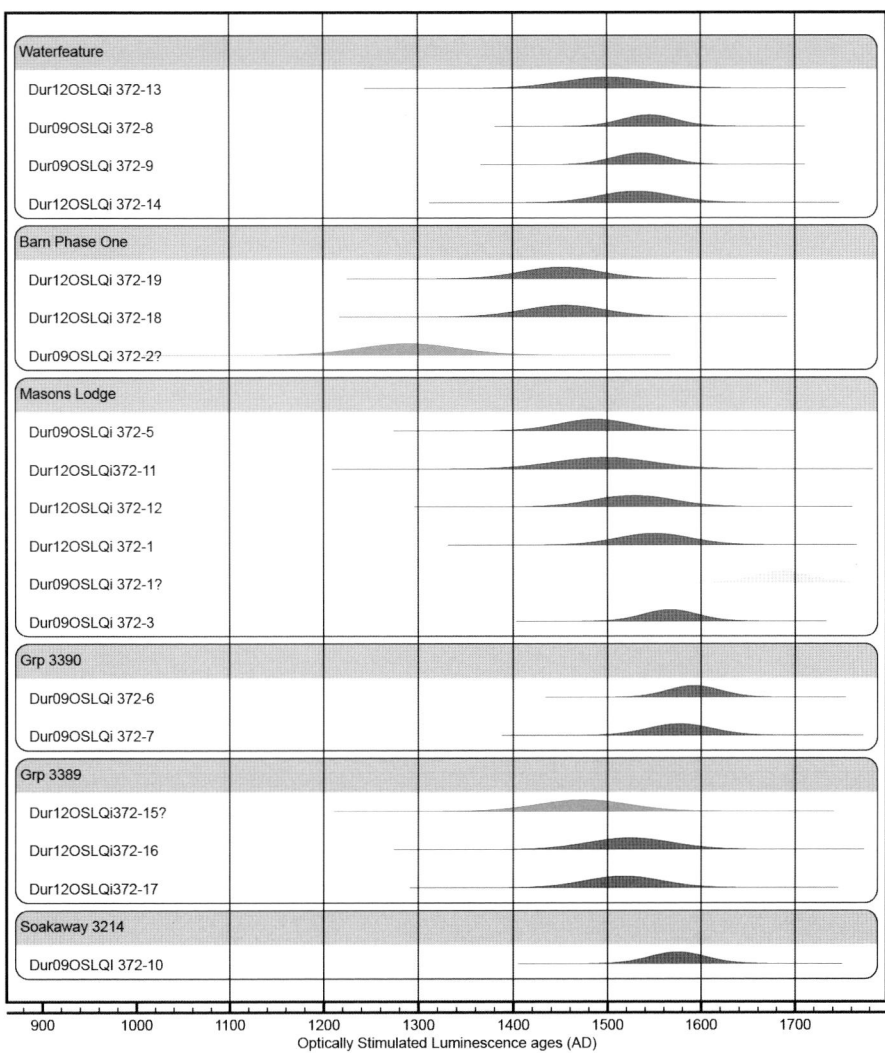

Figure 4.8. OSL results on ceramic building material from work on Base Court at Hampton Court Palace. Full details of the associated radiocarbon measurements and the Bayesian modelling are given in Ford et al. (2009). Results followed by a '?' are in tension with other results from the same structures and may represent reuse of materials, or repair of the structures. Copyright: Seren Griffiths.

associations with the *construction* of the structures but instead provided a chronology for the *use* of the complex; these measurements were also markedly more precise.

Luminescence results

OSL sample preparation and measurement followed the quartz inclusion technique outlined by Aitken (1985; 1998) and developed by Bailiff (2007) for the measurement of brick. Radiation could not be determined on site due to limitations in access but was estimated from samples of the surrounding soil and mortar matrix. Measurement took the form of a single aliquot SAR OSL procedure (Bailiff 2006) similar to that described by Murray and Wintle (2000; 2003), though handled corrections for sensitisation effects and thermal transfer differently because of the nature of the measured samples (Bailiff 2007, 834).

Two results produced a range of age estimates that appeared slightly too early for their position in the stratigraphic sequence. This included an unexpectedly early date range of AD 1185–1400 (Dur09OSLQi372-2; 95% confidence) from the barn/mason's lodge. This result might be associated with early activity on the site that is not well-documented but which may be associated with Knights Hostpitallers use as a grange.

Another result which appears to be earlier than the Wolsey-era structure from which it was recovered (Dur09OSLQi372-15) is in keeping with historically documented activity at the site; this sample may represent re-use of materials from one of these earlier phases of activity. Dur09OSLQi372-1, from the barn/mason's lodge appears to be too young in comparison with the rest of the results from this structure. This is more difficult to interpret; perhaps this sample represented a later repair to the fabric of this building.

Taken together, the other results are consistent with the recorded history of activity at the site and the archaeological phasing. The first phase of the barn was most probably constructed from bricks manufactured in the first half of the 15th century. The mason's lodge was probably constructed from bricks manufactured in the second half of 15th century and the water feature was probably constructed from bricks manufactured in the late 15th or, most probably, in the first half of the 16th century. The OSL results demonstrate a complicated history of construction and modification, including results that indicate work that was not historically documented (Ford *et al.* 2009).

Discussion of the scientific dating considerations
Henry VIII commissioned brick manufacture for specific projects. This has been documented, for example, at the now demolished Nonsuch Palace, on the southern outskirts of London, in 1541 (Moore 2001). Historical sources attest to a John Lawrence who, in 1529–30, supplied bricks to Hampton Court Palace, initially from his kiln at Charing Cross (Moore 2001, 223). However, given the presence of medieval structures at Hampton Court, the scientific dating analysis needed to consider the prospect of re-used ceramic building material.

As with dendrochronological measurements (Chapter 3), building materials may often be stored prior to incorporation in a structure or recovered from one structure and subsequently re-used in another (e.g. Bailiff *et al.* 2010). While stockpiling of bricks prior to construction might only give an interval of several years (which in itself may be critically important for some scientific dating research aims), the *re-use* of ceramic building materials could introduce a really sizeable age difference. Re-use of building materials, for example from Roman to medieval structures, is widely known from across Europe, while medieval bricks were re-used in other structures including in the Tudor period (e.g. Simpson 1960). OSL dating indeed has been the means to identify re-used brick, for example as at Eastbury Manor, Barking (Bailiff *et al.* 2010, 188; 166) when it otherwise might not be easy to identify archaeologically (Gurling 2009, 288).

Case study conclusions

This case study has demonstrated the importance of producing age estimates for a range of samples especially for complex **multi-phase** or **urban** sites. Selecting scientific dating methods based on the association between the dated event and the archaeological event of interest is very important. Using **multi-technique** scientific dating methods, combined with Bayesian statistical modelling (Chapter 8) can create scientific dating programmes that most effectively and eloquently address research aims.

Case study: West Cliffe, St Margaret's, Kent, UK

West Cliffe (51.191310 N, 1.396882 E (WGS84)) is one of a series of associated Palaeolithic sites located on uplands in the south of Britain. The site was surveyed by fieldwalking (Halliwell and Parfitt 1993; Parfitt and Halliwell 1996; Scott-Jackson 2000) and stone tools, including Acheulean handaxes, were recovered. The majority of the assemblage appears on typological grounds to date to the Lower Palaeolithic or the period pre-dating *c.* 300,000 years ago. The finds were located in and around a series of solution holes which were formed where water had eroded the Chalk geology.

The underlying geology means that natural, unmodified flint nodules feature in the overlying soils. These would have represented an important resource for pre-modern human species, which at this time could have included *Homo heidelbergensis* or *H. neanderthalenis*. The solution holes may have held water and formed a pond, potentially explaining the presence of homanins in the vicinity of the feature.

There were two classes of deposit infilling the solution holes: clay-with-flints (a deposit forming at the interface with chalk) and brickearth (a well-sorted sediment with fine-grained silt inclusions), which formed as a wind-blown deposit (or loess). The composition of brickearth means it has potential for OSL dating. Excavation revealed that the brickearth had formed interleaved deposits in some of the solution holes, so OSL measurements on the brickearth deposits could provide *termini post quos* and *termini ante quos* for the formations of deposits containing artefacts.

Sample selection
OSL samples were recovered from three deposits of silty-clay. Two samples came from deposits that clearly underlay the artefact-rich layer and one came from a deposit that clearly overlay the artefact-rich layer (Fig. 4.9).

Luminescence results
Initially SAR measurements were made. The results from these measurements suggested that the parent sediments for these samples might have been partially bleached or the OSL signal not fully zeroed. An alternative scenario could be that, within each of the deposits, material accumulated in more than one phase and that the deposit formation sequence was more complicated than the available stratigraphic evidence. To investigate this further, a series of additional experimental measurements was undertaken. These measurements aimed to better understand the Equivalent Dose with measurements made on very small aliquots of fewer than 100 grains (Table 4.2). The dosimeters were

Figure 4.9. Sample locations for OSL measurements from West Cliffe. The section has been recorded prior to sampling. The sand-rich deposits, making the deposits suitable for OSL measurements, are clearly visible in the section. Copyright: Mark White.

coarse quartz grains which were extracted from the samples and pretreated (see Bailiff *et al.* 2013 for full details).

Even using these very small numbers of grains, the estimates for the Equivalent Dose had a wide range of values. For example, some grains appeared infinitely old (with electron traps that were saturated). As a result, some of the measurements on individual grains within a sample were excluded from the age estimates (Bailiff *et al.* 2013). Following this exploration of the deposit formation, the resultant measurements were used to produce age estimates for the different deposits. The material overlying the artefacts produced OSL age estimates indicating the deposit formed between 87±9 kya and 75±9 kya. The age measurements on the latest deposit underlying the artefacts suggested that this formed in 136±15 kya.

Discussion of the scientific dating considerations
These age estimates are significantly younger than archaeological understandings of the currency of lower Palaeolithic technology in Britain. Several possibilities exist that could help explain these unexpectedly late age estimates. First, the age estimates could be inaccurate. This seems unlikely in this case, the use of very small aliquots provided

Table 4.2: The D_e values for very small aliquots from West Cliffe (reproduced from Bailiff et al. 2013).

Sample	Single aliquot			Dose recovery				Model	Equivalent dose, burial single grain			
	D_e CDM (Gy)	OD (%)	n	D_a (Gy)	De CDM (Gy)	OD (%)	n		OD (%)	n	D_e k1 (Gy)	D_e k2 (Gy)
316-1	355±15	13	10	205	233±8	13	19	CDM	36	18	290±20[55±13%]	560±40[45±13%]
				408	380±13	0	4	FMM	4[1]			
				612	450±24	9	4					
316-2	283±15	26	24	213	218±10	17	19	CDM	17[1]	26	234±12	
316-3	215±17	21	8	208	219±9	12	10	CDM	22	20	210±17[74±26%]	295[26±26%]
								FMM	7[1]			

The values observed indicate that the sediments may have been partially bleached or perhaps buried in more than one phase, with implications for the site chronology. OD: overdispersion, CDM: central dose model, FMM: finite mixtures model, n: number of determinations. K1 and K2 represent different Equivalent Dose (De) values obtained from the samples as part of the analysis. The OD value has been modified in the analysis to account for issues identified in the analysis. For further details of the age calculation see Bailiff et al. (2013).

a means to screen the behaviour of individual grains so that only those with clearly categorised sensitivity and behaviour during laboratory measurements were included in the age estimates. In addition, the two age estimates for deposits that post-date the artefact-rich layer are comparable.

The second potential explanation could be that archaeologists do not have a full picture of the timing of the latest use of lower Palaeolithic artefacts. Generally in archaeology, it is easier to push the chronologies of material culture and sites back *earlier* than it is to provide estimates for the latest use of an artefact or site type.

The third explanation could be that the association between the artefacts and the samples might not be robust. This could be explained by the anthropogenic material being redeposited or reworked within the solution hole. In this case, the artefacts could have been already old when they were deposited in the solution hole. The OSL chronology could therefore provide age ranges for the *redeposition* of these artefacts, not the initial manufacture or use of these artefacts.

Case study conclusions

This case study demonstrates the importance of robust **quality control** methods in all forms of scientific dating. In this case, it was imperative to understand any differences in the results using **small aliquot** measurements. This is especially important when a sequence may have been subject to **complex deposit formation** processes. In such cases we need to think critically about how well we understand any **association** between the dated event and the archaeological event of interest.

Case study: palaeo-environmental modelling, Herm, Channel Islands, UK

Herm has a remarkable concentration of Neolithic monuments located on its very small land mass. At the north of the island, at least 16 Neolithic monuments exist around The Common, a lowland plain (Fig. 4.10). The northern coast of The Common is edged by sand dunes (49.480804 N, 2.452860 W (WGS84)), which cover some of the monuments. Research here (Bailiff *et al.* 2014) aimed to provide evidence for periods of dune development and to estimate the date of burial of the old land-surface. Archaeological trenching was accompanied by an auger survey (Scarre and French 2013) which demonstrated that one of the tombs was constructed on a ridge and that the plain had been subject to periods of marine inundation followed by peat formation. Palaeo-environmental analysis identified evidence for manuring and agricultural activity which was associated with pottery and lithics dated to the regional early Neolithic (*c.* 4000 BC).

Sample selection
OSL samples were selected from a series of eight trenches located in proximity to some of the monuments (Fig. 4.10). Archaeological trenching had to be limited in size because of the sensitivity of the environment. Samples were taken from deposits that were identified as dune sand, wind-blown sand or palaeosol. Most of the samples were recovered from the cleaned and recorded sections by driving opaque plastic tubes of *c.* 40 mm diameter into the section to a depth of *c.* 200 mm. The samples were then sealed. Where compaction meant this process was not viable, blocks were cut from the section and stored in opaque packaging (Bailiff *et al.* 2014, 893). At least two OSL samples were taken from each sequence. The sand-rich deposits and the wind-lain formation processes meant that these sequences had excellent potential for OSL measurements.

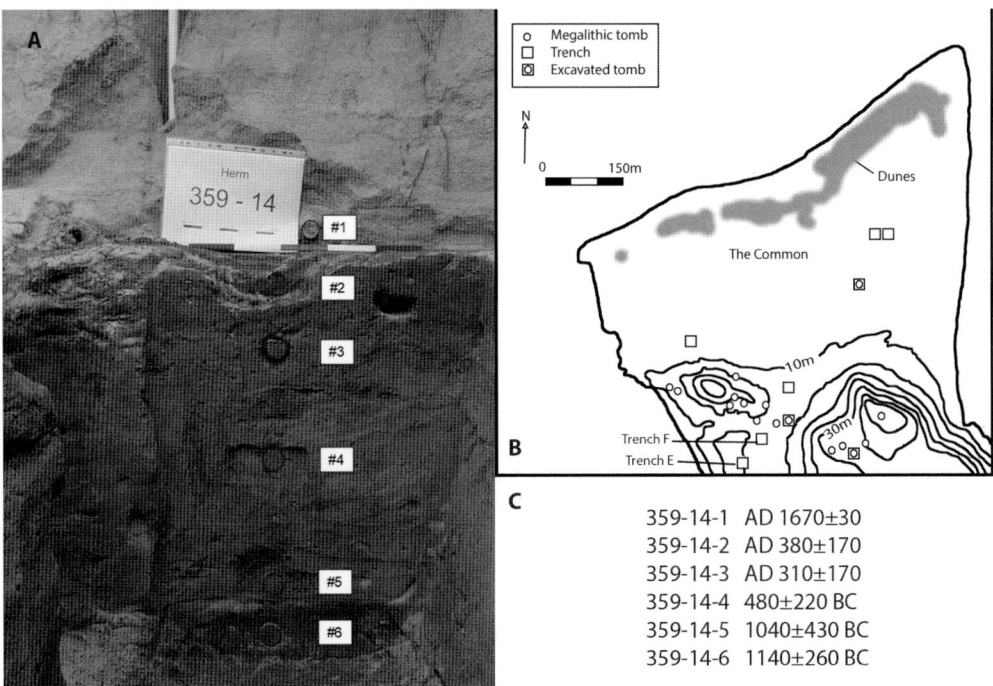

Figure 4.10. (A) In situ OSL sampling tubes from one of the sequence of results 359-14 produced from Herm by Bailiff et al. (2014); (B) location map for the monuments and trenches; (C) the resultant age estimates are shown Copyright: Ian Bailiff and Seren Griffiths.

The samples were processed in the laboratory to extract coarse (200–355 μm) quartz grains. The Equivalent Dose estimate was produced using a SAR protocol (Murray and Wintle 2000; 2003) and with added sensitivity analyses to determine the impact of individual grains on the signal and to ensure consistency of response in grains from a given sample (Bailiff *et al.* 2014, 895). The moisture content required to calculate the dose rate was measured for the individual samples and the background radiation was measured for individual soil samples. Full details of the measurements and modelling are given in Bailiff *et al.* (2014).

Luminescence results
Twenty-six OSL age estimates were produced from the trenches exploring the landscape development. The age estimates produced ranged from the middle 5th millennium BC to the 17th century AD. Distinct phases of wind-lain sand deposits were identified and dune formation events were defined at different times in different trenches. This included dune formation in the near two of the tombs (1210±200 BC near one tomb and 290±170 BC near another site; Bailiff *et al.* 2014, 899). There were also periods of high levels of aeolian sand transportation in the historic period between the 13th and 17th centuries AD.

Discussion of the scientific dating considerations
The deposits available for OSL samples on Herm represent very good sample types because of their aeolian deposition and high quartz content. There are also direct stratigraphic relationships between these deposits and archaeological sites. Results from samples from two of the trenches (Trench E and F) produced date estimates for palaeosol formation in the middle 5th millennium BC which may provide a *terminus post quem* for the construction of some of the Neolithic monuments. The other results show a wide chronological range for wind-lain deposits forming on the island. The evidence for medieval dune formation could be associated with storms creating wind-lain sand deposits which are historically documented (Bailiff *et al.* 2014, 902). This research project produced a wealth of data and a complex picture of palaeo-environmental change over time (Chapter 6).

Case study conclusions
This case study highlights the importance of good OSL samples for palaeo-environmental reconstruction. This project investigated wind-lain, quartz-rich deposits that ensured **full bleaching**. The trenches resulted in a wide-ranging sample of landscape history. Sampling from **open faces** across this area compensated for the limited area of individual trenches. Fewer trenches would have resulted in a more confused, more chronologically and geographically constrained narrative. The range of OSL results demonstrates the **complexity** of landscape change here.

Case study: Cava Petrilli, Gargo peninsula, south-east Italy

Neolithic enclosures on the Tavolier Plain of the Gargano Promontory in south-east Italy were identified via aerial photography in the 1940s during the Second World War and they are interpreted as settlements (Bradford 1949; Whittle 1996; Whitehouse 2014). The sedimentary deposits on this plain include Quaternary alluvial and terrace deposits, overlying Middle Pliocene to Lower Pleistocene shallow water marine deposits and hemipelagic deposits (De Santis *et al.* 2014).

Cava Petrilli (41034.6 N, 15019.1 E (WGS84)) is one of hundreds of sites with sections of ditch enclosures (Jones 1987). Sanderson and Murphy (2010) produced OSL measurements on two features from part of the same main ditch enclosure: Feature 1 and Feature 2. The sediment within the lower fill of the main enclosure ditch had a slightly darker colour, associated with organic content, and was thought to indicate agronomic land-use, while the upper fill was drier with a stony base and thought to represent a post-abandonment fill (Fig. 4.11).

Sample selection
In this case, field-assessment of deposits in terms of their suitability for OSL measurement was undertaken using a portable luminescence reader (port-OSL). Port-OSL is a useful field tool which can assess relative age and help identify stratigraphic inconsistencies within sedimentary profiles (e.g. Sanderson and Murphy 2010; Stone *et al.* 2015; Gray *et al.* 2018). These measurements can be 'calibrated' to provide low-fidelity age estimate (Stone *et al.* 2019). Full luminescence measurements and radiocarbon results were also produced from features (Sanderson and Murphy 2010; Fig. 4.11).

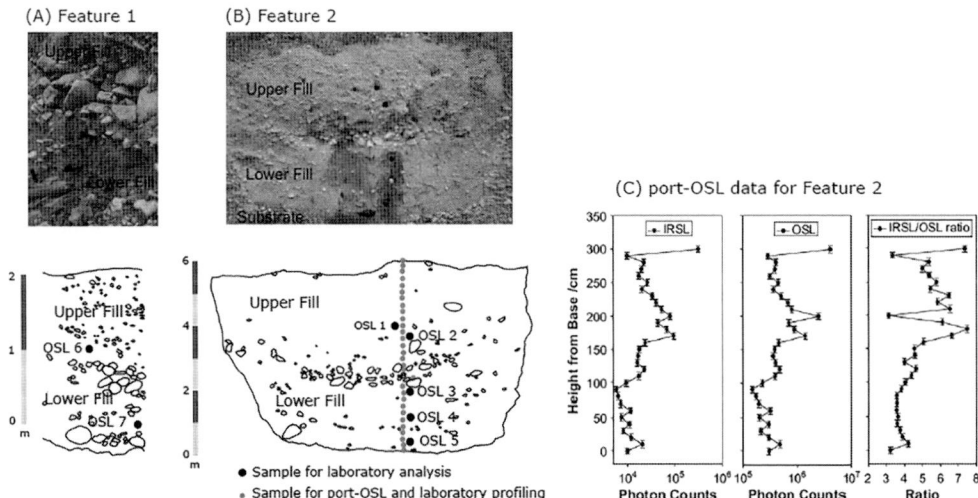

Figure 4.11. (A, B) Photos and schematics of two Cava Petrilli ditch features showing the position of sampling for port-OSL profiling and for full laboratory measurements; (C) port-OSL data for Feature 2, showing IRSL (red diode stimulated) and OSL (blue diode stimulated) signal size and the ratio of the two signals dating. The results suggested the upper deposits redeposited and/or insufficiently bleached and might therefore not produced accurate OSL age estimates for the deposit formation. Modified from Sanderson and Murphy (2010).

Luminescence results

The luminescence results are shown together with two radiocarbon results in Table 4.3. The radiocarbon measurements were produced on cattle bone samples from the lower and upper ditch fills of Feature 2. These results do not have a functional association with the infilling of the feature but they were intended to compare distinctly different dated events from the ditch fill chronology and to help evaluate if the Port-OSL could be usefully used in the field to screen potential OSL samples.

Port-OSL measurements made during excavation demonstrated that the upper fill of Feature 2 had a larger luminescence signal than the lower fill, suggesting that the upper deposit included material that was older in terms of the OSL signal (Sanderson and Murphy 2010). This suggested that the upper fill contained redeposited material, or material that had not been completely bleached. In addition, the ratio of IRSL (infrared stimulated) to OSL (blue stimulated) port-OSL signals was higher in the upper fill than the lower fill, which suggests a different sediment composition (particularly the amounts of quartz compared to feldspar). These measurements suggested that the lower fills would provide luminescence measurements where the association between the dated event and the archaeological event of interest were better understood.

Eight full OSL measurements were produced, using a SAR protocol to establish the Equivalent Doses (Sanderson and Murphy 2010, 304). The age estimates range from 5790±530 BC to 6940±570 BC for the lower fill, while the OSL measurements for the upper fill ranged from 6980±600 BC to 10,620±960 BC (Table 4.3; Fig. 5.12).

Table 4.3: Quartz SAR measurements from samples from Cava Petrilli (Sanderson and Murphy 2010).

Field sample no.	SUTL no	Sample context	Height above basal datum (cm)	Date (BC)
		Feature 2		
OSL 1	2139	Upper fill	197	6980±600
OSL 2	2140	Also produced radiocarbon measurement SUERC-4535 6180±35 BP	168	7970±620
OSL 3	2141	Lower fill	89	5790±780
OSL 4	2142	Also produced radiocarbon measurement SUERC-4536 6415±35 BP	55	6320±410
OSL 5	2143		14	5830±720
		Feature 1		
OSL 6	2144	Upper fill	117	1062±960
OSL 7	2145	Lower fill	10	5790±530
OSL 8	2146		10	6490±570

The results are consistent with the interpretation that the upper deposits had been redeposited and/or not fully bleached, an assessment first identified in the field measurements using the portable reader.

Discussion of the scientific dating considerations

In Figure 4.12, we have combined the results from the radiocarbon and full OSL measurements from the lower and upper deposits in Feature 2 (Chapter 8). We can see the range of age estimates produced using OSL and radiocarbon for the upper fill; these suggest that material has been redeposited. In contrast, the lower fill produced much more consistent results, suggesting that these measurements may provide accurate age estimates for the timing of the deposit formation. This suggests that the Port-OSL screening was effective at differentiating more reliable samples in the field.

The ways in which ditch fills form means that there can be issues producing accurate OSL age estimates for the timing of infilling. There is the chance that insufficiently bleached material may erode immediately back into negative features. Because mineral grains cannot be identified as having a functional association with the deposits from which they were recovered it can be challenging to identify which age estimates may be the most appropriate for the formation of a deposit overall. Port-OSL measurements used in this case study appear to provide a means for screen potential OSL samples.

Together, the field port-OSL measurements, the full laboratory OSL analysis and the radiocarbon measurements suggest that only the lower fill represent accurate OSL age estimates. The upper fill appears to be redeposited material that was not fully zeroed.

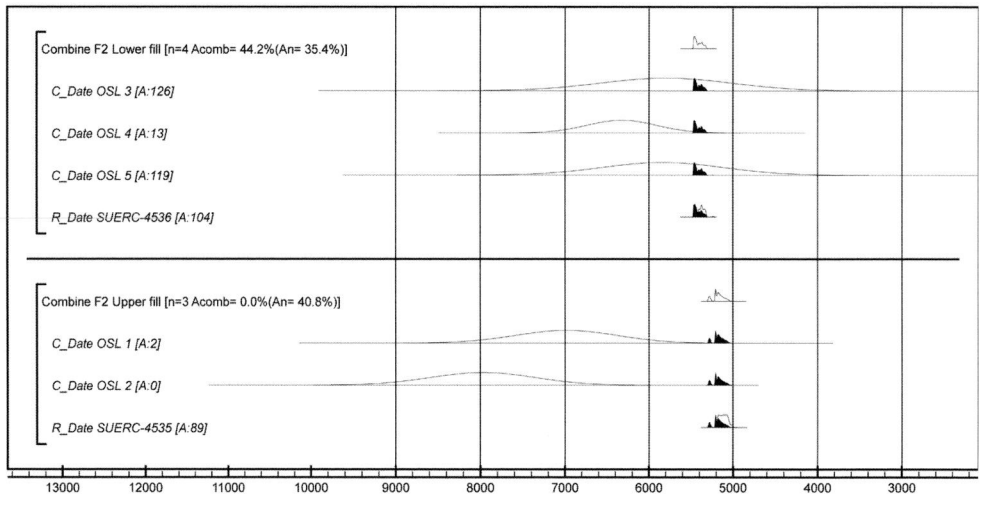

Figure 4.12. At Cava Petrilli field-assessment of deposits' suitability in Feature 2 suggested the upper deposits may have been redeposited and/or insufficiently bleached. The radiocarbon results and laboratory OSL measurements support the field-profiling results from the port-OSL. This approach can provide an invaluable approach to sample selection in the field. Combining results from different techniques is discussed in Chapter 8.

Case study conclusions
This case study emphasises the importance of considering **deposit formation** processes using a range of approaches. Negative features may contain grains that had not been zeroed before deposition. It also highlights the value of using a **port-OSL** reader during fieldwork to guide the laboratory OSL dating strategy. Having identified the upper fill as less appropriate for dating, a greater number of samples from the lower fill could be chosen to be the focus of dating. This is particularly important in making the most effective use of resources.

Chapter conclusions

Luminescence dating allows archaeologists to explore the date of the **deposition** of a **sedimentary deposit** (its last exposure to daylight). This can be very important in terms of thinking about how a site has developed over time. TL is also extremely useful for archaeologists, for example by facilitating the direct dating of the point in time when a sample is heat affected. Luminescence measurements on ceramic building materials provide a useful means to re-evaluate **historic buildings**.

The uptake of luminescence dating within archaeology has been uneven across different time slices, and settings, within archaeological research. There is longstanding and widespread application for time frames that exceed ~50 ka (the upper limit of radiocarbon), and particularly in dryland settings with limited preservation of organic carbon (outside the scope of this chapter). Current exciting developments within rock surface dating is pushing the frontiers of luminescence into the direct dating of surface lithics (see Gliganic *et al.* 2021). Luminescence techniques offer archaeologists a unique ability to provide age estimates for a **sample type** that do not contain organic, or inorganic, carbon.

Bibliography

Aitken, M. 1985. *Thermoluminescence Dating*. London: Academic Press
Aitken, M. 1990. *Science-based Dating in Archaeology*. London: Longman
Aitken, M. 1998. *An Introduction to Optical Dating*. Oxford: Oxford University Press
Bailiff, I. 2006. Development of single grain OSL dating of ceramic materials: spatially resolved measurement of absorbed dose. *Radiation Measurements* 41, 744–9
Bailiff, I. 2007. Methodological developments in the luminescence dating of brick from English late-medieval and post-medieval buildings. *Archaeometry* 49, 827–51
Bailiff, I. 2009. Luminescence dating of bricks from Hampton Court Palace. Durham: unpublished report, Luminescence Dating Laboratory, Department of Archaeology, University of Durham
Bailiff, I. 2012. Luminescence dating of bricks from Hampton Court Palace. Durham: Unpublished report, Luminescence Dating Laboratory, Department of Archaeology, University of Durham
Bailiff, I. 2019. Applications in archaeological contexts. In M. Bateman (ed.), *Handbook of Luminescence Dating*, 321–49. Dunbeath: Whittles
Bailiff, I. and Holland, N. 2000. Dating bricks of the last two millennium from Newcastle upon Tyne: a preliminary study. *Radiation Measurements* 41, 744–9

Bailiff, I., Scarre, C. and French, C. 2014. Application of luminescence dating and geomorphological analysis to the study of landscape evolution, settlement and climate change on the Channel Island of Herm. *Journal of Archaeological Science* 41, 890–903

Bailiff, I., Lewis, S., Drinkall, H. and White, M. 2013. Luminescence dating of sediments from a Palaeolithic site associated with a solution feature on the North Downs of Kent, UK. *Quaternary Geochronology* 18, 135–48

Bailiff, I., Blain, S., Graves, C., Gurling, T. and Semple, S. 2010. Uses and recycling of brick in medieval and Tudor English buildings: insights from the application of luminescence dating and new avenues for further research. *Archaeological Journal* 167, 165–96

Bøtter-Jensen, L., Andersen, C., Duller, G. and Murray, A. 2003. Developments in radiation, stimulation and observation facilities in luminescence measurements. *Radiation Measurements* 37, 535–41

Bradford, J. 1949. 'Buried Landscapes' in southern Italy. *Antiquity* 23, 58–72

Cano, N., Munita, C., Watanabe, S., Barbosa, R., Chubaci, J., Tatumi, S. and Neves, E. 2014. OSL and EPR dating of pottery from the archaeological sites in Amazon Valley Brazil. *Quaternary International* 352, 176–80

Chithambo, M., Preusser, F., Ramseyer, K. and Ogundare, F. 2007. Time-resolved luminescence of low sensitivity quartz from crystalline rocks. *Radiation Measurements* 42 (2), 205–12

Cramp, R., Everson, P. and Hall, D. 1977. Excavations at Brixworth, 1971 and 1972. *Journal of British Archaeological Association* 130, 55–132

De Santis, V., Massimo, C. and Luigi, P. 2014. The marine and alluvial terraces of Tavoliere di Puglia plain (southern Italy). *Journal of Maps* 10(1), 114–25

Duller, G. 2003. Distinguishing quartz and feldspar in single grain luminescence measurements. *Radiation Measurements* 37, 161–5

Duller, G. 2015. Luminescence dating. In J. Rink and J. Thompson (eds), *Encyclopaedia of Scientific Dating Methods*, 390–404. Dordrecht: Encyclopaedia of Earth Sciences Series

Duller, G. and Wintle, A. 2012. A review of the thermally transferred optically stimulated luminescence signal from quartz for dating sediments. *Quaternary Geochronology* 7, 6–20

Durcan, J., King, G. and Duller, G. 2015. DRAC: dose rate and age calculator for trapped charge dating. *Quaternary Geochronology* 28, 54–61

Ford, B., Gruszczynski, J. and Sykes, D. 2009. The Resurfacing Project, Base Court, Hampton Court. An Archaeological Post-Excavation Assessment Report. Oxford: unpublished report, Oxford Archaeology

Gliganic, L., Meyer, M., May J-H., Aldenderfer, M. and Tropper, P. 2021. Direct dating of lithic surface artifacts using lumienscence. *Science Advances* 7(23) DOI: 10.1126/sciadv.abb3424

Goedicke, C., Slusallek, K. and Kubelik, M. 1981. Thermoluminescence dating in architectural history: Venetian villas. *Journal of the Society of Architectural Historians* 40(3), 203–17

Gray, H., Mahan, S., Springer, K. and Pigati, J. (2018). Examining the relationship between portable luminescence reader measurements and depositional ages of paleowetland sediments, Las Vegas Valley, Nevada. *Quaternary Geochronology* 48, 80–90

Gurling, T. 2009. Luminescence dating of medieval and early modern brickwork. Unpublished doctoral thesis, Durham University.

Halliwell, G. and Parfitt, K. 1993. Non-river gravel lower and middle palaeolithic discoveries in east Kent. *Kent Archaeological Review* 114, 80–9

Huntley, D. and Lamothe, M. 2001. Ubiquity of anomalous fading in K-feldspars and the measurement and correction for it in optical dating. *Canadian Journal of Earth Sciences* 38(7), 1093–106 [https://doi.org/10.1139/e01-013]

Hütt, G. Göksu, H., Jaek, I. and Hiekkanen, M. 2001. Luminescence dating of Somero sacristy, SW Finland using the 210° peak in quartz. *Quaternary Science Reviews* 20, 773–7

Jain, M. and Akærgaard, C. 2011. Towards a non-fading signal in feldspar: insight into charge transport and tunnelling from time-resolved optically stimulated luminescence. *Radiation Measurements* 46, 292–309

Jones, G. 1987. *Neolithic Settlement in the Tavoliere*, Volume I. London: Society of Antiquaries Research Report 44

Li, B. and Li, S-H. 2011. Luminescence dating of K-felds par from sediment: a protocol without anomalous fading correction. *Quaternary Geochronology* 6, 468–79

Moore, N. 2001. Brick. In J. Blair and N. Ramsey (eds), *British Medieval Industries*, 211–36. London: Hambledon Press

Murray, A. and Roberts, R. 1998. Measurement of the equivalent dose in quartz using a regenerative-dose single-aliquot protocol. *Radiation Measurements* 29, 503–15

Murray, A. and Wintle, A. 2000. Luminescence dating of quartz using an improved single-aliquot regenerative-dose protocol *Radiation Measurements* 32, 57–73

Murray, A. and Wintle, A. 2003. The single aliquot regenerative dose protocol: potential for improvements in reliability. *Radiation Measurements* 37, 377–81

Parfitt, K. and Halliwell, G. 1996. More palaeolithic discoveries in East Kent. *Kent Archaeological Review* 123, 58–64

Prescott, J. and Hutton, J. 1988. Cosmic ray and gamma ray dosimetry for TL and ESR. *Nuclear Tracks and Radiation Measurements* 14, 223–7

Prescott, J. and Hutton, J. 1994. Cosmic ray contributions to dose rates for luminescence and ESR dating: large depths and long-term time variations. *Radiation Measurements* 23(2/3), 497–500

Preusser, F. and Degering, D. 2007. Luminescence dating of the Niederweningen mammoth site, Switzerland. *Quaternary International* 164–5, 106–12

Reimann, R., Thomsen, K., Jain, M., Murray, A. and Frechen, M. 2012. Single-grain dating of young sediments using the pIRIR signal from feldspar. *Quaternary Geochronology* 11, 28–41

Richter, D. 2015. Luminescence, flints and stones. In J. Rink and J. Thompson (eds), *Encyclopaedia of Scientific Dating Methods*, 460–5. Dordrecht: Encyclopaedia of Earth Sciences Series

Roberts, R. and Jacobs, Z. 2015. Luminescence dating, single-grain dose distribution. In J. Rink and J. Thompson (eds) *Encyclopaedia of Scientific Dating Methods*, 435–40. Dordrecht: Encyclopaedia of Earth Sciences Series

Sanderson, D. and Murphy, S. 2010. Using simple portable OSL measurements and laboratory characterisation to help understand complex and heterogeneous sediment sequences for luminescence dating. *Quaternary Geochronology* 5, 299–305

Scarre, C. and French, C. 2013. The palaeogeography and Neolithic archaeology of Herm. *Journal of Field Archaeology* 38, 1–15

Scott-Jackson, J. 2000. *Lower and Middle Palaeolithic Artefacts from Deposits Mapped as Clay-with-flints: a new synthesis with significant implications for the earliest occupation of Britain*. Oxford: Oxbow Books

Simpson, T. 1960. *The Building Accounts of Tattershall Castle 1434–1472*. Hereford: Lincoln Record Society

Spooner, N. 1994. The anomalous fading of infrared-stimulated luminescence from feldspars. *Radiation Measurements* 23(2–3), 625–32

Stone, A. and Fenn, K. 2020. Dating aeolian deposits. In J. Shroder, N. Lancaster, D. Sherman and A. Baas (eds), *Treatise on Geomorphology* (2nd edn), 320–65. San Diego, CA: Academic Press [https://doi.org/10.1016/B978-0-12-818234-5.00016-X]

Stone, A., Bateman, M. and Thomas, D. 2015. Rapid age assessment in the Namib Sand Sea using a portable luminescence reader. *Quaternary Geochronology* 30(B), 134–40

Stone, A., Bateman, M., Burrough, S., Garzanti, E., Limonta, M., Radeff, G. and Telfer, M. 2019. Using a portable luminescence reader for rapid age assessment of aeolian sediments for reconstructing dunefield landscape evolution in southern Africa. *Quaternary Geochronology* 49, 57–64

Thomsen, K. 2015. Luminescence dating, instrumentation. In J. Rink and J. Thompson (eds) *Encyclopaedia of Scientific Dating Methods*, 422–5. Dordrecht: Encyclopaedia of Earth Sciences Series

Thomsen, K., Murray, A., Jain, M. and Bøtter-Jensen, L. 2008. Laboratory fading rates of various luminescence signals from feldspar-rich sediment extracts. *Radiation Measurements* 43, 1474–86

Thomsen, K., Murray, A., Jain, M. and Buylaert, J.-P. 2012. Re 'Luminescence dating of K-feldspar from sediments: a protocol without anomalous fading correction' by Bo Li and Sheng-Hua Li. *Quaternary Geochronology* 8, 46–8

Trauerstein, M., Lowick, S., Preusser, F. and Veit, H. 2017. Testing the suitability of dim sedimentary quartz from northern Switzerland for OSL burial dose estimation. *Geochronometria* 44, 66–76 [https://doi.org/10.1515/geochr-2015-0058]

Wang, X. and Miao, X. 2006. Weathering history indicated by the luminescence emissions in Chinese loess and palaeosol. *Quaternary Science Reviews* 25, 1719–26

Westaway, K., Roberts, R., Sutikna, T., Morwood, M., Drysdale, R., Zhao, J. and Chiva, A. 2009. The evolving landscape and climate of western Flores: an environmental content for the archaeological site of Ling Bua. *Journal of Human Evolution* 57, 450–64

Whitehouse, R. 2014. The chronology of the Neolithic ditched settlements of the Tavoliere and the Ofanoto Valley. *Accordia Research Papers* 13, 57–77

Whittle, A. 1996. *Europe in the Neolithic: the creation of new worlds*. Cambridge: Cambridge University Press

Wintle, A. and Murray, A. 2006. A review of quartz optically stimulated luminescence characteristics and their relevance in single-aliquot regeneration dating protocols. *Radiation Measurements* 41(4), 369–91

Wood, R., Jacobs, Z., Vannieuwenhuyse, D., Balne, J., O'Connor, S. and Whitau, R. 2016. Towards and accurate and precise chronology for the colonisation of Australia: the example of Riwi, Kimberly, Western Australia. *PloS One.* 11(9), e0160123 [https://doi.org/10.1371/journal.pone.0160123]

5. Archaeomagnetic dating

Sam Harris and Seren Griffiths

Archaeomagnetic dating depends on a very different series of underlying principles than those other scientific dating techniques discussed in this volume. Rather than measuring a signal that changes proportionally to the passage of time, as with the radiocarbon method or for luminescence measurements, archaeomagnetic dating uses a signal that should not change once it is preserved in a sample.

The Earth is surrounded by a very weak magnetic field known as the geomagnetic field. This field is understood to have existed as far back as *c.* 3.5 billion years ago (Biggin *et al.* 2011) with evidence remaining contentious for any dated record before that age (Tang *et al.* 2019). The north and south magnetic poles are the points where the magnetic field lines converge (Fig. 5.1). The simplest way to describe the geomagnetic field is as a dipole with the two opposing geomagnetic poles – almost like a giant bar magnet. As a result, a north seeking compass in the northern hemisphere will always point to the magnetic north pole, providing that there are no local anomalies which could affect the dipole behaviour of the geomagnetic field (such as, for example, the South Atlantic Anomaly; Campuzano *et al.* 2019). Magnetic north is independent of geographic north, with geographic north representing the northern axis about which the Earth rotates.

The Earth's geomagnetic field has varied over time, mainly as a result of the movement in convection currents in the Earth's molten outer core. This variation means that the location of magnetic north also changes over time, as does the intensity of the signal of magnetic north

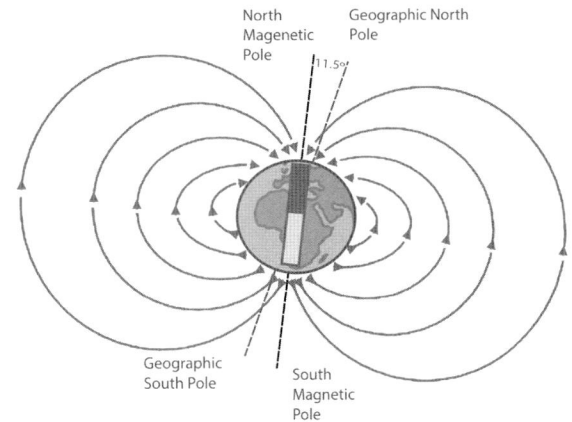

Figure 5.1. The magnetic poles and field lines. Copyright: Seren Griffiths.

at any particular location. This phenomenon is known as secular variation. Secular variation means that if you were able to make a series of readings using a north seeking compass in the northern hemisphere over several centuries you would see the needle change its orientation as it described the process of secular variation over time.

Both natural and anthropogenic materials can record signals that correspond to the geomagnetic conditions of the times when they were formed. Archaeomagnetic dating relies on identifying this preserved signal and relating this signal to known variations in magnetic north over time.

Anthropogenic materials that can preserve this geomagnetic signal include fired objects, deposits or structures such as hearths or kilns (Gallet *et al.* 2009; Tema *et al.* 2012). Natural deposits or geological forms can also preserve a geomagnetic signal from the point of their creation. Water-lain sediments, lava flows and rock formations are among the natural materials that can retain geomagnetic signals (Snowball *et al.* 2007; Peña *et al.* 2014; Avery *et al.* 2017). Both anthropogenic fired materials and natural deposits preserve a geomagnetic signal because they include iron-bearing minerals. These materials preserve within their structures both a record of the *direction* and a record of the *intensity* of the geomagnetic conditions at the point of formation. The preserved magnetic signal is known as a remanent magnetisation or magnetic remanence.

The geomagnetic field can be defined at a single point in time as a vector by its directional component (declination or 'D' and inclination or 'I') and its strength (or intensity given the notation 'F'). All three parameters vary over time. Quantifying these components in archaeomagnetic samples defines the past geomagnetic field at the point in time and location when the material that carries the signal was formed. Archaeomagnetic dating is therefore possible based on both the changes in the directional components or intensity of signal in a sample. However, *directional* archaeomagnetic dating studies are much more commonly applied in archaeology. It is this method on which this chapter will focus. For more in-depth discussions on archaeointensity studies see Pavón-Carrasco *et al.* (2021).

What is a magnetic remanence?

There are a variety of mechanisms in both natural and anthropogenic settings which can preserve a record of the ancient geomagnetic field and how it has changed through time. There are three signals which are particularly relevant to archaeomagnetic studies:

- thermoremanent magnetisation,
- detrital/depositional remanent magnetisation, and
- post-depositional remanent magnetisation.

There are several other mechanisms which could be relevant to archaeomagnetic and palaeomagnetic study. These include chemical remanent magnetisation (CRM) which is the acquisition of a remanence by crystal growth at a constant temperature (Tarling 1983, 29). CRM is rarely relevant for archaeomagnetic studies and is more prevalent in palaeomagnetic studies (Larson and Walker 1975), though has shown recent promise for the elucidation of palaeosecular variation (Ponte *et al.* 2018). An exciting relatively recent mechanism that was discovered and utilised as a form of archaeomagnetic dating is pictorial remanent magnetisation (PiRM). This method relies on the red pigments in mural paintings containing hematite grains which acquire the remanence by the alignment of the free moving magnetic grains as the paint dries on the substrate (Chiari and Lanza 1997; Goguitchaichvili *et al.* 2016; 2018). However, PiRM applications are dependent on very exact sample types which mean that they can only be used in very specific situations.

In this chapter we focus on thermoremanent magnetism as this is most frequently employed in archaeological work but we briefly introduce detrital/depositional remanent magnetisation and post-depositional remanent magnetisation below.

Thermoremanent magnetisation

Thermoremanent magnetisation (TRM) is particularly useful for archaeologists as suitable deposits are widely preserved on a range of different types of sites (e.g. Catanzariti *et al.* 2008; Gómez-Paccard *et al.* 2013; Carrancho *et al.* 2016). The dated event in this context is the heating of iron-bearing minerals to very high temperatures. Critically for archaeologists, this can include the use of archaeological deposits and structures such as hearths, kilns, and furnaces etc. As well as the potential to use TRM measurements on a range of commonly preserved deposit or structure types, a key advantage of TRM is the close association between the dated event and anthropogenic activity. Often the dated event and the archaeological event of interest – for example the use of a hearth – are the same.

There are several types of magnetic minerals that act as recorders of the magnetic field and retain a remanent magnetisation. Primarily these are haematite or magnetite but can also contain admixtures of other magnetic minerals depending on the underlying lithology and the firing conditions. Characterising a sample's magnetic properties is an important part of any archaeomagnetic study as it can aid the determination of the conditions present at the time of firing. During the firing of any soil or clay, the iron bearing oxides (magnetite, haematite etc) and hydroxides (goethite, lepidocrocite etc) can be oxidised or reduced to magnetite, maghaemite, titanomagnetite, and haematite depending on the conditions. A number of major reviews explore the magnetic properties of rocks and soils (Tarling 1983; Dunlop and Özdemir 1997; Walden *et al.* 1999; Liu *et al.* 2012; Roberts 2015).

Each magnetic mineral has a Curie temperature, the temperature above which materials undergo a significant change in their magnetic properties. When magnetic minerals exceed their Curie temperatures they lose all prior permanent magnetic moments. During the cooling phase each magnetic mineral will re-acquire a remanent magnetisation. This remanent magnetisation will be parallel and proportional to the prevailing ambient field, which is normally the Earth's geomagnetic field (Tarling 1983, 26; Linford 2006), though local disturbance to this orientation can be created by iron-rich objects or deposits. If the relevant Curie temperature is not exceeded the material will not be fully reset and only the magnetic minerals with Curie temperatures below the firing temperature will acquire a new magnetic remanence. The temperature to which any material was heated can also influence the stability of the magnetic remanence.

The higher the temperature and the uniformity of the firing across the archaeological deposit or feature, the higher likelihood of a single stable magnetic remanence.

This temperature threshold therefore proves an important practical consideration in selecting samples for archaeomagnetic measurement on site. A layer of clay or soil containing iron bearing magnetic minerals would need to have been heated to high enough temperature consistently across the deposit to be suitable for archaeomagnetic analysis. A good indicative temperature through which samples might pass is c. 580°C, the Curie temperature of magnetite, a common magnetic mineral found in clays and soils.

The effect of secular variation means that the location and intensity of magnetic north will appear to vary in different places at different times. Because these changes are relative to the sample location, archaeomagnetic age calculations require the calibration of the average TRM recorded from a sample against a local record of the changes in the archaeomagnetic direction (see below). There are varying levels of detail in this calibration data for different parts of the world. For example, the United Kingdom dataset currently contains the largest collection of independently dated archaeomagnetic directions acquired through the TRM mechanism (Batt *et al.* 2017).

Detrital/depositional remanent magnetisation (drm) and post-depositional remanent magnetisation (pDRM)
Detrital (or depositional) remanent magnetisation relies on the ability of magnetic grains in sedimentary environments which are already magnetised to align themselves with the ambient geomagnetic field. Although this chapter does not focus on material which has come from sedimentary environments, this can be a useful sample type as ancient geomagnetic field signals are preserved in sediments across many site types and periods (e.g. Avery *et al.* 2017; Lund *et al.* 2017; Gogorza *et al.* 2018). Moreover, these deposits are a crucial avenue for expanding our knowledge of the past geomagnetic field.

Post-depositional remanence is best defined as the acquiring of a magnetic signal after deposition of the sediment has taken place. This is due to the re-alignment of the magnetic grains gradually during compaction and dewatering of the sediment until they are no longer free to move and become locked in by the non-magnetic matrix (Hamano 1980; Mellström *et al.* 2015). The depth at which the pDRM becomes locked in varies depending on the environment and the particle size; resulting in a large body of discussion and research into this mechanism (Demenocal *et al.* 1990; Roberts and Winklhofer 2004; Suganuma *et al.* 2010; 2011; Snowball *et al.* 2013; Pulley *et al.* 2015).

The DRM and pDRM mechanisms have remained the subject of contention for many years due to the ambiguity over which mechanism causes sediments to develop a magnetic remanence (Carter-Stiglitz *et al.* 2006; Mitra and Tauxe 2009; Zhao and Roberts 2010; Zhao *et al.* 2016). Despite the uncertainties that arise from studying sediments, crucially, they have the potential to retain a near-continuous record of the past geomagnetic field proving invaluable for building the secular variations curves, which are necessary to calibrate TRM archaeomagnetic measurements (see below). In Britain for example, lake sediments have been studied to create secular variation curves (Mackereth 1971; Turner and Thompson 1979; 1981). Recent work by Avery and colleagues produced a new British master curve for secular variation covering the Holocene (Avery *et al.* 2017). They produced age estimates for sediment from Lake Windermere through both radiocarbon measurements and archaeomagnetic measurements to identify the past secular variation, or 'palaeosecular variation'.

Applications of DRM or pDRM in archaeological settings are less frequent than in geological or palaeo-environmental studies. However, negative archaeological features such as ditches and water courses can be sampled for pDRM or DRM archaeomagnetic dating. Hounslow and Karloukovski (2013) provide a summary of the processes of pDRM and DRM archaeomagnetic dating in archaeological contexts.

In the following sections we focus on archaeomagnetic directional studies of fired materials.

History of development

Underlying principles

In directional archaeomagnetic studies, to use the preserved magnetic signal four key criteria are required to calculate age estimates for the last firing of a deposit. First it needs to be possible to record accurately the orientation of the sample during the sampling process (Fig. 5.2). Secondly, this orientation needs to be unchanged from the moment of heating. Thirdly, the different positions of magnetic north or the palaeosecular variation over time (*in situ* since the last firing event) need to be understood accurately. Fourthly, the sample needs to record only the thermoremanent magnetic signal from the point of formation of the deposit and not include any residual signal or signal incurred from the burial environment. Given these key criteria, it is possible to produce an age estimate for the firing of a deposit by calibrating the direction of the remanent magnetic signal preserved in a sample against the different positions of magnetic north over time.

However, if a sample has moved since the firing event the orientation of the remanent magnetic signal will have changed and any age calculation will therefore be inaccurate. This means that portable fired artefacts (such as pottery) are not suitable for directional studies. It is possible to produce archaeomagnetic age estimates on portable material using archaeomagnetic intensity studies calibrated against palaeosecular variation (e.g. Stillinger *et al.* 2015), however these are relatively uncommon. The essential principle that deposits measured by TRM archaeomagnetic studies must remain undisturbed and *in situ* also means that deposits that may have been truncated or that were formed on unstable or subsiding footings may not be suitable for archaeomagnetic dating (see discussion below).

Sample types

In terms of TRM, the wide range of potential samples from archaeological contexts is one of the key strengths of the method. Any deposit that has been fired to a sufficient temperature, contains minerals capable of taking on a stable remanent magnetism and has not been subject to disturbance since firing could be suitable for measurement. In archaeological terms, this means that any *in situ* burnt deposit or structure is a potential archaeomagnetic sample. This can include kilns, hearths, ovens, corn dryers, destruction layers, furnaces, and many more deposits associated with high-temperature industrial or domestic activities.

Sample association

The benefit of using archaeomagnetic dating on fired material is that the association between the archaeological event of interest and the dated event should be clear; the dated event should be the last firing of a deposit *in situ*. The robustness of this association for archaeomagnetic measurements means that the technique is ideal to use in combination with other scientific dating techniques to produce multi-technique scientific dating chronologies (see below and Chapter 8).

Applied sampling considerations and field measurements

As with luminescence measurements, archaeomagnetic dating requires specialist sampling on site. Because archaeomagnetic dating requires undisturbed deposits a chronometric sampling strategy needs to be developed between the fieldwork team and the archaeomagnetic specialist before fieldwork begins (Chapter 7). If multiple deposits require archaeomagnetic measurements the deposits will either need to be preserved *in situ* as the excavation progresses or a specialist may be required to undertake multiple site visits. Depending on the features in question, it may be possible to sample two or three in a day – sample recovery is time consuming – a key issue for site management. As the method of sampling is destructive all standard practices of archaeological recording need to be completed before the archaeomagnetist can undertake sampling.

Practically speaking, archaeomagnetic samples should preferably be well-compacted or well-consolidated, though it is possible to sample friable material by modifying the sampling technique. Potential samples also need to be safely accessible for the specialist and of sufficient extent that a series of samples can be recovered from a single deposit. As low levels of unstable magnetism can be introduced by heating of deposits around a potential sample, or by proximity to a local magnetic field, the surrounding environment of any potential sample needs to be assessed to ensure the only magnetic signal preserved in the sample derives from the last, direct firing.

Because magnetic disturbance or irregularities can occur within a deposit as a result of the minerals present in the deposit, or localised magnetic fields, a series of samples is taken from an individual deposit in order to produce an average signal measurement. This series can come from large samples that are identified, recorded, recovered and then sub-sampled in the laboratory. Using this approach, a minimum number of *c.* 12 samples might be required (Fig. 5.2). Alternatively, a series of smaller samples can be recovered after identification and recording. If smaller samples are recovered then the minimum recommended number is no less than 20. The method of sampling will depend on the size, accessibility and consolidation of the deposit that is to be measured.

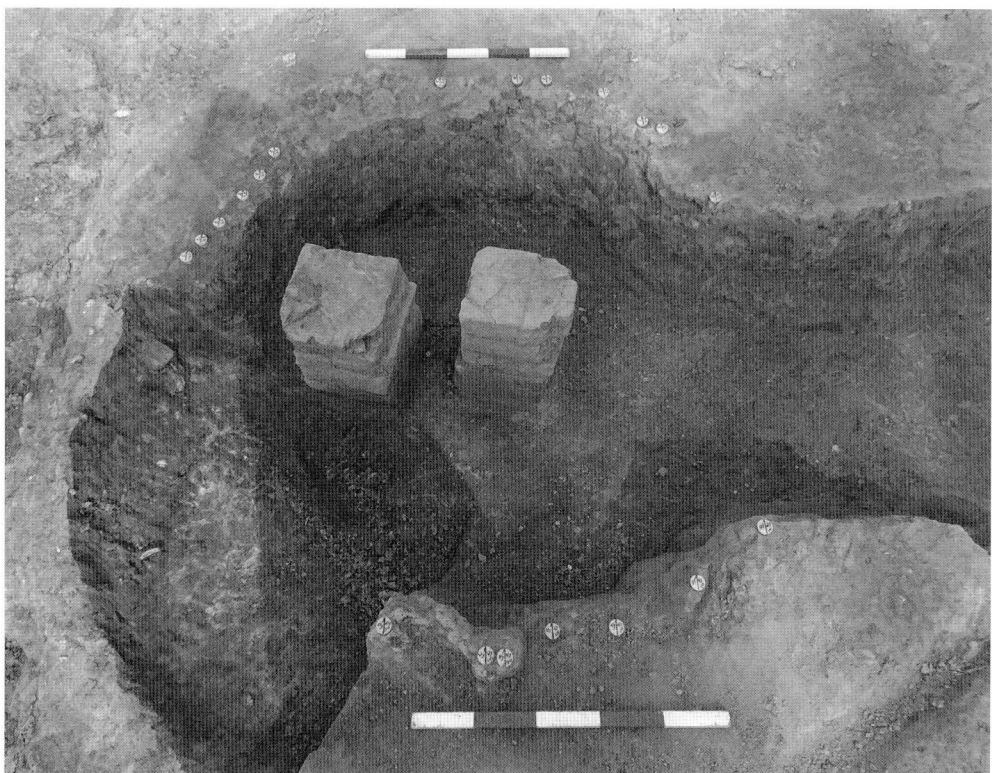

Figure 5.2. Sampling on site using the button method. This method is used to recover well-consolidated samples from the heat-effected sides of a kiln. The scale is 50 cm. Copyright: Sam Harris.

There are three main methods of taking field samples: the Plaster of Paris method which can take large samples of friable material; the button method which takes small samples of hardened material (Figs 5.3 and 5.4); or the tube method which takes small samples of soft material with a plastic sample pot (Fig, 5.5). See Linford (2006) and Trapanese *et al.* (2008) for further description and assessment of the sampling methods. The most appropriate method is usually chosen based on the quantity of available material and the compactness of the matrix. Friable and loose material require Plaster of Paris to encapsulate the material to allow consolidation in the laboratory. Hard fired clays are most suited to the button method. By far the easiest and least time-consuming is the tube method which requires soft soils and clays (Fig. 5.6). If required, samples can be consolidated in the laboratory by applying either polyvinyl acetate (PVA) or a dilution of sodium silicate (liquid glass).

Prior to sampling, the exact orientation of each of the samples relative to a known reference direction needs to be measured *in situ*. It is extremely important that this takes place prior to any disturbance associated with either excavation or sample recovery. To record the sample a level, horizontal surface is created on the top of the deposit and the orientation of the sample recorded with a reference direction. This can be true north

Figure 5.3. Sampling on site using the Plaster of Paris method in order to recover large quantities of friable sample material. Here the heat-effected material at the bottom of a ditch cut is being recovered and a magnetic compass being used to record the bearing for orientation correction. Copyright: Sam Harris.

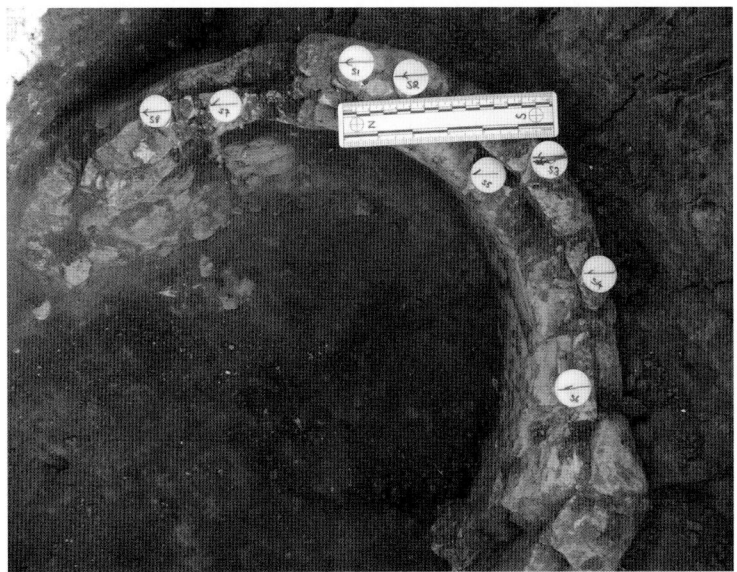

Figure 5.4. Sampling a furnace on site using the button method on well-consolidated deposits. Each sample has been given an identifier and orientation. The scale is 50 cm. Copyright: Sam Harris.

or contemporary magnetic north in cases where there is likely to be little magnetic disturbance on a site. In any case, the reference direction needs to be accurately and permanently recorded physically on the sample's surface. The sample can then be removed for measurement in the laboratory.

Laboratory measurements

In the laboratory, there are several stages of analysis that archaeomagnetic samples must undergo to establish an archaeomagnetic age estimate. The first is to measure the natural remanent magnetisation (NRM) of a sample which informs the archaeomagnetist on the strength of the magnetic minerals present. Commonly, the measurements are carried out on a spinner magnetometer, originating from the model built by Molyneux (1971). The sample is placed inside a magnetically shielded chamber which is surrounded by a coil. The spinning sample induces an electromagnetic force in the coil which is measurable as an AC current. This current is directly proportional to the remanent

Figure 5.5. Sampling on site using the tube method. This method is used here to sample relatively soft heat-effected deposits. Copyright: Manca Vinazza.

magnetisation of the sample. The measurement process involves placing the sample in a defined number of positions to calculate the sample's complete magnetic vector (Walden *et al.* 1999, 66). The spinner magnetometer requires calibration with a known standard (in most laboratories these are samples with a known value that is very stable). Incrementally, the equipment requires recalibration to account for machine drift.

Measurement of the magnetisation of the sample in the laboratory also needs to assess how stable a sample's magnetic signal is and therefore whether an age estimate produced from a given sample could be robust. The NRM can contain multiple signals as well as the TRM which might be acquired through natural processes over time.

Identifying mixed signals where the remanent magnetism has not been fully overprinted are especially relevant for archaeomagnetic samples that were incompletely fired. In the cases of complex magnetisations where a signal is mixed, the resultant signal could not be clearly related to any single dated event.

Tto investigate the stability of a signal and how much of a magnetisation relates to a single, high-intensity burning event, a number of measurements can be undertaken in the laboratory. In some cases signals resulting from the background environmental conditions are less stable than those produced by high-intensity burning. Partially demagnetising a sample can remove the low-level magnetisation resulting from the burial environment. This partial demagnetisation can be achieved through heating a sample (thermal demagnetisation), or by exposing it to an alternating magnetic field (alternating field demagnetisation). After partial demagnetisation the only signal remaining in a sample should be that produced from the high-intensity burning dated event. Variation in a series of sample behaviours during demagnetisation can indicate that the deposit as a whole was insufficiently fired, and that may not give an accurate measurement. Once a sample has been partially demagnetised, the directions of the remanent magnetism can be measured.

The behaviour of different samples in a series will depend on:

- their mineral composition;
- the intensity of burning to which they are exposed;
- the proximity of the sample to other materials that might exhibit a magnetic field;
- and the physical stability of the deposit over its burial history.

As noted above, exploring the behaviour of a series of samples from the same deposit allows a qualitative appraisal of any signals. These multiple measurements provide an assessment of the accuracy of any age calculation from the series. Individual samples that behave as outliers can be rejected from this age calculation, or if the whole series of samples behave very differently, the deposit may be deemed not suitable to produced accurate age estimates.

Age calculation and calibration

Archaeomagnetic measurements from the series of samples from a deposit or structure are averaged using Fisher (1953) statistics (the Fisher mean) which is more suited for dealing with vector based datasets than another statistical method. This Fisher average is then the basis for calibration to provide the archaeomagnetic date range for the last firing event. The age estimate will be quoted with an error term or alpha-95 (α_{95}). The alpha-95 value represents the 95% likelihood that the true mean direction lies within this range. Having established the mean direction of magnetic north when the deposit was fired a calibrated date range needs to be produced using an appropriate local calibration curve.

Reference curves

An archaeomagnetic TRM date for the last time a feature was fired can be obtained by comparison with a reference curve. These reference curves show the secular variation of geomagnetic north over time. Reference curves contain data of the archaeomagnetic direction and associated age estimates produced by an independent dating method that isn't archaeomagnetic. Reference curves can include data on geomagnetic field change from archaeological deposits, lava flows or sedimentary deposits. However, they tend to focus on data from the first two of these (e.g. Batt *et al.* 2017; Tema *et al.* 2018; Zanella *et al.* 2018) which are appended with regional stacks of sediment records where there are hiatuses (e.g. Pavón-Carrasco *et al.* 2011; Korte *et al.* 2019).

Because the direction of magnetic north is relative to the sample location, archaeomagnetic age estimates need to be produced with a regionally specific reference curves to reflect this geographical variability. There are multiple approaches to constructing reference curves. These regional datasets are mostly country specific and are known as palaeosecular variation curves (PSVCs). Their resolution varies internationally due to the differing quantities and qualities of the data which form each one. There is also variation in the quality assurance criteria that are used to select data for inclusion in different curves (cf. De Marco *et al.* 2013; Kovacheva *et al.* 2014; Tema *et al.* 2018). For example, for Britain, several calibration curves have been created (Clark *et al.* 1988; Tarling and Dobson 1995; Batt 1997; Zananiri *et al.* 2007; Batt *et al.* 2017) for the central geographic reference point (Meriden). The curve constructed by Zananiri *et al.* (2007) only allowed directional components of the past geomagnetic field to be calibrated. Thanks to new approaches and techniques, the most recent calibration curve by Batt *et al.* (2017) has incorporated geographically wide-ranging palaeo-intensity data to produce a full vector PSVC for Britain.

To produce accurate age estimates, as well as using the most appropriate regional PSVC, it is necessary to relate the sample site relative to the spatial location for which the curve was built. In Britain, for example, the PSVC (Batt *et al.* 2017) is located at Meriden. Archaeomagnetic measurements therefore need to be relocated to this geographical location This is typically done via the virtual geomagnetic pole method (Noel and Batt 1990). However, relocating archaeomagnetic directions with reference to the PSVC can introduce error, perhaps of as much as 7° (Casas and Incoronato 2007), which can translate into an error in the age estimate. A way round this error is to use geomagnetic field models which can produce PSVCs for any location within the constraints of that model (Pavón-Carrasco *et al.* 2009; 2011; Korte *et al.* 2011; 2019). However, as noted above, geomagnetic data are not evenly distributed around time and space, and there are some periods and regions that are over-represented or under-represented by data in these models. For example, much of the archaeomagnetic data for the geomagnetic field model for the period 6000–10,000 BC comes from the Balkans and the Near East (Tema and Kondopoulou 2011; Kovacheva *et al.* 2014; Yutsis-Akimova *et al.* 2018). There may be periods or regions where relocating site samples relative to the PSVC incorporates uncertainty.

After correcting for the difference between the sample location and that of the regional calibration curve, age estimate can be achieved by plotting the measured mean direction of remanent magnetism and the associated alpha-95 error term against the archaeomagnetic calibration curve.

Interpreting age estimates

In practice, there are several additional difficulties in establishing the date at which a deposit was fired. Archaeomagnetic calibration curves may include multiple points in time where the magnetic field was in the same or very similar positions. This is because the secular variation of the Earth's magnetic field does not fit any regular pattern (for the purpose of archaeomagnetic studies) and coincidentally can have similar behaviour at more than one point in the past. This means that in some cases multiple date ranges could be produced when a single archaeomagnetic measurement is calibrated (Fig. 5.6). For example, a measurement could produce two possible, quite chronologically discrete estimates for the firing of a deposit from a site in Britain, in the 9th or 17th century cal. AD. In many cases, archaeological prior information about a site, for example from pottery or other material culture in use, could help us evaluate these ranges but this may not always be the case (see case studies below). This means that archaeomagnetic dating can be very powerfully used in conjunction with other scientific dating methods.

Computer modelling

Archaeomagnetic age estimates are commonly produced using specific software to compare the known archaeomagnetic vector to the chosen PSVC or geomagnetic field model. The two most common software programmes are RenCurve (Lanos 2004) and MATLAB's archaeo_dating programmes (Pavón-Carrasco *et al.* 2011). Both modes of calibration rely on the conversion of the observations to probability density functions

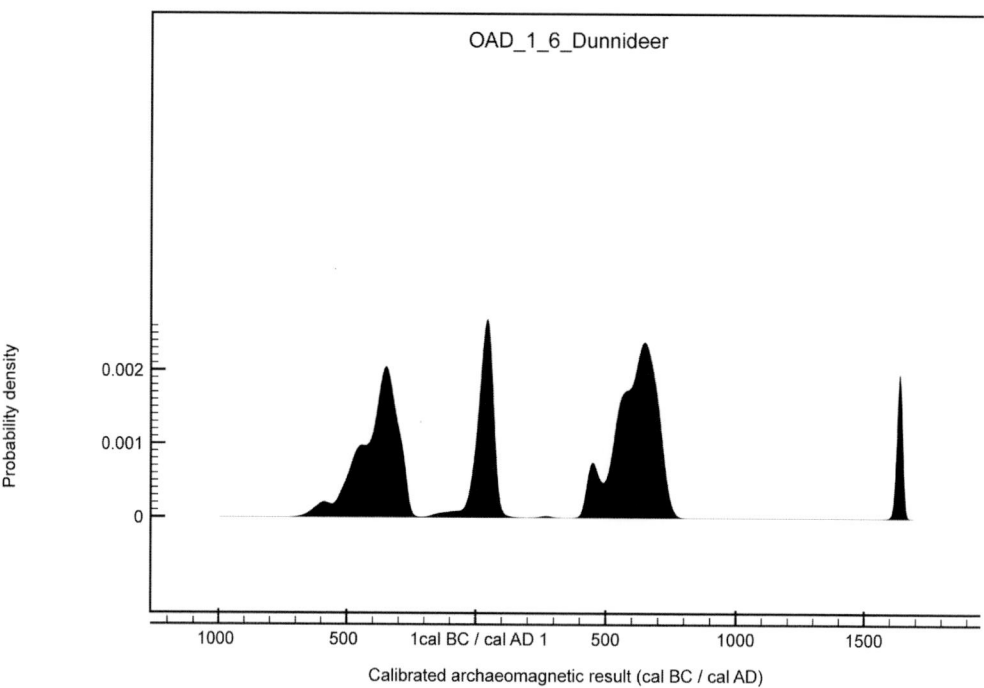

Figure 5.6. A multimodal distribution for a calibrated archaeomagnetic measurement from Dunnideer vitrified hillfort. Copyright: Seren Griffiths.

and can allow the inclusion of the associated experimental error. The computation of secular variations curves in RenCurve is based on Bayesian frameworks (Hervé and Lanos 2017), utilising Monte Carlo Markov Chains to minimise the misfit of each data point with respect to the curve. The archaeo_dating programme (Pavón-Carrasco *et al.* 2011) converts archaeomagnetic data to the relevant PSVC through the conversion via pole method (Noel and Batt 1990). The archaeo_dating programme allows users to constrain the time interval for the analysis to exclude multiple date ranges (cf. Pavón-Carrasco *et al.* 2014). The probability density functions calculated from comparing the declination and inclination values (with associated errors and intensity when available) are then combined to provide a set of date ranges at 95% probability.

Quality indicators: being a critical consumer

Laboratory quality assurance

As with luminescence measurements, there have been no recent archaeomagnetic inter-comparisons. All measurements should be reported in full and archived at a relevant repository.

Reporting results

As with radiocarbon measurements, it will be possible to recalibrate archaeomagnetic measurements with new revisions to the regional calibration curve. The publication of archaeomagnetic results therefore needs to include quality assurance indicators that demonstrate the method and present the calibrated results, details of the raw measurements so that these can be recalibrated in the future and included in new analyses, and the archaeological details of the measured sample. The archaeologist who commissioned the results should expect to receive the measurement details from the laboratory as listed below and should include the raw result, measurement details *and* the archaeological contextual information for each measurement in the publication.

For the robustness of measurements to be assessed, and for measurements to be recalibrated in the future, the following information should be reported for each result in the publication:

- The laboratory code;
- The archaeology context, and sample information;
- The location of the sample site expressed in longitude and latitude;
- The number of subsamples taken, and the number used to calculate the date of the deposit, including a discussion in the report of the reasons that any of the samples were rejected from the age calculation;
- The method and degree of demagnetisation applied to samples;
- Any analysis taken into account before the calculation of the average archaeomagnetic direction of a sample set for example the Maximum Angular Deviation, or distortion correction;

- The declination and inclination of the averaged archaeomagnetic direction for the location of the calibration curve (in the UK, for example, Meriden);
- The inclination from an established local geographic reference point (in the United Kingdom, for example, Meriden);
- Both the values used in the estimate of precision: the alpha-95 reported in degrees, and the Fisher precision parameter (k);
- Date ranges at quoted confidence levels (68% and 95% confidence);
- The received date range for the firing of the deposit, and the archaeological information used to revise the quoted ranges if this has occurred. For example, the accepted range on a site might involve rejecting one of two potential date ranges based on specific archaeological evidence.

Because archaeomagnetic calibration curves are constructed from relatively few data – in comparison with the radiocarbon calibration curve for example – it means that each new archaeomagnetic measurement is important in developing the discipline and the various regional calibration curves. Archiving full data in publicly accessible databases is therefore very important, therefore the archaeologist should publish all the laboratory details noted above and the archaeological contextual information in the archaeological publication.

Case studies

Case study: Tipping Street, Stafford, UK

The excavations at Tipping Street in Stafford were introduced in Chapter 2 as the location of a key settlement in the 9th–10th centuries AD. Here an archaeomagnetic result from the site is considered; the analysis of these results is discussed in more detail in Chapter 8 (see Dodd *et al.* 2014; Hamerow *et al.* 2020 for details).

Archaeomagnetic sample selection
One kiln from the site was well-preserved and an archaeomagnetic age estimate was produced to provide a date its last firing and the production of Saxon Stafford Ware pottery. The radiocarbon results estimate different dated events, the date of the formation of the plant tissues from the fuel used to fire the kiln. These results are not only produced by different methods but define different dated events.

Archaeomagnetic dating results
Figure 5.7 shows calibrated archaeomagnetic results using the Batt *et al.* (2017) calibration curve, together with calibrated radiocarbon results using the IntCal20 curve (Reimer *et al.* 2020; Chap. 8). We can see that there is the potential that the radiocarbon results are slightly older than the last firing of the feature as dated by the archaeomagnetic measurements. In the model that we develop in Chapter 8, we have presented the archaeomagnetic result (GPR3408_2020) as slightly later than the radiocarbon results on fuel from the feature. This reflects our understanding of the different dated events that these measurements sample. This may indicate

that these measurements related to different dated events with different associated archaeological events of interest.

Discussion of the scientific dating considerations

The archaeomagnetic result may represent slightly later activity than radiocarbon results on the kiln fuel. Here it is important to think critically about what the measurements actually represent archaeologically in terms of an assessment of the underlying principles that define the method. Using multiple radiocarbon measurements from this site allowed more scientific dating measurements to be produced than would have been the case if only the archaeomagnetic measurement was available. Here the radiocarbon measurements were used in conjunction with the archaeomagnetic measurement, which had a very secure association in terms of the site chronology, but for which there were fewer samples available. Multiple techniques here allowed a more developed chronology of the site to be created.

Case study conclusions

This case study has demonstrated the benefit of thinking critically about what scientific dating measurements represent in terms of archaeological chronologies. The archaeomagnetic measurement provides a very strong functional **association** between the archaeological event of interest (the last firing of the kiln to produce Stafford Ware) and the dated event. The use of additional radiocarbon measurements provided a more **representative** sample of activity at the site, and another **independent method of age estimate**. That the results are internally consistent means we can start to analyse them with regard to other evidence of Saxon activity in this part of the world (Chapter 8).

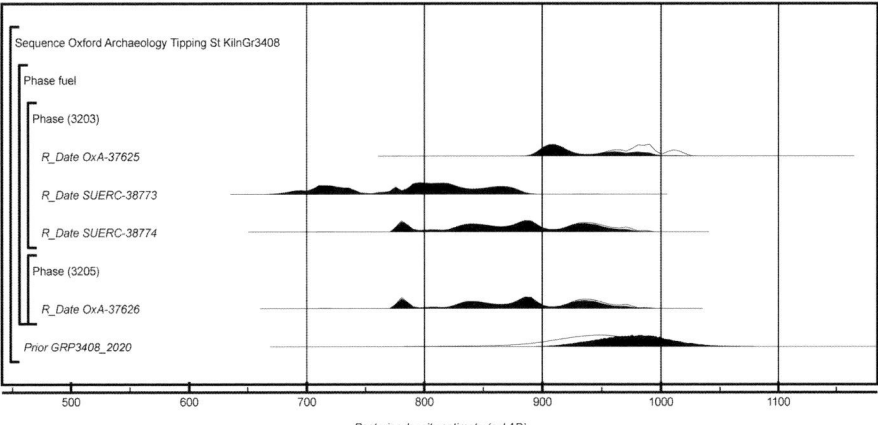

Figure 5.7. Posterior density estimates from an archaeomagnetic measurement and associated radiocarbon measurements that were produced on the same kiln feature from Tipping Street, Stafford (Dodd et al. 2014; Hamerow et al. 2020). The archaeomagnetic result is denoted 'Prior GRP3408_2020' and shown towards the bottom of the figure. Bayesian modelling of these results and others from Saxon Stafford are dsicussed in Chapter 8. Copyright: Seren Griffiths.

Case study: Dunnideer Vitrified Fort, Insch, Aberdeenshire, UK

Dunnideer vitrified fort (57.342356 N, -2.646019 W; Fig. 5.8) is an example of one of over 50 such sites from Scotland which date from the Iron Age into the early historic period, although the actual chronology of these sites has been debated (cf. Ralston 2006). These structures take their name from the vitrified remains of the hillfort ramparts which have been produced as a result of high-temperature firing. These stones are not mortared together but the firing results in a fused structure that, in some cases, includes a significant glassy matrix. To produce this vitrification the structures would have to have been subjected to purposefully managed firings. This requirement suggests that the vitrification does not result from a short-lived attack.

Systematic studies of these sites have been undertaken since the last quarter of the 18th century (Williams 1777; Anderson 1779; 1782). However, both the functions and

Figure 5.8. Dunnideer vitrified hillfort. The sampling location on a vitrified stone rampart is shown in the mid-ground. Copyright: Mark Hounslow.

chronologies of these sites remain unclear. Many different scientific dating methods have been applied to vitrified forts across Scotland, including radiocarbon dating at Langwell and Craig Phadrig (Mackie 1969; 1976) and thermoluminescence dating at Langwell, Craig Phadrig, Knock Farril, Finavon and Tap O'Noth (Sanderson *et al.* 1988). These different studies have produced results which range from 1000 cal. BC–cal. AD 1000. Due to the number of contradictory dates and the large errors associated with them, chronology remains a subject of active debate (e.g. Alexander 2002; Kresten *et al.* 2003; Ralston 2006).

Archaeomagnetic dating was applied to several of these sites in the 1980s (Gentles 1989; 1993). More research has also occurred into the vitrification process (Friend *et al.* 2007; 2008; Suttie and Batt 2020). Archaeomagnetic study of a vitrified hillfort at Dunnideer was undertaken by Harris and Hounslow (2010). A more recent study re-evaluated the directional data from seven hillforts and utilised a new Bayesian method of calibration was able to unpick the chronology of the firing events (Suttie and Batt 2020).

The defences at Dunnideer comprise a tripled ditched enclosure with an inner oblong rampart 73 × 30 m in area. The rampart is formed of vitrified stonework and fragments of timber structures which would have supported the wall. The inner and outer defences probably represent at least two main structural phases but no evidence exists to indicate whether the vitrified fort preceded the unfinished outer works or vice versa. More obvious on the hill are the remains of a later rectangular castle thought to be one of the earliest castles in Scotland, dating to AD 1260.

Sample selection
Samples for archaeomagnetic measurements were selected from a low section of wall in the south-east of the fort (Fig. 5.8) from near an area of collapse, which allowed the section through the wall to be inspected in order to aid sampling. The section chosen appeared to represent an area of wall that had not been moved or disturbed and that had been fired *in situ*. The block work had been strongly bonded together during this firing. As a result, the areas between the stone block work had been filled with melted stone which took the form of a semi-glassy, highly vesicular substance.

The samples selected for archaeomagnetic dating were all fired gabbro stone. Gabbro is high in ferromagnetic minerals so represents a very suitable sample type for archaeomagnetic measurements. This material was homogeneous to allow sub-sampling for the multiple measurements required for archaeomagnetic age estimate. The nature of this material however, meant that it had to be levelled (to record the orientation) using a hammer and chisel in the field. This presented quite a difficult process; the practicalities of sampling are very important in the production of accurate chronologies.

Archaeomagnetic dating results
Five samples provided a reliable specimen based mean direction (Harris and Hounslow 2010; Fig. 5.9). This mean direction was used with the archaeomagnetic calibrated European magnetic field model for the present-day to 1000 BC (Pavòn-Carrasco *et al.* 2009).

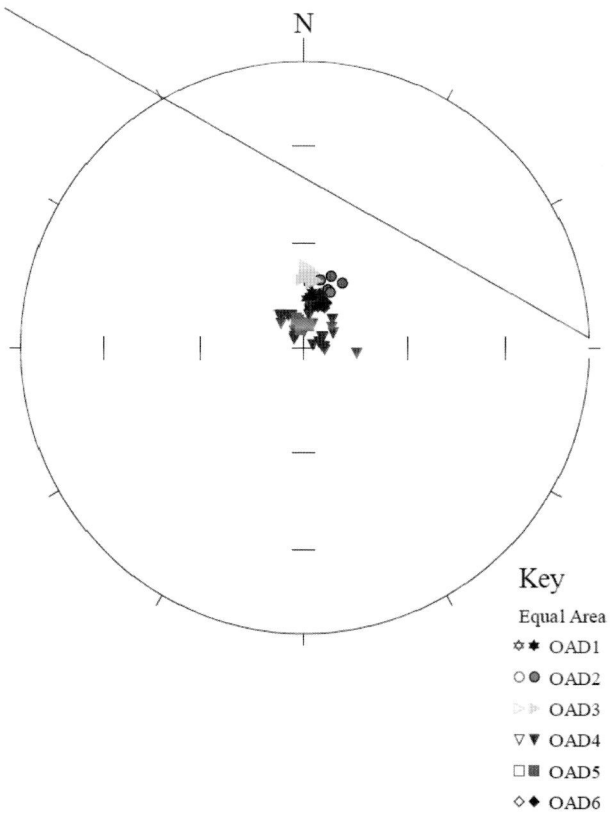

Figure 5.9. Measurements of the NRM from samples from Dunnideer vitrified hillfort. The measurements are shown on a stereographic projection (uncorrected for magnetic deviation) which provides a visualisation of how scattered the results are with implications for assessing measurements in order to produce accurate age estimates. Modified from Harris and Hounslow (2010). Copyright: Sam Harris.

Discussion of the scientific dating considerations

We can compare the archaeomagnetic results with two radiocarbon results that were produced on charcoal from the structure (Cook *et al.* 2011; Fig. 5.10). Both results were produced on hazel charcoal which originated from burnt wood within the collapsed rampart (Noble *et al.* 2013; supplementary information). The archaeological interpretation is that this wood may have provided fuel for the burning. Because this was a relatively short-lived species there should therefore be relatively limited interval between the dated radiocarbon events and the firing of the fort wall. Because we understand the close association between the two archaeological events of interest – the firing of the fort measured by the archaeomagnetic result, and the short-life fuel samples for this event measured by radiocarbon – we can suggest that

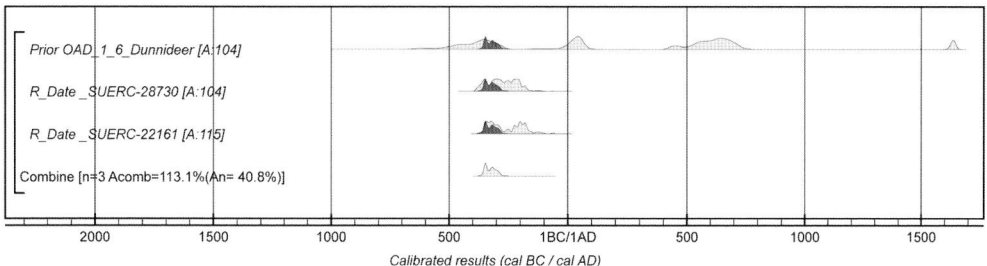

Figure 5.10. Calibrated radiocarbon and archaemagnetic results from the firing event at Dunnideer vitrified hillfort, together with a revised estimate for the timing of that event using the Combine *function in OxCal. Copyright: Seren Griffiths.*

these are accurate estimates. Using the Combine function of OxCal we can compare these results produced by different measurement techniques. This revised estimate suggests that the Dunnideer fort was fired in 365–275 cal. BC (95% confidence; or 355–300 cal. BC 68% confidence; Fig. 5.10). This estimate is also much more precise than either of the ranges produced by the archaeomagnetic or radiocarbon measurements alone.

Case study conclusions
This case study demonstrates the importance in thinking **critically** about suitable samples for archaeomagnetic measurements and suitable **calibration curves**. Assessment of **disturbance** was important here in trying to think about the association between the measurement and the archaeological event of interest. Here using **multi-technique** approaches for age estimates helps us explore the timing of what is probably closely-related dated events; that the results are internally consistent provides added importance given the consideration of which calibration curve might be most appropriate. With a well-defined dated event it is possible to produce **precise** and **accurate** age estimates even with relatively few data.

Chapter conclusions

Archaeomagnetic **TRM measurements** are arguably under-employed in archaeological chronologies. They provide a great deal of potential in that they provide **direct age estimates** for deposit or feature types (including fired clays) that are frequently of great interest for archaeologists. Archaeomagnetic measurements on *in situ* undisturbed deposits can be very useful for producing chronologies on stratigraphic sequences of clearly defined events. Archaeomagnetic TRM results can be used in complementary chronology building with radiocarbon measurements, especially in the production of **Bayesian site-specific stratigraphic chronological models** (Chapter 8).

Bibliography

Alexander, D. 2002. An oblong fort at Finavon, Angus: an example of the over-reliance of the appliance of science. In B. Ballin Smith and I Banks (eds), *In the Shadow of the Brochs*, 45–54 Stroud, Tempus

Anderson, J. 1779. An account of ancient monuments and fortifications in the Highlands of Scotland. *Archaeologia* 5, 241–66

Anderson, J. 1782. A further description of ancient fortifications in the North of Scotland. *Archaeologia* 6, 87–99

Avery, R., Xuan, C., Kemp, A., Bull, J., Cotterill, C., Fielding, J., Pearce, R. and Croudace, I. 2017. A new Holocene record of geomagnetic secular variation from Windermere, UK. *Earth and Planetary Science Letters* 477, 108–22

Batt, C. 1997. The British archaeomagnetic calibration curve: an objective treatment. *Archaeometry* 39(1), 153–68

Batt, C., Brown, M., Clelland, S.-J., Korte, M., Linford, P. and Outram, Z. 2017. Advances in archaeomagnetic dating in Britain: new data, new approaches and a new calibration curve. *Journal of Archaeological Science* 85, 66–82

Biggin, A., de Wit, J., Langereis, C., Zegers, T., Voûte, S., Dekkers, M. and Drost, K. 2011. Palaeomagnetism of Archaean rocks of the Onverwacht Group, Barberton Greenstone Belt (southern Africa): evidence for a stable and potentially reversing geomagnetic field at ca. 3.5Ga. *Earth and Planetary Science Letters* 302(3–4), 314–28

Campuzano, S., Gómez-Paccard, M., Pavón-Carrasco, F. and Osete, M. 2019. Emergence and evolution of the South Atlantic Anomaly revealed by the new paleomagnetic reconstruction SHAWQ2k. *Earth and Planetary Science Letters* 512, 17–26

Carrancho, Á., Herrejón Lagunilla, Á. and Vergès, J. 2016. Three archaeomagnetic applications of archaeological interest to the study of burnt anthropogenic cave sediments. *Quaternary International* 414, 244–57

Carter-Stiglitz, B., Valet, J.-P. and LeGoff, M. 2006. Constraints on the acquisition of remanent magnetization in fine-grained sediments imposed by redeposition experiments. *Earth and Planetary Science Letters* 245(1), 427–37

Casas, L. and Incoronato, A. 2007. Distribution analysis of errors due to relocation of geomagnetic data using the 'Conversion via Pole' (CVP) method: implications on archaeomagnetic data. *Geophysical Journal International* 169(2), 448–54

Catanzariti, G., McIntosh, G., Monge Soares, A., Díaz-Martínez, E., Kresten, P. and Osete, M. 2008. Archaeomagnetic dating of a vitrified wall at the Late Bronze Age settlement of Misericordia (Serpa, Portugal). *Journal of Archaeological Science* 35(5), 1399–1407

Chiari, G. and Lanza, R. 1997. Pictorial remanent magnetization as an indicator of secular variation of the Earth's magnetic field. *Physics of the Earth and Planetary Interiors* 101(1), 79–83

Clark, A., Tarling, D. and Noël, M. 1988. Developments in archaeomagnetic dating in Britain. *Journal of Archaeological Science* 15(6), 645–67

Cook, M., Kdolska, H., Dunbar, L., Engl, R., Sagrott, S. and Druce, D. 2011. New light on oblong forts: excavations at Dunnideer, Aberdeenshire. *Proceedings of the Society of Antiquaries of Scotland* 140, 79–91 [http://journals.socantscot.org/index.php/psas/article/view/9753]

De Marco, E., Tema, E., Lanos, P. and Kondopoulou, D. 2013. An updated catalogue of Greek archaeomagnetic data for the last 4500 years and a directional secular variation curve. *Studia Geophysica et Geodaetica* 58(1), 121–47

Demenocal, P., Ruddiman, W. and Kent, D. 1990. Depth of post-depositional remanence acquisition in deep-sea sediments: a case study of the Brunhes-Matuyama reversal and oxygen isotopic Stage 19.1. *Earth and Planetary Science Letters* 99, 1–13

Dodd, A., Goodwin, J., Griffiths, S., Norton, A., Poole, C. and Teague, S. 2014. Excavations at Tipping Street, Stafford, 2009–10: possible Iron Age roundhouses, three Stafford-type Ware kilns, and medieval and post-medieval urban remains. *Staffordshire Archaeological and Historical Society Transactions* 47, 1–114

Dunlop, D. and Özdemir, Ö. 1997. *Rock Magnetism: fundamentals and frontiers*. Cambridge: Cambridge University Press

Fisher, R. 1953. *Dispersion on a sphere.* Proceedings of the Royal Society A. Mathematical, Physical and Engineering Sciences. 217, 295–305

Friend, C., Dye, J. and Fowler, M. 2007. New field and geochemical evidence from vitrified forts in south Morar and Moidart, NW Scotland: further insight into melting and the process of vitrification. *Journal of Archaeological Science* 34(10), 1685–1701

Friend, C., Charnley, N., Clyne, H. and Dye, J. 2008. Experimentally produced glass compared with that occuring at The Torr, NW Scotland, UK: vitrification through biotite melting. *Journal of Archaeological Science* 35, 3130–43

Gallet, Y., Genevey, A., Le Goff, M., Warmé, N., Gran-Aymerich, J. and Lefèvre, A. 2009. On the use of archeology in geomagnetism, and vice-versa: recent developments in archeomagnetism. *Comptes Rendus Physique* 10(7), 630–48

Gentles, D. 1989. Archaeomagnetic Directional Studies of Large Fired Structures in Britain. Unpublished PhD thesis, Plymouth Polytechnic.

Gentles, D. (1993). Vitrified forts. *Current Archaeology* 133, 18–20

Gogorza, C., Irurzun, M., Orgeira, M., Palermo, P. and Llera, M. 2018. A continuous Late Holocene paleosecular variation record from Carmen Lake (Tierra del Fuego, Argentina). *Physics of the Earth and Planetary Interiors* 280, 40–52

Goguitchaichvili, A., Morales, J., Urrutia-Fucugauchi, J., Soler Arechalde, A., Acosta, G. and Castelleti, J. 2016. The use of pictorial remanent magnetization as a dating tool: state of the art and perspectives. *Journal of Archaeological Science: Reports* 8, 15–21

Goguitchaichvili, A., Torres, G., Cejudo, R., Ortega, V., Archer, J., Calvo-Rathert, M., Morales, J. and Urrutia Fucugauchi, J. 2018. From empirical considerations to absolute ages: how geomagnetic field variation may date Teotihuacan mural paintings. *Physics of the Earth and Planetary Interiors* 284, 10–16

Gómez-Paccard, M., Beamud, E., Mc Intosh, G. and Larrasoana, J. 2013. New archaeomagnetic data recovered from the study of three Roman klilns from north-east Spain: a contribution to the Iberian palaeosecular variation curve. *Archaeometry* 55(1), 159–77

Hamano, Y. 1980. An experiment on the post-depositional remanent magnetization in artificial and natural sediments. *Earth and Planetary Science Letters* 51(1), 221–32

Hamerow, H., Bogaard, A., Charles, M., Forster, E., Holmes, M., McKerracher, M., Neil, S., Bronk Ramsey, C., Stroud, E. and Thomas, R. 2020. An integrated bioarchaeological approach to the medieval 'Agricultural Revolution': a case study from Stafford, England, c. AD 800–1200. *European Journal of Archaeology* 23(4), 585–609

Harris, S. and Hounslow, M. 2010. Dunnideer Hillfort, Insch, Aberdeenshire: Archaeomagnetic dating of the vitrified remains. Unpublished laboratory report, Lancaster University, Centre for Envrionmental Magnetism and Palaeomagnetism, Lancaster Environmental Centre

Hervé, G. and Lanos, P. 2017. Improvements in archaeomagnetic dating in western Europe from the Late Bronze to the Late Iron Ages: an alternative to the problem of the Hallsttattian radiocarbon plateau. *Archaeometry* 60(4), 870–83

Hounslow, M and Karloukovski, V. 2013. Archaeomagnetic dating. In J. Zant and C. Howard-Davies (eds), *Scots Dyke to Turnpike: the archaeology of the A66, Greta Bridge to Scotch Corner*, 191–9. Lancaster: Oxford Archaeology

Korte, M., Constable, C., Donadini, F. and Holme, R. 2011. Reconstructing the Holocene geomagnetic field. *Earth and Planetary Science Letters* 312(3), 497–505

Korte, M., Brown, M., Gunnarson, S., Nilsson, A., Panovska, S., Wardinski, I. and Constable, C. 2019. Refining Holocene geochronologies using palaeomagnetic records. *Quaternary Geochronology* 50, 47–74

Kovacheva, M., Kostadinova-Avramova, M., Jordanova, N., Lanos, P. and Boyadzhiev, Y. 2014. Extended and revised archaeomagnetic database and secular variation curves from Bulgaria for the last eight millennia. *Physics of the Earth and Planetary Interiors* 236, 79–94

Kresten, P., Goedicke, C. and Manzano, A. 2003. TL-dating of vitrified material. *Geochronometria* 22, 9–14

Lanos, P. 2004. Bayesian inference of calibration curves: application to archaeomagnetism. In C. Buck, and A. Millard (eds), *Tools for Constructing Chronologies: crossing disciplinary boundaries*, 43–82. London: Springer

Larson, E. and Walker, T. 1975. Development of chemical remanent magnetization during early stages of red-bed formation in late Cenozoic sediments, Baja, California. *Geological Society of America Bulletin* 86, 639–50

Linford, P. 2006. *Archaeomagnetic Dating. Guidelines on Producing and Interpreting Archaeomagnetic Dates*. Swindon: English Heritage

Liu, Q., Roberts, A., Larrasoaña, J., Banerjee, S., Guyodo, Y., Tauxe, L. and Oldfield, F. 2012. Environmental magnetism: principles and applications. *Reviews of Geophysics* 50(4), 1–50

Lund, S., Oppo, D. and Curry, W. 2017. Late Quaternary paleomagnetic secular variation recorded in deep-sea sediments from the Demerara Rise, equatorial west Atlantic Ocean. *Physics of the Earth and Planetary Interiors* 272, 17–26

MacKie, E. 1969. Radiocarbon dates and the Scottish Iron Age. *Antiquity* 43, 15–26

MacKie, E. 1976. The vitrified forts of Scotland. In D. Harding (ed.), *Hillforts. Later prehistoric earthworks in Britain and Ireland*, 205–35. London: Academic Press

Mackereth, F. 1971. On the variation in direction of the horizontal component of remanent magnetisation in lake sediments. *Earth and Planetary Science Letters* 12(3), 332–8

Mellström, A., Nilsson, A., Stanton, T., Muscheler, R., Snowball, I. and Suttie, N. 2015. Post-depositional remanent magnetization lock-in depth in precisely dated varved sediments assessed by archaeomagnetic field models. *Earth and Planetary Science Letters* 410, 186–96

Mitra, R. and Tauxe, L. 2009. Full vector model for magnetization in sediments. *Earth and Planetary Science Letters* 286(3), 535–45

Molyneux, L. 1971. A complete result magnetometer for measuring the remanent magnetization of rocks. *Geophysical Journal International* 24, 429–33 [http://dx.doi.org/10.1111/j.1365-246X.1971.tb02188.x]

Noble, G., Gondek, M., Campbell, E. and Cook, M. 2013. Between prehistory and history: the archaeological detection of social change among the Picts. *Antiquity* 87, 1136–50 [doi:10.1017/S0003598X00049917]

Noel, M. and Batt, C. 1990. A method for correcting geographically separated remanence directions for the purpose of archaeomagnetic dating. *Geophysical Journal International* 102(3), 753–6

Pavón-Carrasco, F., Osete, M., Torta, J. and De Santis, A. 2014. A geomagnetic field model for the Holocene based on archaeomagnetic and lava flow data. *Earth and Planetary Science Letters* 388, 98–109

Pavón-Carrasco, F., Osete, M., Torta, J. and Gaya-Piqué, L. 2009. A regional archeomagnetic model for Europe for the last 3000 years, SCHA.DIF.3K: applications to archeomagnetic dating. *Geochemistry, Geophysics, Geosystems* 10(3), 1–22

Pavón-Carrasco, F., Rodríguez-González, J., Osete, M. and Torta, J. 2011. A Matlab tool for archaeomagnetic dating. *Journal of Archaeological Science* 38(2), 408–19

Pavón-Carrasco, F., Campuzano, S., Rivero-Montero, M., Molina-Cardín, A., Gómez-Paccard, M. and Osete, M. 2021. SCHA.DIF.4k: 4,000 years of paleomagnetic reconstruction for Europe and its application for dating. *Journal of Geophysical Research: Solid Earth* 126, e2020JB021237 [https://doi.org/10.1029/2020JB021237]

Peña, R., Goguitchaichvili, A., Guilbaud, M.-N., Martínez, V., Rathert, M., Siebe, C., Reyes, B. and Morales, J. 2014. Paleomagnetic secular variation study of Ar–Ar dated lavas flows from Tacambaro area (central Mexico): possible evidence of Intra-Jaramillo geomagnetic excursion in volcanic rocks. *Physics of the Earth and Planetary Interiors* 229, 98–109

Ponte, J., Font, E., Veiga-Pires, C. and Hillaire-Marcel, C. 2018. Speleothems as magnetic archives: palaeosecular variation and a relative paleointensity record from a Portuguese speleothem. *Geochemistry, Geophysics, Geosystems* 19(9), 2962–72

Pulley, S., Rowntree, K. and Foster, I. 2015. Conservatism of mineral magnetic signatures in farm dam sediments in the South African Karoo: the potential effects of particle size and post-depositional diagenesis. *Journal of Soils and Sediments* 15(12), 2387–97

Ralston, I. 2006. *Celtic Fortifications*. Stroud: Tempus

Reimer, P., Austin, W., Bard, E., Bayliss, A., Blackwell, P., Bronk Ramsey, C., Butzin, M., Cheng, H., Edwards, R., Friedrich, M., Grootes, P., Guilderson, T., Hajdas, I., Heaton, T., Hogg, A., Hughen, K., Kromer, B., Manning, S., Muscheler, R., Palmer, J., Pearson, C., van der Plicht, J., Reimer, R., Richards, D., Scott, E., Southon, J., Turney, C., Wacker, L., Adolphi, F., Büntgen, U., Capano, M., Fahrni, S., Fogtmann-Schulz, A., Friedrich, R., Köhler, P., Kudsk, S., Miyake, F., Olsen, J., Reinig, F., Sakamoto, M., Sookdeo, A. and Talamo, S. 2020. The IntCal20 Northern Hemisphere radiocarbon age calibration curve (0–55 cal. kBP). *Radiocarbon* 62, 725–57

Roberts, A. 2015. Magnetic mineral diagenesis. *Earth-Science Reviews* 151, 1–47

Roberts, A. and Winklhofer, M. 2004. Why are geomagnetic excursions not always recorded in sediments? Constraints from post-depositional remanent magnetization lock-in modelling. *Earth and Planetary Science Letters* 227(3), 345–59

Sanderson, D., Placido, F. and Tate, J. 1988. Scottish vitrified forts: TL results from six study sites. *Nuclear Tracks and Radiation Measurements* 14, 307–16

Snowball, I., Zillén, L., Ojala, A., Saarinen, T. and Sandgren, P. 2007. FENNOSTACK and FENNORPIS: varve dated Holocene palaeomagnetic secular variation and relative palaeointensity stacks for Fennoscandia. *Earth and Planetary Science Letters* 255(1), 106–16

Snowball, I., Mellström, A., Ahlstrand, E., Haltia, E., Nilsson, A., Ning, W., Muscheler, R. and Brauer, A. 2013. An estimate of post-depositional remanent magnetization lock-in depth in organic rich varved lake sediments. *Global and Planetary Change* 110, 264–77

Stillinger, M., Feinberg, J. and Frahm, E. 2015. Refining the archaeomagnetic dating curve for the Near East: new intensity data from Bronze Age ceramics at Tell Mozan, Syria. *Journal of Archaeological Sciences* 53, 345–55

Suganuma, Y., Okuno, J., Heslop, D., Roberts, A., Yamazaki, T. and Yokoyama, Y. 2011. Post-depositional remanent magnetization lock-in for marine sediments deduced from 10Be and paleomagnetic records through the Matuyama–Brunhes boundary. *Earth and Planetary Science Letters* 311(1), 39–52

Suganuma, Y., Yokoyama, Y., Yamazaki, T., Kawamura, K., Horng, C.-S. and Matsuzaki, H. 2010. 10Be evidence for delayed acquisition of remanent magnetization in marine sediments: implication for a new age for the Matuyama–Brunhes boundary. *Earth and Planetary Science Letters* 296 (3), 443–50

Suttie, N. and Batt, C. 2020. Re-evaluating archaeomagnetic dates of the vitrified hillforts of Scotland. *Journal of Archaeological Science: Reports* 30, 102233 [https://doi.org/10.1016/j.jasrep.2020.102233]

Tang, F., Taylor, R., Einsle, J., Borlina, C., Fu, R., Weiss, B., Williams, H., Williams, W., Nagy, L., Midgley, P., Lima, E., Bell, E., Harrison, T., Alexander, E., and Harrison, R. 2019. Secondary magnetite in ancient zircon precludes analysis of a Hadean geodynamo. *Proceedings of the National Academy of Sciences* 116(2), 407–12 [doi: 10.1073/pnas.1811074116]

Tarling, D. 1983. *Palaeomagnetism: Principles and Applications in Geology, Geophysics and Archaeology*. London: Chapman and Hall

Tarling, D. and Dobson, M. 1995. Archaeomagnetism: an error assessment of fired material observations in the British directional database. *Journal of Geomagnetism and Geoelectricity* 47, 5–18

Tema, E. and Kondopoulou, D. 2011. Secular variation of the Earth's magnetic field in the Balkan region during the last eight millennia based on archaeomagnetic data. *Geophysical Journal International* 186(2), 603–14

Tema, E., Gómez-Paccard, M., Kondopoulou, D. and Almar, Y. 2012. Intensity of the Earth's magnetic field in Greece during the last five millennia: new data from Greek pottery. *Physics of the Earth and Planetary Interiors* 202–3, 14–26

Tema, E., Hedley, I., Fasnacht, W. and Peege, C. 2018. Insights on the geomagnetic secular variation in the Eastern Mediterranean: first directional data from Cyprus. *Physics of the Earth and Planetary Interiors* 285, 1–11

Trapanese, A., Batt, C. and Schnepp, E. 2008. Sampling methods in archaeomagnetic dating: a comparison using case studies from Wörterberg, Eisenerz and Gams Valley (Austria). *Physics and Chemistry of the Earth, Parts A/B/C* 33(6–7), 414–26

Turner, G. and Thompson, R. 1979. Behaviour of the earth's magnetic field as recorded in the sediment of Loch Lomond. *Earth and Planetary Science Letters* 42(3), 412–26

Turner, G. and Thompson, R. 1981. Lake sediment record of the geomagnetic secular variation in Britain during Holocene times. *Geophysical Journal of the Royal Astronomical Society* 65(3), 703–25

Walden, J., Oldfield, F. and Smith, J. 1999. *Environmental Magnetism: a practical guide*. London: Quaternary Research Association Technical Guide 6

Williams, J. 1777. *An account of some remarkable ancient ruins, lately discovered in the highlands, and northern parts of Scotland. In a series of letters to G. C. M. Esq; By John Williams*. Edinburgh: William Creech

Yutsis-Akimova, S., Gallet, Y. and Amirov, S. 2018. Rapid geomagnetic field intensity variations in the Near East during the 6th millennium BC: new archaeointensity data from Halafian site Yarim Tepe II (northern Iraq). *Earth and Planetary Science Letters* 482, 201–12

Zananiri, I., Batt, C., Lanos, P., Tarling. D. and Linford, P. 2007. Archaeomagnetic secular variation in the UK during the past 4000 years and its application to archaeomagnetic dating. *Physics of The Earth and Planetary Interiors* 160(2), 97–107

Zanella, E., Tema, E., Lanci, L., Regattieri, E., Isola, I., Hellstrom, J., Costa, E., Zanchetta, G., Drysdale, R. and Magrì, F. 2018. A 10,000 yr record of high-resolution paleosecular variation from a flowstone of Rio Martino Cave, northwestern Alps, Italy. *Earth and Planetary Science Letters* 485, 32–42

Zhao, X. and Roberts, A. 2010. How does Chinese loess become magnetized? *Earth and Planetary Science Letters* 292(1), 112–22

Zhao, X., Egli, R., Gilder, S. and Müller, S. 2016. Microbially assisted recording of the Earth's magnetic field in sediment. *Nature Communications* 7, 10673 [https://doi.org/10.1038/ncomms10673]

6. Ecofactual chronologies

Seren Griffiths and Ben Gearey

One of the central research questions that archaeologists often seek to explore – regardless of when or where their work is focused – is the relationships between past human societies, plants and other animal communities and landscapes. The conditions in which people, plants and animals lived have huge implications for how we imagine societies in the past. Central research themes may include how people made their living, got food and survived in different environments. Comparing the timing of signals from proxies of palaeo-environmental sequences and the timing of changes in anthropogenic material culture or sites is often important in thinking about resilience or the impacts of climate change or palaeo-environmental events (Griffiths forthcoming).

In many projects working in the Holocene chronologies are often provided by radiocarbon measurements, with other techniques such as Optically Stimulated Luminescence and dendrochronology employed to lesser degrees. There are a number of key considerations in working to produce accurate and robust palaeo-environmental chronologies. This chapter discusses approaches to constructing chronologies for palaeo-environmental research projects, before considering some case studies.

Thinking about ecofactual chronologies

We can identify two key types of ecofactual chronologies. First, we have those chronologies where direct age estimates are produced on ecofacts which are of interest. For example, if the research question concerns the introduction or extinction of a species in a region, direct radiocarbon measurements on the remains of members of that species are intrinsically relevant to that research question. In a recent study, for example, direct radiocarbon measurements on cereal seeds helped explore the introduction of these resources to Ireland and Britain (Griffiths 2018).

A related development of this approach is the use of 'dates as data'. In dates as data approaches, the numbers of scientific dating measurements are taken as an indication of the size of a population of a species of humans, animals or plants. There are lots of issues with these approaches including, perhaps most importantly, the research history of a region which may determine how many chronometric measurements have been produced (see discussion in Bronk Ramsey 2017; see also Shennan *et al.* 2013; Contreras and Meadows 2014; Griffiths *et al.* 2022).

Even if the presence of a species is not the primary objective of a research programme, providing age estimates for the presence of introduced species, species of economic importance, or those that became extinct can add value to chronological research projects with another primary research aim. Producing a radiocarbon measurement on a sample that is both a species of archaeological interest and was recovered from an important archaeological deposit on a site means the measurement is useful for several research questions.

Our second class of palaeo-environmental chronology moves beyond direct age estimates on samples. We can think about these analyses as proxy chronologies. Chronologies in this class are more complicated to build because the association between the measurement and the palaeo-environmental signal needs to be determined. When we have lots of ecofacts recovered from a sequence (for example pollen, plant macrofossils, beetle remains and so on) with very different taphonomies, the associations between different ecofacts and the scientific dating measurements may vary. The underlying processes that cause signals in the proxies also have to be considered. In these proxy chronologies there are lots of places where uncertainties can be introduced.

As well as the complexity of thinking about past ecosystems, the construction of robust proxy chronologies requires a significant degree of practical consideration. This can include issues surrounding sampling for these chronologies in the field, in the choice of scientific dating techniques employed, in the analytical definition of palaeo-environmental events (see below) and in constructing analytic models of the chronometric data. In this chapter, we will cover each of these issues concerning the creation of proxy palaeo-environmental chronologies in turn before turning to our case studies. First, we begin by thinking about sampling.

Sampling for proxy chronologies

The recovery of ecofacts requires specific sampling strategies in order that assemblages are produced in a standardised and meaningful way. So, when constructing palaeo-environmental chronologies it is important to consider *both* how sampling strategies contributed to the recovery of ecofacts under analysis and how sampling strategies produce chronometric measurements. The relationship between these sampling strategies is critical to subsequent interpretation and analysis. As noted in Chapter 2, the development of Accelerator Mass Spectrometry means that radiocarbon measurements can be produced on small ecofacts, which means that chronologies can be produced on samples from vertical soil monoliths (Fig. 6.1), corers (Fig. 6.2) or boreholes (Fig. 6.3). In these cases, there may be practical considerations about how specialists sub-sample limited material or multiple sampling strategies may be required to recover a range of different ecofacts. In terrestrial contexts, potential ecofacts may include: pollen and other microscopic non-pollen polymorphs such as fungal spores; beetles and other insects; terrestrial molluscs; and phytoliths from plants. From aquatic environments additional microscopic ecofacts can be used to inform on past environmental conditions. These may include: microscopic algae or diatoms; simple marine animals or foraminifera; and tiny aquatic crustaceans or ostracods. Not all proxies are present in different preservation environments, so depending on where and when research is focused, it may be possible to use land molluscs to inform about the degree of tree-cover at a specific sample site for highly calcareous contexts, but evidence from the study of pollen grains may not be available to you due to poor preservation in such environments. The volume in this series by Allen (2017) covers the analysis of molluscs as palaeo-environmental proxies.

Sampling strategy

In order that robust chronologies are produced for environmental archaeology or palaeo-environmental research, a sampling strategy for different palaeo-environmental proxies and ecofacts, as well as different types of scientific dating measurements, needs to be developed in advance of fieldwork. Any sampling strategy needs to start with the research aims for a project and should be developed in consultation with palaeo-environmental specialists, material culture specialists and specialists in scientific dating. In Britain, in large infrastructure projects, it is becoming increasingly common to employ a designated specialist to lead the scientific dating aspects of the project design in the field and in post-excavation. For large infrastructure projects, the project design may therefore include written technical strategies for a range of specialisms, such as: osteoarchaeological work, palaeo-environmental work, geoarchaeological work and scientific dating, with site-specific Written Schemes of Investigation for individual areas.

Figure 6.1. Recovering palaeo-environmental evidence from intertidal deposits to the south of Ferriter's Cove, Co. Kerry, Ireland. Here deposits of peat are overlain by freshwater silts and then dune or beach deposits. Producing accurate estimates for the timing of change indicated by sediments and ecofacts is important for palaeo-environmental reconstruction. Copyright: Ben Gearey.

The sampling strategy needs to consider the likelihood that palaeo-environmental proxies and samples suitable for different chronometric techniques will be preserved given the underlying geology and hydrological regime. It is very important to ensure that the correct types of samples of sufficient size are recovered for both palaeo-environmental analysis and scientific dating. It may not be sufficient to select material for scientific dating from samples taken for palaeo-environmental purposes – this is true of radiocarbon as well as the other dating techniques covered in this volume (which of course require dating specialists to recover the samples). For example, taking samples for palynological or molluscan reconstruction may not provide sufficient suitable material for radiocarbon measurements. In the case of pollen work, it may be necessary to recover a separate series of parallel bulk samples to recover plant macrofossils for radiocarbon measurements. If parallel sequences are employed, the stratigraphic relationships between these sequences need to be directly related and clearly recorded *in situ* prior to sampling. Consideration should be given to standard sampling sizes for different ecofacts, for example 40 litres or more for charred plant remains as is recommended in Britain (see Chapter 7). In the rest of this chapter, we focus on producing proxy radiocarbon chronologies, as this is the most common palaeo-environmental Holocene chronological dataset.

Chronologies from cores

There are several challenges in producing robust radiocarbon chronologies from cores (augers, boreholes etc). First, only a very small volumes of sediment will be recovered from any depth. This means that it is difficult to assess whether any potential radiocarbon sample is likely to be intrusive or residual. Secondly, without an open section it may not be possible to judge if the lithology or sedimentary sequence at a particular sample location is representative of the wider sequence across an area. Systematic coring programmes can provide ways of evaluating the wider sequence in an area, however, generally ensuring robust palaeo-environmental proxy radiocarbon chronologies from cores is more difficult than from open sections. Certain conditions preclude the use of open sections (see below) and interpreting results from such situations may be challenging.

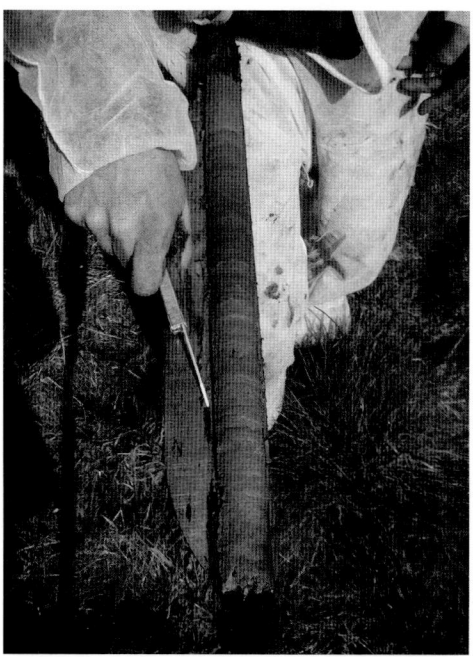

Figure 6.2. Recovering palaeo-environmental evidence using coring equipment. Here a Russian Corer is used to extract late Glacial lake marl from Newrath, Co. Waterford, Ireland. Copyright: Ben Gearey.

Chronologies from open sections

Palaeo-environmental reconstruction from open sections offers a number of advantages. By looking that the deposit sequence, a geomorphologist can assess how representative a proposed sample sequence would be of the section as a whole. Open sections allow us to have more information about deposit formation processes in different parts of a sequence. For example, if you were researching tsunami events, you might wish to focus on parts of a section which looked as if they had been subject to high energy storm events. If researching conditions associated with more gradual sea level change you might wish to avoid these areas.

A further advantage of sampling from an open section is that you can ensure that sufficient ecofactual and scientific dating samples are recovered from the same deposits. This can be especially useful when working with multiple palaeo-environmental proxies. Open sections of course also allow the use of OSL measurements which can be very important in palaeo-environmental research although certain hydrological regimes may not be suitable for this (Chapter 4).

Whatever the research questions for palaeo-environmental reconstruction and the scientific dating technique employed, the ability to see the full sequence through an exposed section therefore provides a number of important advantages. These can be summarised as ensuring that:

- a representative sample sequence can be taken,
- samples for a variety of ecofacts and for scientific dating are recovered from the same deposits,
- types of deposits relevant to the research aims (for example marine transgressions) are represented in the sequence,
- the full sequence of relevant deposits can be recovered,
- sufficient material can be recovered for the relevant ecofactual and scientific dating technique (including for example bulk sampling for plant macrofossils, or hydrological and *in situ* radiation measurements for OSL).

Documenting samples

Whatever technique of sample recovery is employed samples need detailed recording. If sampling from an open section, sections should be recorded prior to sampling and with the monolith or other sample recovery equipment *in situ* in the section. This means that there is a record of exactly what was recovered in each sample (Chapter 7).

Sub-sampling cores and monoliths

For samples recovered in cores, a detailed description of the sediment sequence will need to be produced in the laboratory. This could be accompanied by a measured drawing, or sketch, or a photographic record of the surface of the core. Depending how many proxies are going to be analysed, and how the samples were recovered, it may then be necessary to sub-sample cores so that the different proxies can be assessed (perhaps by several different specialists). At this point, it is important to consider whether you need to record, extract and preserve some suitable samples for radiocarbon measurements (e.g. short-life, single entity plant macrofossils) as specialist sub-sampling occurs.

Analytical definition of palaeo-environmental events

A significant proportion of palaeo-environmental work investigates the correlation of palaeo-environmental events observed in individual site sequences with similar events that have been identified over large geographic areas. Investigating the timing of similar proxy signals can provide evidence about the underlying processes of palaeo-environmental change.

Palaeo-environmental events could include for example:

- the deposition of volcanic ash or tephra across large ranges,
- the extinction or marked decline in a species of plant or animal over time,
- the inundation of a specific sample site after a storm.

Importantly, palaeo-environmental events are defined in spatial as well as temporal terms. Even very short-lived events do not occur everywhere *at the same time*, even though the underlying causes may be related. They also usually have some time duration attached to them; they have a temporal magnitude. Finally, palaeo-environmental events are defined by an analyst from specific patterns in the proxy evidence. In this sense, such events are subjective and this subjectivity needs to be considered in any synthesis across sites. Different analysts might recognise and define palaeo-environmental events in different ways and, in this sense, palaeo-environomental events are conceptual constructions that are observed through patterns in ecofactual evidence (Parnell *et al.* 2008; Griffiths and Gearey 2017). As such, when comparing palaeo-environmental events identified in different locations and by different analysts it is important to be very specific about how these events have been defined. By thinking critically about how these events are defined we can engage more meaningfully with the potential underlying processes (see discussion below).

Constructing models

As discussed in Chapter 8, a variety of programs exist for the analysis of chronometric data from palaeo-environmental sequences. These can include software with additional specialist capabilities useful for palaeo-environmental researchers, for example in the analysis of sea-level change in the program Bchron (Parnell and Gehrels 2015).

The analyses presented in the case studies below all make use of the Bayesian statistical age-depth modelling provided by OxCal (Bronk Ramsey 2008). In these models, chronometric data are plotted against the depth of the radiocarbon sample location. Sample depth provides one form of prior information that we have about the relationships between measurements (see Chapter 8 for a case study).

Bayesian chronological modelling of radiocarbon results from palaeo-environmental sequences offers significant advantages over traditional linear interpolation models, as it allows changes in the rate of deposit formation to be included in analysis (see Chapter 8). Such models also allow estimates to be made for the timing of palaeo-environmental events of interest at specific depths, even when we may not have direct chronometric measurements for these events.

Case studies

The case studies presented here compare measurements for the timing of palaeo-environmental events from different sample locations. In both these case studies, the analysis faces issues with sampling for proxies in the field, the analytical definition of the event in question and the choices about the most appropriate models. While these concerns are specific to the research projects detailed below, these kinds of considerations are made routinely in palaeo-environmental reconstruction work using a range of ecofacts. All the case studies discussed below have been recalculated with the calibration data in Reimer *et al.* (2020) using the original analytical approaches cited in the publications.

Case study: marine palaeoenvironmental reconstruction, Sea-Level Index Points: Hinkley Point, Somerset, UK

Hinkley Point (51.2064992221033 N, 3.14526165072327 W (WGS84)) is a location on the coast near the western edge of Bridgwater Bay (Fig. 6.3), on the edge of the tidal Bristol Channel. In advance of work to build a new power station, considerable inter- and sub-tidal archaeological work was undertaken. The bay specifically, and the Bristol Channel more generally, has been subject to considerable sea-level change since the last glacial maximum as a result of eustatic change (the melting of the glaciers) and isostatic rebound (a change in elevation of the part of the Earth's crust resulting from a shift in pressure after the last glaciation). The area under what is now Bridgwater Bay was identified as of importance for early- and mid-Holocene archaeology because of a number of finds of stone tools on the seashore and in the adjacent inland area. The area is also of interest in terms of human responses to environmental change. Changes in sea-level have been identified as especially important in understanding the local Mesolithic cultural sequence associated with hunter-gatherer-fisher lifeways, who lived in this area in the early- to mid-Holocene (*c.* 10,000 to *c.* 39th century BC). The challenges for both recovering

Figure 6.3. Recovering vibrocores from Bridgwater Bay for sub-tidal palaeo-environmental reconstruction including exploring the chronology of early Holocene sea-level change in this part of the world. Copyright: Fraser Sturt.

evidence and providing secure chronologies for palaeo-environmental change from this area are, however, considerable.

In 2009–2010 a series of 24 boreholes and 63 vibrocores (a technique for recovering underwater and wetland deposits) was collected from submerged deposits in the bay area (Fig. 6.3). From these, lithological recording identified peat deposits associated with silty, water-lain deposits. These parts of the sequence are of key importance for understanding sea-level change as they can indicate a very specific class of palaeo-environmental event: Sea Level Index Points (SLIPs). SLIPs are estimates of the relative sea-level and the sea-level tendency (i.e. rising or falling sea-level) at a specific sampling location at a specific time. Radiocarbon measurements on samples from peat can provide *termini post quos* or *termini ante quos* for changes in sea-level identified in related deposits. Peat forms in waterlogged contexts where plant material can only partially decompose because of the anoxic conditions. As a result, bits of twig, leaf matter and other plant macrofossils get preserved along with other ecofacts. The combination of the waterlogged burial environment and the partial decay of plant material results in a very acidic deposit that is ideal for palynology for example.

New analysis

In the development around Hinkley Point (Sturt *et al.* 2014), 26 radiocarbon measurements were produced from six vibrocores. These measurements were made on samples from peat deposits associated with sea-level change. The samples selected for radiocarbon measurement included plant macrofossils and different chemical fractions from the peats. The depths of all the sub-samples for radiocarbon measurements were recorded so that Bayesian deposit models could be built.

The identification of the plant macrofossils for radiocarbon measurements was important here. If species were selected that fixed carbon from submerged contexts they might be subject to an inbuilt marine offset (see Chapter 2). Results on these samples would need to be calibrated using a marine curve with an appropriate offset to produce accurate age estimates. Short-lived plant macrofossils with atmospheric photosynthetic pathways were therefore selected for radiocarbon measurement. Twig or leaf fragments were selected where possible, to exclude intrusive rooty material. Because of the level of preservation, plant macrofossils could be hand-picked from the vibrocores to ensure that they looked as if they had been deposited as the peat formed – the leaves and twigs were arranged in horizontal layers of terrestrial plant detritus. These ecofacts are believed to have ceased carbon exchange very shortly before they were deposited. The dated event (end of carbon exchange) should therefore have very little time difference with the event of interest (deposition in the sequence and formation of peat).

Where such plant macrofossils were not available from the peat, 10 mm thick samples of the peat itself were sub-sampled from the vibrocore. The location of these sub-samples was determined by the changes identified in the lithology, with samples of the top and bottom of the same peat horizon selected to provide estimates to chronologically bracket the peat formation.

For the peat samples, two measurements were made on different chemical fractions extracted in the radiocarbon laboratory. After manual cleaning of rooty material, samples were subjected to chemical pretreatment, in this case, an acid-base-acid wash.

During this pretreatment the humic acid fractions (the acid-insoluble/alkali-soluble fraction) and the humin fractions (the alkali-/acid insoluble fractions) were extracted.

The association between these fractions and the age of the deposit formation presents some uncertainty. Within peat bodies, humic acid fractions are thought to be potentially mobile in water while humin fractions are thought to be less mobile. Ideally, radiocarbon measurements from both the humin and humic acid fractions from the same peat sample would be of the same age, in which case we might suggest that we have a robust estimate for the formation of peat at a particular depth. However, in many cases these fractions produce varying radiocarbon ages. Direct measurements of the radiocarbon age of soil or sediment are equally problematic. In these cases it can be very unclear how carbon enters a sample of soil or sediment (Brock *et al.* 2011; Griffiths *et al.* 2015) and therefore what the dated event represents.

The results showed that there was considerable variation between some of the age estimates produced on samples of humic acid, humin and plant macrofossils from the same depths (Fig. 6.4). In this case study, many of the humic acid fractions were older than the humin fractions. Because humic acids are thought to be more likely to be mobile in peat in terrestrial sequences they often return *younger* dates than the comparable measurement produced on humin fractions. In this sub-marine case study, we suggested that the generally *older* humic acid fractions may have resulted from the upward movement of humic acid from older, underlying deposits as the environment became increasingly waterlogged, associated with elevated and more brackish ground water in advance of sea-level change. However, these fractions cannot be thought of as ideal samples exactly because we are not sure how and when carbon isotopes enter the sediment and whether these sample therefore represent closed systems.

Evidence from a number of ecofacts from three cores suggested that the lower peat deposits encountered in these sequences represented the transition from freshwater to full marine conditions. The interface between the peat and the overlying marine deposits in one of the cores (VC06) seemed to have preserved a full depositional sequence of this transition, whereas in other cores there was evidence for erosive contacts, meaning that part of the sequence might have been lost. An estimate for the end of the process of peat formation suggested that fully marine conditions might have been achieved in *8830–8150 cal. BC (95% probability)* or *8740–8470 cal. BC (68% probability*; End Hinkley Point Lower Peat; Fig. 6.5). However, this process took place over a long time. From the three vibrocores with this lower peat, the estimates for the formation of peats indicate that this took place over some *650–1130 years (95% probability,* or *780–1020 years 68% probability*; Duration Hinkley lower peat; figure not shown).

Case study conclusions
From the case study at Hinkley Point, we see the importance of thinking about a strategy for **sub-sampling** cores where limited material exists in order that all specialists can complete their work. This case study also shows the importance of avoiding carbon fractions from peat or other sediment. Here, the different chemical fractions extracted often produced different radiocarbon ages. Looking at multiple cores in this instance helped us to think about the **complexities** of this landscape where marine conditions may have developed as a localised **mosaic** over a very

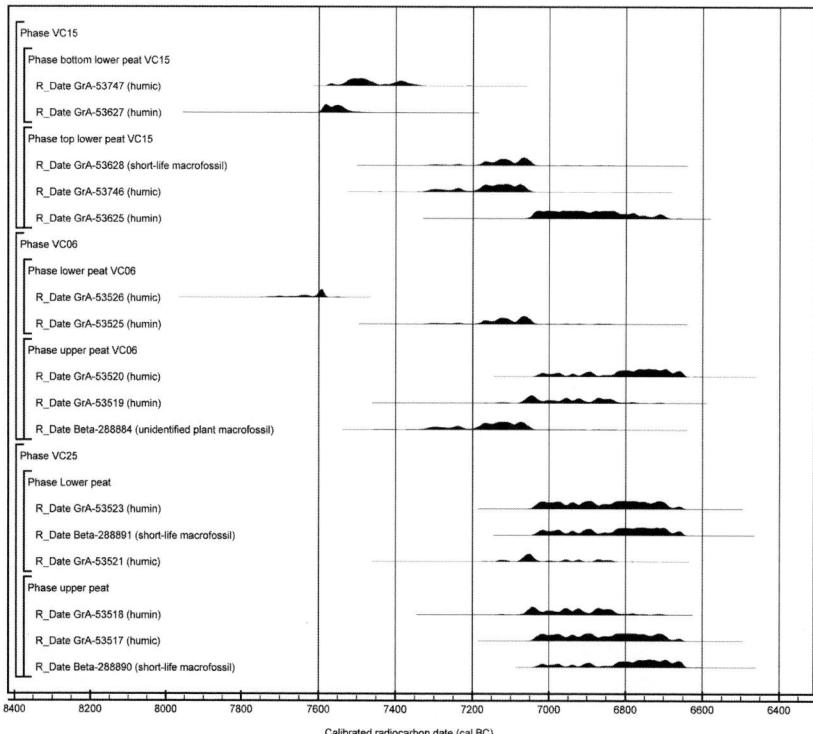

Figure 6.4 Calibrated radiocarbon results on different types of samples recovered from Bridgwater Bay. A range of radiocarbon ages has been produced on different sample types. Working with chemical fractions from sediment poses a number of challenges as plant macrofossils with well-understood taphonomies, and carbon reservoirs, may often represent preferable samples. Full details in Griffiths et al. (2015). Copyright: Seren Griffiths.

long time. In contrast, constructing a model for relative sea level change on only one radiocarbon measurement or from one core could have provided an overly simplistic impression of environmental change.

Case study key themes
This case study demonstrates the importance of thinking critically about the **association** of the dated event with the palaeo-environmental event of interest. For palaeo-environmental reconstruction based on radiocarbon measurements on peat it may be necessary to investigate age differences between different types of radiocarbon samples. In proxy chronologies, thinking about the **taphonomy** of the dated samples and the palaeo-environmental evidence is vital. **Comparing results** from multiple cores or other vertical samples can provide an insight into change at a landscape scale. Use of **multi-proxy** palaeo-environmental data will always provide a more comprehensive picture of change.

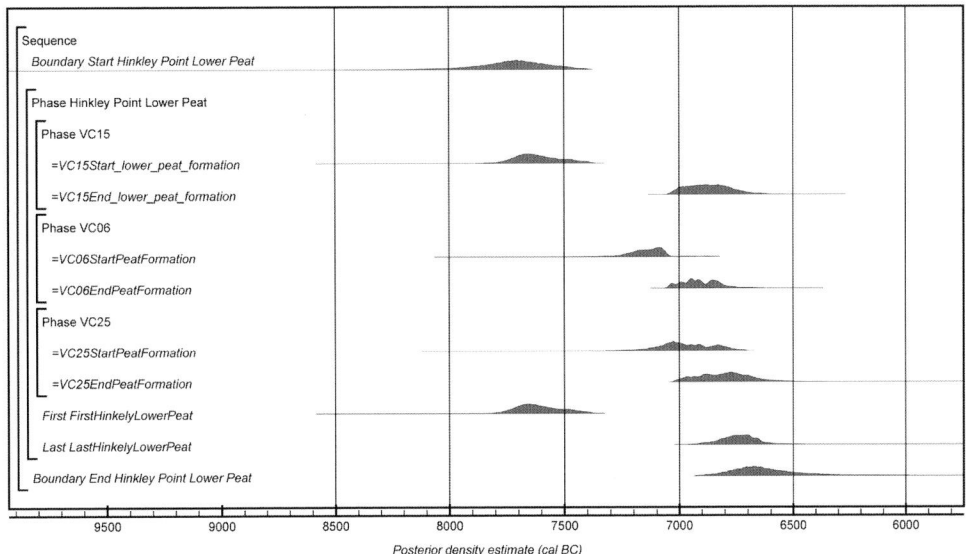

Figure 6.5. Posterior density estimates from the deposit models that estimate the timing of peat formation from Bridgwater Bay. Results from palaeo-environmental analysis are discussed further in Chapter 8. Full details in Griffiths et al. *(2015). Copyright: Seren Griffiths.*

Case study: terrestrial palynological palaeo-environmental reconstruction: the elm decline on the Yorkshire Moors, UK

The mid-Holocene elm decline is a widely identified palaeo-environmental event in pollen records across north-west Europe. In this sense, the elm decline is a classic palaeo-environmental event. The causes of the decline in pollen records for elm trees has been the subject of considerable debate in palaeoecological and archaeological circles for decades (e.g. Huntley and Birks 1983; Edwards and Hirons 1984; Hirons and Edwards 1986; Parker *et al.* 2002). However, the nature of the palaeo-environmental signals that are interpreted as the elm decline can actually be quite variable.

The 'elm decline' pollen signal often takes the form of an initial sustained fall in elm pollen percentage, that represents a major reduction in the population of the trees. In many cases, this reduction is followed by a recovery in pollen counts, only to be followed by a sustained second decrease in frequencies.

In the UK the elm decline seemed to broadly coincide chronologically with a number of changes in the archaeological record, including the first evidence for the use of most domestic animal and plant resources, as well as the first evidence for the local Neolithic practices. The duration of time over which the elm decline occurred has been recognised as important in identifying the possible causes. Was this a very short-lived, widely occurring event as a result of a single primary cause, as we might imagine the effects of human activity associated with the start of farming? Or perhaps a similar fungal infection to that of the 1980s' Dutch Elm Disease? Or did the elm decline occur in a much more time-transgressive manner? Was this a more gradual process and, if so, what would this indicate about the underlying cause – or perhaps *causes*? To investigate this we (Griffiths and Gearey 2017) undertook a re-analysis of the chronological evidence for the elm decline in the heavily studied North Yorkshire Moors and surrounding regions.

New analysis
Thirty-one paleoenvironmental sequences with palynological evidence for elm declines and radiocarbon measurements were identified from Lincolnshire, the Humber area and the North Yorks Moors. Much of this work had been undertaken by Jim Innes and Ian Simmons and colleagues. The sequences from this region with evidence for the elm decline including blanket, intertidal and floodplain peats, from lowland and upland sites.

Each of the sites that had good evidence for an elm decline – and consistent radiocarbon measurements – was subject to Bayesian deposit modelling using functions in OxCal (Bronk Ramsey 2008; Griffiths and Gearey 2017), which allowed estimates for the elm decline to be compared from across the region. In some cases, the material that had been used for radiocarbon measurements meant that the result could only be regarded as a *terminus post quem* for the elm decline. The different estimates for elm declines are shown in Figure 6.6. As can be seen there is considerable variability in the chronological estimates for 'the' elm decline.

One of the critical considerations in this analysis was how different specialists sub-sampled their cores, identified the elm decline and produced pollen counts. This synthesis includes data collected over a long period by many researchers who used different sampling intervals, employing a range of approaches to producing pollen sums and who therefore had a range of approaches to identifying the elm decline event itself. In the sites included in this analysis, approaches to calculating pollen sums included the total land pollen method (%TLP), the percentage total arboreal pollen method (%AP), and in some cases the total land pollen method excluding the species of hazel, alder and birch that are over-represented at these locations.

Case study conclusions
As can be seen in Figure 6.6 there is considerable variation in the timing of elm declines identified in different sample sites. In this part of the world we have reasonably good estimates for that start of the regional Neolithic material culture package (Griffiths 2014). The results of the elm decline analysis show that there is lots of evidence for elm declines that pre-date the earliest evidence we have for Neolithic practices, including the presence of plant and animal domesticates. Moreover, the data presented here suggest that the elm declines identified at individual sites occurred over a very long period of time, over *2900–3620 years (95% probability; or 2990–3320 years 68% probability; duration elm decline;* figure not shown). Sites around North Gill on the North Yorks Moors (which represents one of the most intensively studied regions in terms of pollen analysis in the UK) show this temporal variability. Here seven cores were studied in detail from a series of sampling points some several hundred metres apart (Fig. 6.7). The elm declines identified in these different cores occurred over *2540–2820 years (95% probability; or 2600–2740 years 68% probability;* figure not shown). The timing of the elm decline shows considerable

6. Ecofactual chronologies

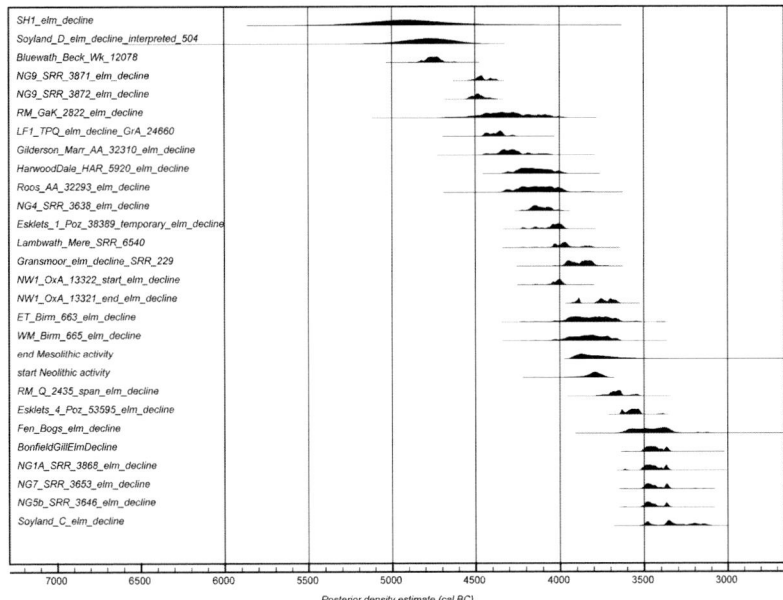

Figure 6.6. A comparative plot showing posterior density estimates for the timing for elm decline signals from sample sites from across Yorkshire and Humberside calculated following method in Griffiths and Gearey (2017). There is considerable variability in the estimates for the elm decline. Many elm declines appear to take place before the first evidence for farming and associated Neolithic material culture (distribution 'start Neolithic activity'), and before the last evidence for Mesolithic material culture (distribution 'end Mesolithic activity'). Copyright: Seren Griffiths.

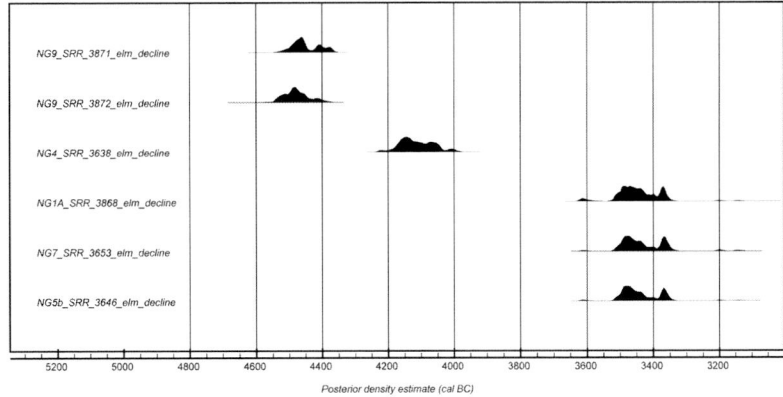

Figure 6.7. Posterior density estimates for the timing of 'elm decline' from sample sites a few hundred metres apart at North Gill, calculated following method in Griffiths and Gearey (2017). The elm declines identified in these different cores occur over long periods of time. Copyright: Seren Griffiths.

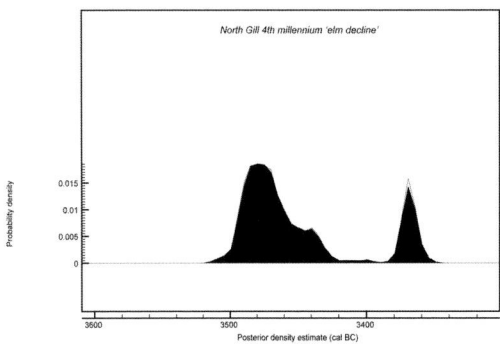

Figure 6.8. A combined estimate for the timing of the 4th millennium 'elm decline' identified at North Gill. Full details in Griffiths and Gearey (2017). Copyright: Seren Griffiths.

chronological variability even in this restricted sampling area.

The variability in the estimates for the elm decline may be telling us something important about the underlying processes. Three of the North Gill sequences have very similar estimates for its timing. Combining these three estimates suggest that the signal they are identifying occurred in 3510–3420 cal. BC (76% probability) or 3380–3350 cal. BC (19% probability; Fig. 6.8). This may represent the timing of the local North Gill elm decline, recognised in classic palynological terms as a second sustained reduction in elm (Hirons and Edwards 1986, 138). The other estimates may, therefore, represent the start of a very long, drawn out process, which had multiple contributions, but probably did not include the immediate impact from the use of domestic plants and animals.

Case study key themes
This elm decline case study emphasises that the identification and interpretation of **palaeo-environmental events** are critical in palaeo-environmental reconstructions. In this case not all the elm declines appeared to be synchronous. Here the **noise** or **time-transgressive** pattern in elm decline signals might actually be telling us something about the underlying causal mechanisms and are important aspects of the interpretation.

Chapter conclusions

Interaction between people, plants and animals is often a central research theme in archaeology. Proposing any kind of **relationship between signals** identified from the palaeo-environment and anthropogenic activity requires robust chronologies for both types of evidence. This means that consideration needs to be paid in the field to **integrated sampling** strategies. Human-environment interaction may be **complicated** and a considered approach to chronological evidence may be required to produce narratives that are not overly simplistic. We discuss site-based issues more broadly in Chapter 7.

Bibliography

Allen, M. 2017. *Molluscs in Archaeology: methods, approaches and applications*. Oxford: Studying Scientific Archaeology 3

Brock, F., Lee, S., Housley, R. and Bronk Ramsey, C. 2011. Variation in the radiocarbon age of different fractions of peat: a case study from Ahrenshöft, northern Germany. *Quaternary Geochronology* 6, 505–55

Bronk Ramsey, C. 2008. Deposition models for chronological records. *Quaternary Science Reviews* 27(1–2), 42–60

Bronk Ramsey, C. 2017. Methods for summarizing radiocarbon datasets. *Radiocarbon* 59(2), 1809–33

Contreras, D. and Meadows, J. 2014. Summed radiocarbon calibrations as a population proxy: a critical evaluation using a realistic simulation approach. *Journal of Archaeological Science* 52, 591–608

Edwards, K. and Hirons, K. 1984. Cereal pollen grains in pre-elm decline deposits: implications for the earliest agriculture in Britain and Ireland. *Journal of Archaeological Science* 11, 71–80

Griffiths, S. 2014. A Bayesian radiocarbon chronology of the early Neolithic of Yorkshire and Humberside. *Archaeological Journal* 171, 2–29

Griffiths, S. 2018. A cereal problem? What the current chronology of early cereal domesticates might tell us about changes in late fifth and early fourth millennium cal. BC Ireland and Britain. *Environmental Archaeology* 27(1), 73–9 [doi: 10.1080/14614103.2018.1529945]

Griffiths, S. forthcoming. Cataclysmic events, long-term processes and human responses: identifying causal relationships in Holocene human-environment interaction. In C. Goudge (ed.), *Archaeologies of Adaptation and Resilience*. Gainesville FL: University of Florida Press

Griffiths, S. and Gearey, B. 2017. The Mesolithic–Neolithic transition and the chronology of the 'elm decline'. *Radiocarbon* 59, 1321–45 [https://doi.org/10.1017/RDC.2017.73]

Griffiths, S., Sturt, F. Dix, J. Gearey, B. and Grant, M. 2015. Chronology and palaeoenvironmental reconstruction in the sub-tidal zone: a case study from Hinkley Point. *Journal of Archaeological Science* 54, 237–53 [https://doi.org/10.1016/j.jas.2014.12.008]

Griffiths, S., Johnson, R., May, R., McOmish, D., Marshall, P., Last, J. and Bayliss, A. 2022. Dividing the land: time and land division in the English North Midlands and Yorkshire. *European Journal of Archaeology* 25(2), 216–37 [doi:10.1017/eaa.2021.48]

Hirons, K. and Edwards, K. 1986. Events at and around the first and second *Ulmus* declines: palaeoecological investigations in Co. Tyrone, Northern Ireland. *New Phytologist* 104, 131–53

Huntley, B. and Birks, H. 1983. *An Atlas of Past and Present Pollen Maps for Europe 0–13, 000 Years Ago*. Cambridge: Cambridge University Press

Parker, A., Goudie, A., Anderson, D., Robinson, M. and Bonsall, C. 2002. A review of the mid-Holocene elm decline in the British Isles. *Progress in Physical Geography* 26(1), 1–45

Parnell, A. and Gehrels, W. 2015. Using chronological models in late Holocene sea-level reconstruction from saltmarsh sediments. In I. Shennan, A. Long and B. Horton (eds), *Handbook of Sea-Level Research*. Hoboken NJ: Wiley-Blackwell, 500–13

Parnell, A., Haslett, J., Allen, J., Buck, C. and Huntley, B. 2008. A flexible approach to assessing synchroneity of past events using Bayesian reconstructions of sedimentation history. *Quaternary Science Reviews* 27, 1872–85

Reimer, P., Austin, W., Bard, E., Bayliss, A., Blackwell, P., Bronk Ramsey, C., Butzin, M, Cheng, H., Edwards, R., Friedrich, M., Grootes, P., Guilderson, T., Hajadas, I., Heaton, T., Hogg, A., Hughen, K., Kromer, B., Manning, S., Muscheler, R., Palmer, J., Pearson, C., van der Plicht, J., Reimer, R., Richards, D., Scott, E., Southon, J., Turney, C., Wacker, L., Adolphi, F., Büntgen, U., Capano, M., Fahrni, S., Fogtmann-Schultz, A., Friedrich, R., Köhler, P., Kudsk, S., Miyake, F., Olsen, J., Reinig, F., Sakamoto, M., Sookdeo, A. and Talamo, S. 2020. The IntCal20 Northern Hemisphere radiocarbon age calibration curve (0–55 cal. kBP). *Radiocarbon* 62(4), 725–57

Shennan, S., Downey, S., Timpson, A., Edinborough, K., College, S., Kerig, T., Manning, K. and Thomas, M. 2013. Regional population collapse followed initial agriculture booms in mid-Holocene Europe. *Nature Communications* 4, 2486 [https://doi.org/10.1038/ncomms3486]

Sturt, F., Dix, J., Grant, M., Steadman, S., Scaife, R., Edwards, R., Griffiths, S., Cameron, N. Thompson, C., Bray, S. and Jones, J. 2014. Life below the waves: palaeolandscapes preserved within the subtidal Bristol Channel. *Archaeology in the Severn Estuary* 22, 41–66

7. On-site: designing and implementing chronometric sampling strategies

Seren Griffiths

Applications of scientific dating in the field

The previous four chapters have provided an introduction to the underlying principles associated with common scientific dating techniques. Understanding these principles is essential in designing an appropriate chronometric sampling strategy in the field and in managing an excavation effectively. All too often scientific dating specialists are presented with samples after excavations have finished and asked to produce a site chronology to address very specific research aims. In these cases, sample recovery may have violated some of the essential aspects of age calculation with the result that chronologies are compromised. It is for this reason that this chapter on sampling strategies comes *after* the chapters introducing the principles underpinning the methods. In this chapter I discuss how to design a site sampling strategy systematically and outline considerations that may need to be made for different techniques to manage a sampling strategy effectively. Involving a scientific dating specialist in project design stages will usually improve research outputs and add value.

The recovery of samples in the field creates the space for scientific dating chronologies and it will also therefore impact on the types of interpretations and narratives that it is possible to build about a site. To produce the most effective chronologies we need to consider the practical limitations on any project in terms of time, resources, personpower for recovering samples and other constraints on site management. We also need to consider the potential that suitable samples for different scientific dating techniques will be encountered on different types of archaeological site. Finally, we need to think about how different potential samples and dating methods will relate to our research aims. In this chapter, I look at approaches to designing a sampling strategy, how you can ensure quality in the field and various practical considerations for different scientific dating methods.

Approaches to designing chronometric sampling strategies

If suitable samples for scientific dating measurements are not recovered in the field it may not be possible to produce the chronologies with the required precision to answer specific research aims. Given that fieldwork is always time consuming, expensive and labour intensive it is very worthwhile thinking about how to devise a sampling strategy that will satisfy specific research aims prior to starting a project. The importance of a systematic and considered approach to sampling for scientific dating – which has been clearly communicated to the whole field team and other specialists working on a project – cannot be under-estimated. This is especially true on large infrastructure projects.

The 'A, B, C, D' of scientific dating

Research aims in site-based archaeological work often revolve around establishing when things happened:

- When was this structure built?
- When was this person buried?
- When did this site flood?
- When did this pottery start to be used here?
- When was this kiln last fired?
- When did this building go out of use?
- When was this town destroyed?

In all these cases, these temporal questions also have an implicit space-dimension:

- When was this structure built [here]?
- When was this person buried [here]?
- When was this site flooded [here]?
- When did this pottery start to be used here?
- When was this kiln last fired [here]?
- When did this building go out of use [here]?
- When was this town destroyed [here]?

Archaeological events of interest should always be understood as site-specific. We need well-defined archaeological events of interest on individual sites in order address research aims and to relate these site-specific events to wider patterns of activity beyond individual sites. To answer these kinds of questions we need to think critically both about the available samples at specific locations and how different measurement techniques can be applied to these samples to provide age estimates. On site, it can be helpful to frame these considerations in terms of the 'A, B, C, D' of scientific dating (Fig. 7.1; Table 7.1). This mnemonic provides a way to devise sampling strategies systematically. We start with:

A: Aim. What do I want to know in my research **aims**? For example: 'what do the funerary traditions suggest about the treatment of the dead at this site and how did this change over time?'. By defining the aim of any chronometric work we can start to think about the *archaeological event of interest*.

B: Beginning or ending? How do you define the archaeological event of interest that you are trying to provide chronological data for? Often archaeologists are especially

7. On-site: designing and implementing chronometric sampling strategies 137

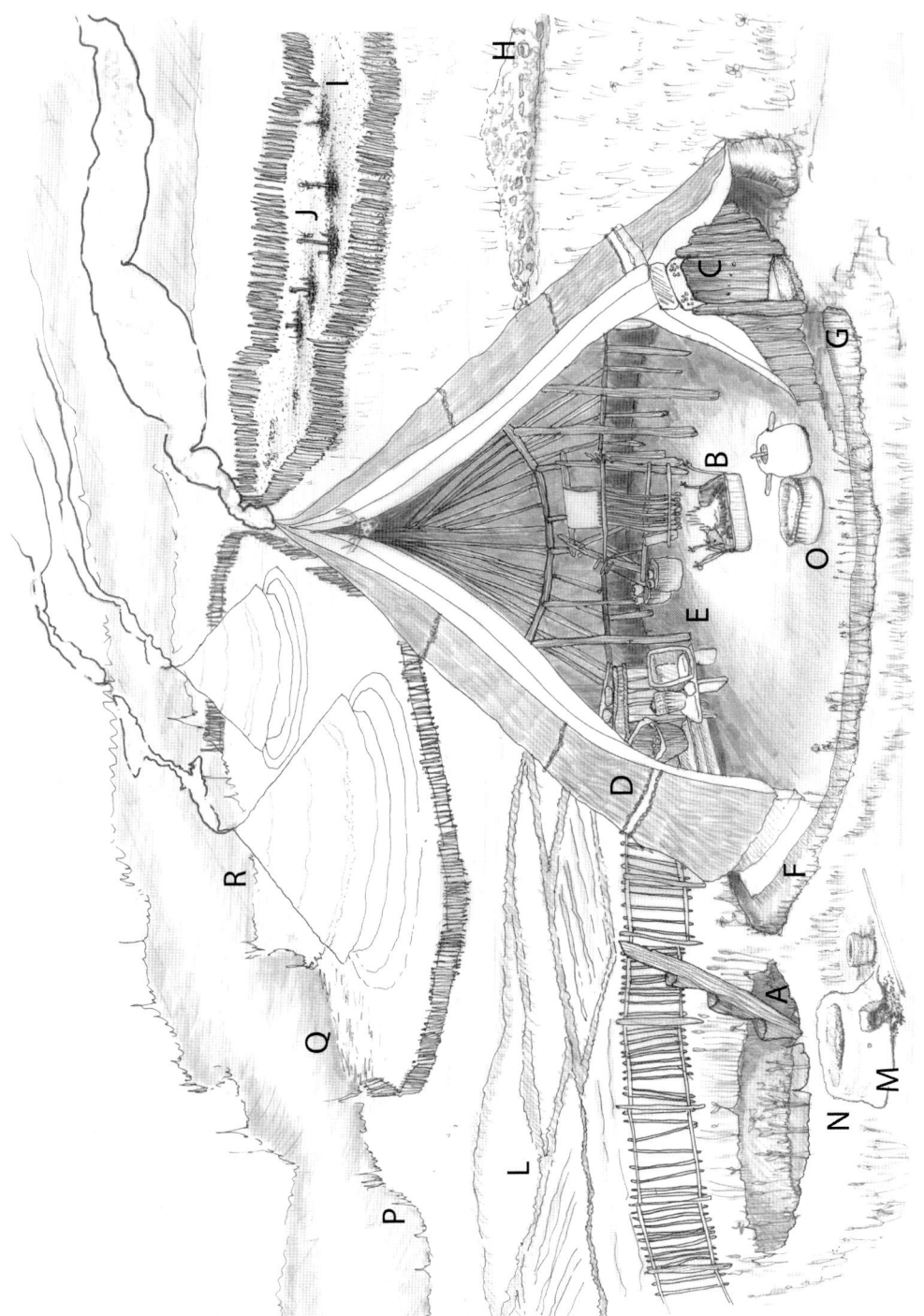

Figure 7.1. A range of potential samples for chronometric measurements exist on any archaeological site. Issues associated with these potential samples are detailed using an 'A, B, C, D' approach in Table 7.1. Copyright: Seren Griffiths.

Table 7.1: An 'A, B, C, D' approach to evaluating potential chronometric samples from the site shown in Figure 7.1.

Archaeological event of interest	Potential sample	Scientific dating method	Dated event	Archaeological interpretation of association of dated event to archaeological event interest
Use of waterhole	Waterhole log ladder (A)	Radiocarbon Dendrochronology	Wood formation (oak heartwood)	*Terminus post quem* use of waterhole
Use of round-house	Deer antler found on top of hearth (unburnt) (B)	Radiocarbon	Annual tissue formation	Stratigraphic *terminus ante quem* hearth?; dates anthropogenic activity
Use of round-house	Charred oak board: ?door furniture (C)	Radiocarbon (legacy measurement on bulk charred material)	Radiocarbon content across all rings, including heartwood	*Terminus post quem* activity at the site
Use of round-house	Honeysuckle ropes from thatch (desiccated/preserved by smoking) (D)	Radiocarbon	Last roof repair	Dates the archaeological event of interest
Construction of round-house	Outer ring (bark edge) round-house post (E)	Radiocarbon	Felling date	Dates the archaeological event of interest
Infilling ditch	Sediment in penannular ditch (F)	Light-stimulated luminescence	Deposition sediment	Dates the archaeological event of interest
	Isolated short-life charcoal (twig) frag., upper fill in penannular ditch (G)	Radiocarbon	Formation tissue	Uncertain association with ditch infilling; could be residual (therefore *terminus post quem* infilling), or intrusive (isolated frag.)
Use of midden	Charred food crusts on pottery vessel from midden (H)	Radiocarbon	Use of vessel	Date for pottery use ?*Terminus post quem* (pottery could be curated prior to deposition)/dates the midden formation

(Continued)

Table 7.1: (Continued)

Archaeological event of interest	Potential sample	Scientific dating method	Dated event	Archaeological interpretation of association of dated event to archaeological event interest
Use of the cemetery	Cremated human bone from urned cremation burial (I)	Radiocarbon	Date of cremation of bone	Date of cremation
	Short-life charcoal sample from urned cremation burial (J)	Radiocarbon	Formation of wood tissue	
Infilling field boundary ditch	Disarticulated human finger bone (L)	Radiocarbon	Formation of tissue	Date of death of individual Uncertain association with ditch infilling; could be residual (therefore *terminus post quem* infilling), or intrusive (isolated frag)
Firing of furnace	Oak heartwood charcoal from slag-rich dump next to furnace (M)	Radiocarbon	Formation tissue	*Terminus post quem* burning event
	Fired clay furnace structure (N)	Archaeomagnetic dating	Firing of furnace	Dates the archaeological event of interest
Introduction of cereal species	Charred grain (O)	Radiocarbon	Tissue formation	Dates the archaeological event of interest
Deposit formation in palaeochannel	Horizontally bedded waterlogged leaf remains (P)	Radiocarbon	Formation of leaf tissue	Dates the archaeological event of interest
	Mature timbers with bark edge (Q)	Dendrochronology	Felling date timber	?*Terminus post quem* infilling, timber already old when deposited
	In situ charcoal-rich burnt horizon after channel infilled, above water table (R)	Archaeomagnetic dating	Formation of burnt horizon	*Terminus ante quem* channel infilling

interested in the beginning or ending of phases of activity on a site, for example: 'when did this type of funerary tradition begin at this site?'. Events defined at specific sites might be related to wider patterns of practice in the past, for example: 'how do the apparently early funerary traditions *here* relate to the burial traditions at another site?'. Archaeological events of interest may also relate to trends in the use of material culture, as part of a wider pattern of distribution beyond an individual site, for example: 'is a general hypothesis about the relative use of cremation urns over time supported by independent scientific dating evidence at this specific site?'.

C: Choice? What potential samples are likely to be encountered that are suitable for different scientific dating techniques? How does the underlying geology and hydrology impact on these methods? What precision will these techniques offer? Is this sufficient precision to answer the research questions? For example, in investigating a cemetery site, we might encounter:

- Human skeletal remains from inhumation burials suitable for radiocarbon measurements,
- organic grave goods suitable for radiocarbon measurements (including the organic adhered or absorbed residues from pottery),
- pyre debris, charcoal and human and animal cremated remains suitable for radiocarbon measurements,
- *in situ* pyre deposits suitable for archaeomagnetic measurements,
- grave backfills suitable for luminescence measurements.

The choice of which measurement techniques to employ will require consideration of a range of factors including:

- the precision needed to answer the research question effectively,
- the costs of the measurements; including access to specialist sampling services where required,
- the physical constraints of excavating and recording deposits,
- the timetable for excavation of that area or site.

D: Dated event? Is the dated event closely defined chronologically? For example, do we understand very clearly how the carbon in any potential radiocarbon sample became incorporated into that sample? Based on the underlying principles of the scientific dating technique, what is the association between the measurement we are thinking of using and the archaeological event of interest? Is the association between this dated event and the archaeological event of interest close enough as to answer the research question effectively?

We can think about the cemetery example above in terms of how we might start to take an 'A, B, C, D' approach to devising a chronometric sampling strategy. Direct radiocarbon measurements on the human skeletal remains from the inhumation burials might represent an obvious place to start. These types of measurements should provide reasonably close estimates for the dates of deaths of the individuals though we might want to think about the potential for diet-derived offsets, for example from marine fish resources. With enough measurements on individuals from the cemetery we should achieve a relatively good sample for the time over which the cemetery was in use – providing burial occurred relatively quickly after death. Here we might want to think about the prospect of secondary burial or disturbance to the burials that might indicate more complex cultural processes. We could consider light-stimulated luminescence samples from the grave fills here. If suitable deposits were identified light-stimulated luminescence measurements on the fills might help us explore whether the date of death of the individual and the date of burial were the same. We might want to think about the precision of light-stimulated luminescence and if this would be sufficient to address this research question. In terms of what the sample of individuals means for the cemetery as a whole, we might want to think about producing measurements on people buried in a variety of different ways. This might help us explore the development or overlap of different burial traditions or the use of different mortuary treatments for different types of social person.

So, direct radiocarbon measurements on the human skeletal remains should help us explore the use of the cemetery for inhumation burials. However, if we are interested in the funeral traditions more broadly, perhaps we also want to think about the age of the pottery or other material culture at the time of burial? Some of these accompanying objects might represent curated artefacts. Direct age estimates on these things would help us explore this idea. Perhaps we might also want measurements on pyre deposits associated with the *in situ* cremation evidence. Does this represent activity at different points in time from the inhumation burials? Archaeomagnetic measurements on the *in situ* fired clay deposits produced during cremation and radiocarbon measurements on the cremated bone or short-life charcoal from the pyres would help us explore the chronologies of these practices.

Thinking about what measurements represent in terms of which types of activity is very important in building a holistic site narrative. In the case study outlined above, if we only sampled cremation burials we may not explore the full range of funerary activity. Similarly, if our sample of chronological measurements only came from a particular spatial area of the cemetery our chronology might not represent the full history of use over time; chronology will only be as representative of a site's history as the samples that are submitted for scientific dating measurements.

Multi-technique scientific dating programmes offer much in these terms because of their ability to provide age estimates for different types of dated event. Moreover, incorporating different techniques may help demonstrate the accuracy of resultant chronologies as well as improving precision. If different methods – based on different underlying principles – produce a consistent chronology then we have an equifinal solution.

Especially when working on a multi-phase site, or when trying to build a multi-technique chronology, it is very important to develop a written sampling strategy for scientific dating that can be disseminated to the team of excavators, scientific dating specialists and other specialists. This needs to highlight to the excavation team the range of deposits that we might be interested in identifying before they are removed. It also needs to identify those sampling techniques – in this example luminescence and archaeomagnetic work – that would require external specialists on site. Identifying key materials for scientific dating and when external specialists are needed on site is critical in managing excavations and available resources.

Practical considerations of different methods in the field

Considering which sample types we might encounter and their suitability to produce different chronometric measurements (Table 7.2) is only one aspect of chronological work that needs to take place in the field. There is a whole series of practical considerations that need to be made for effective chronologies, some general considerations for ensuring quality, followed by some specific considerations for different techniques are detailed below.

Ensuring quality

Working with national research frameworks and to international standards

Prior to commencement of fieldwork it is important to ensure that appropriate national and international standards are observed. Scientific dating projects could come into contention with a range of ethical issues. These might include ownership of looted cultural heritage, the ethical treatment of human remains and acts of vandalism against the historic environmental. There could also be issues in the legality of sending samples of cultural heritage items overseas for destructive scientific dating measurements. Different jurisdictions will have different statutory requirements. It is always essential to ensure that permission to excavate or sample has been granted by the owner of a site or item of material culture and by the relevant national heritage agency if required. Scientific dating laboratories or specialists may be able to advise on their own ethics policies.

Some methods of scientific dating have developed international standards. In radiocarbon, laboratories take part in an international inter-comparison that ensures reproducibility of results (e.g. Scott *et al.* 2017). Reporting chronometric data also may have national or international standards in best practice, for example Millard (2014) and Bayliss (2015) for radiocarbon data and Jansma *et al.* (2010) for international standards in the curation of digital dendrochronological data. Similarly, there may be national guidelines produced by historic environment agencies for sampling, analysis and reporting of chronometric results. In Britain, Historic England provides scientific dating advice though guidelines, its scientific dating team and its regional archaeological science advisors; Historic Environment Scotland provides scientific dating advice through its archaeological science team.

Documenting the sampling process

Regardless of which scientific dating methods are applied, the systematic recording of samples recovered for scientific dating is essential. Most methods will sub-sample material recovered in the field to produce chronometric measurements. This could include the disaggregation of charred plant materials from bulk sediment samples using

Table 7.2: Comparison of the different techniques explored in this volume and their utility on different site types.

Technique	Time period & application	Sample types	Limiting factors in accurate measurements	Issues associating measurements with archaeological events of interest	Potential for innovation
Radiocarbon	About 50–60,000 years ago; international	Carbonaceous materials generally. Specifically, short-life, single entity ecofacts or increasingly, chemical compounds	Upper limits constrained by ability to detect ^{14}C isotopes. Measurements can be impacted by contamination or offsets. Association between measurement & archaeological event of interest is critical	Taphonomy of dated sample, & the parent deposit formation need to be clearly explored in interpretation of any measurement	Wiggle matching different skeletal elements (see Chap. 8), organic compound
Dendro-chronology	Holocene; location dependent on species suitability	Timber or tree with sufficient ring counts to 'date' by traditional dendrochronology or in combination with ^{14}C wiggle matching	Presence of a regional chronology that allows different species in different parts of the world is important. The number of rings will impact on the ability of a sample to 'date'. Association between measurement & archaeological event of interest is critical	Re-use or stockpiling of timbers can impact on association between dendrochronological estimate & archaeological event of interest	Integrating measurements on portable material culture as *termini post quos* into site-specific chronological models with other forms of scientific dating measurement

(Continued)

Table 7.2: Comparison of the different techniques explored in this volume and their utility on different site types. (Continued)

Technique	Time period & application	Sample types	Limiting factors in accurate measurements	Issues associating measurements with archaeological events of interest	Potential for innovation
Light Stimulated Luminescence	Holocene & Pleistocene	Quartz or feldspar recovered from sediment samples. Ceramic building materials containing quartz grains	Insufficient bleaching may result in samples that do not behave in predictable manners. High levels of laboratory analysis are undertaken to detect these incidents, though there may be some occasions where this impacts on measurements. Re-exposure to light can overprint signals. Inconsistent hydrological regimes, or other changes to dose rate can make age calculations challenging. Association between measurement & archaeological event of interest is critical	Deposit formation processes need to be critically considered in thinking about what a measurement means in archaeological terms. Accurate age estimates for deposit formation may often provide stratigraphic *termini post* or *ante quos* rather than direct estimates for archaeological event of interest. Re-use of ceramic building materials can affect association between measurements on these materials & archaeological event of interest	Portable measurements may be very useful for thinking about sample selection on site. Use in combination with other techniques to improve precision
Archaeomagnetic	Holocene; location dependent on calibration curve availability	*In situ* burnt materials which contain magnetic minerals & have been exposed to high temperatures	In directional studies, disturbance including slumping or redeposition in the field can lead to inaccurate measurements. Inhomogeneous deposits can respond variably. Refiring of deposits such as hearths should over-print the initial signal, meaning any measurement estimates last firing event. Local magnetic objects can influence signal orientation. Association between measurement & archaeological event of interest is critical	Archaeomagnetic measurements provide excellent association. Often last firing (the dated event) *is* archaeological event of interest. If not, it may be possible to use these measurements as *termini post* or *ante quos* for archaeological events of interest	Highly specific site chronologies using multi-technique approaches, especially in urban or highly stratified sites should lead to unprecedented precision and accuracy

7. On-site: designing and implementing chronometric sampling strategies

flotation, followed by the selection of individual entities for radiocarbon measurement. In OSL for example, individual quartz grains may be sub-sampled for measurements.

It is highly advisable to create a unique identifier on site for materials subsequently used or sub-sampled for chronometric measurements. This 'sample number' is important in tracking the 'data journey' that occurs in the production of site chronologies (Chapter 9). This is the only identifier that will travel with the material from the site, into the site archive and to the specialists undertaking the scientific dating measurement. The sample number not only relates a sample to the site but it can relate a series of measurements to each other. It therefore needs to be clearly recorded and transcribed across records. There are many opportunities for attributed data to be corrupted or information lost, the sample number – as unique identifier – is essential. Sample numbers for materials that will be used for chronometric measurement need to be recorded in a site sample register along with associated information including:

- the sample's parent context or location on site,
- the purpose for which the sample was taken,
- if the sample was part of a series,
- the location in the site archive of the written, photographic and drawn records of the sample prior to recovery and with recovery equipment *in situ*,
- location details to identify if the samples were taken away for analysis by the specialist or retained by the fieldwork team.

Ideally some attempt to relate the archaeological event of interest to the dated event might be given in the interpretation section of the sample register, for example: 'this sample of burnt clay was recovered by the external specialist to estimate the last firing of the hearth using archaeomagnetic directional measurements'. Sample registers can include prompts to get the excavation team to make reference to the written scientific dating strategy to explain why the sample was taken.

General advice on how to package and store samples
Especially on big projects it is very important to ensure that the sample unique identifier remains associated with the material. Clearly label the outside of the sample packaging and, if possible, include labels within the sample packaging (e.g. for bulk sediment samples and dendrochronological samples this should be possible, though it will not be possible for luminescence or archaeomagnetic samples). For dendrochronological samples, the labels should be attached to the material in ways that do not damage the woody tissue (i.e., using string, cable ties or other non-destructive means).

The sample labels should clearly identify: the site code, sample number, context number, purpose the sample was collected for and the number of constituent elements. Samples need to be packaged to ensure the material is in a stable environment that will not compromise the sample utility (e.g. waterlogged wood samples for dendrochronology need to not dry out). If in doubt talk to the relevant materials specialist and laboratory.

For techniques which require specialist sample recovery (i.e., dendrochronology, luminescence, archaeomagnetic dating) it is very important that every sample is recorded in the site sample register (this includes hydrological samples for luminescence). This allows the project management team to keep track of the scale of material recovered and the parts of the site that have been sampled. If a specialist is allocating their own numbering system to chronometric samples, this numbering system needs to be cross-referenced in the site sample register, however, the creation of yet another numbering system is to be strongly discouraged. In the case of dendrochronology, luminescence and archaeomagnetic dating, samples may usually be taken off-site by the relevant specialists. It is essential that a sample transfer register details whether samples have been recovered by a specialist, have been retained by the fieldwork team or have been transferred somewhere else off-site.

Ring-fencing sampling when time is tight

I briefly want to emphasise the importance of recovering samples for scientific dating measurements even at the end of a project. There can be a considerable time pressure to excavate and record the last important features and deposits in an area before it is handed over or the site closed down. At the end of a project or a phase of work it may also be very important to maximise the chronometric potential in two ways, first, by documenting and recovering samples that can be taken by non-specialists for radiocarbon measurements. Bulk samples for the extraction of charred or waterlogged plant macrofossils for radiocarbon measurements can be recovered relatively quickly (see below). It is important not to neglect this aspect of the sampling strategy even at the end of the project. Secondly, for samples that require specialist collection, it is absolutely essential that the project timetable allows specialists sufficient time to visit and collect samples on a site. Involving the scientific dating specialists in the project design and development of the sampling strategy (and revising this over the project lifespan) will improve research quality by identifying key targets to satisfy the project aims. It can be advisable to 'bookmark' external specialists and ask them to block out some time for the penultimate weeks on site in order that representative specialist samples can also be recovered.

When working on large, complicated, and/or multi-phase sites, it may be advisable to appoint a member of the excavation team to check that sampling of key deposits has been undertaken and to take additional samples if deposits have been missed. This member of the team may also be tasked with identifying and highlighting potential materials that require specialist sampling for chronometric dating as the excavation proceeds.

Getting help

Thinking through the scientific dating problem in terms of the 'A, B, C, D' approach outlined above is a useful way to break down what you are trying to understand through fieldwork and the scientific dating sampling strategy. Contacting relevant laboratories or scientific dating specialists is a good place to start to get help. National and regional heritage agencies may offer scientific dating support, and independent academics in universities may also be able to advise.

Sampling considerations by method

Sampling for radiocarbon measurements in the field

How to take samples: can I do this myself?

Samples for radiocarbon measurements could include peat, marine or terrestrial shells, plant macrofossils, faunal remains, human remains including cremated bone, lime mortar, absorbed residues in pottery, timbers and other carbonaceous materials. Generally, single entity, short-life organisms that have absorbed carbon in equilibrium with terrestrial ecosystems make the simplest samples, both in terms of measurement and in understanding the definition of the dated event. If a potential radiocarbon sample is not a terrestrial ecofact, you might be advised to consult with a dating specialist or a radiocarbon laboratory. This is especially true for samples requiring complicated measurement techniques such as lime mortar, absorbed pottery residues or organic samples which fixed carbon through marine or other aquatic reservoirs.

Most radiocarbon measurements will probably be produced on osseous or plant material which is relatively simple to recover and store. Osseous material may be hand recovered or bulk sampled depending on the advice of the osteoarchaeologist. Plant remains will be recovered from bulk samples based on the environmental archaeologist's advice. Such materials can be happily stored in plastic tubs or bags until processed. Different sized samples and sampling increments will be applied for waterlogged and charred plant remains. In Britain, bulk samples for charred plant remains are generally taken at a minimum of 40 litres of the parent deposit but could be larger for specific research questions or may be a smaller volume if this represents the whole of a context. In Britain, bulk samples for waterlogged plant remains are generally in the order of 10–20 litres but, again, this may be adjusted depending on the deposit and research questions. Do not hand collect individual items of charred or waterlogged plant remains for radiocarbon measurements; this compromises our ability to assess taphonomy (Chapter 2).

For osteological remains, samples can either be recovered by hand or through bulk sampling for the recovery of smaller bones. Human skeletal remains should be recovered in line with international best practice, the guidelines of the relevant national heritage agency and under the supervision of the project osteologist. Generally, we might want to think about the taphonomy of any potential osteological sample. Disarticulated material might have been through a complex taphonomic journey. Articulated material should have entered the archaeological record relatively recently after the death of the individual (there are potential atypical exceptions, for mummified material for example). Articulated remains therefore provide a very useful potential radiocarbon sample because both the dated event (date of tissue formation) and an archaeological event of interest (date of deposition) are clearly defined. Similarly, groups of dumped osteological material or associated bone groups suggest that material entered the burial environment as a result of anthropogenic activity rather than representing isolated redeposited elements. In these cases, recovering the entirety of the assemblage is important for osteological work and for radiocarbon sample selection.

For osseous and plant remains, where ecofacts are identified as of high potential for radiocarbon dating in the field (because they are articulated, dumped or have a functional association with an archaeological event of interest; Chapter 2) it is advisable to photograph materials *in situ* prior to recovering the sample.

Recovery and storage of pottery for radiocarbon measurements (on either adhering or absorbed residues) is slightly more complicated. Adhering residues may be very delicate so careful recovery and sub-sampling in control conditions is advisable. They may be contaminated by lipids present on the hands of the excavator (for example from sunscreen), so nitrile gloves may be useful to minimise contamination; if this is not possible cleaning hands prior to handling sherds is advisable. Avoid storing sherds in plastic or cling film, instead consider acid-free paper. As this is a relatively specialised dating technique it is a good idea to contact the laboratory for advice if considering measurements on absorbed residues.

What size is required for scientific dating measurement?
There are many factors that contribute to making a radiocarbon measurement. Giving the laboratory a reasonable sample size to pretreat may help ensure there is sufficient material to achieve a measurement. For example, for plant macrofossils, it is possible to produce measurements on single seeds of domesticated cereals. However, it may be advisable to submit larger samples if possible. For bone, which is more chemically complex in terms of pretreatment, laboratories may be able to make measurements on samples of as little as 1 g but larger sample sizes might be preferable (depending on preservation). It is always a good idea to contact the laboratory prior to undertaking any destructive sampling to ensure you have received up-to-date advice.

If you are struggling to find a sample of sufficient size from a context it may mean that you should be asking yourself questions about the taphonomy of that material in the first place. If there is only one fragment of bone or item of charred plant remains in the whole of a ditch fill sequence do you understand how that ecofact entered the feature? You might need to consider other samples from different contexts. Never mix ecofacts from across contexts or areas of the site to achieve sufficient material for a measurement; in so doing the definition of the dated event has been compromised.

What will limit the value of a sample?
The chemical pretreatment mechanisms undertaken by radiocarbon laboratories are effective at removing most soil-derived chemical contaminants. This, together with physical pretreatment mechanisms (to remove roots etc), will ensure accurate measurements. Any form of site-derived contamination could have implications for radiocarbon age estimates produced on samples. This might include the presence of hydrocarbons in the soil (though hopefully this would be identified in the site risk assessment). During post-excavation work and museum conservation work try to avoid adding contaminant carbon of any form (solvents, petrol, paraffin, cigarette ash, glue, chemicals containing carbon to disaggregate the soil and so on). If chemical contaminants have been added during post-excavation or conservation make sure to give the laboratory as much detail as possible prior to submitting the sample.

7. On-site: designing and implementing chronometric sampling strategies

Sampling for dendrochronology measurements in the field

How to take samples, can I do this myself?

While it is possible for a non-specialist to sample for dendrochronology it is not advisable. Identifying samples that are likely to 'date' against a regional master curve is a specialist skill. It includes considering how many rings are preserved. Beyond successfully matching a timber, selecting samples that satisfy an 'A, B, C, D' approach to scientific dating requires specialist training. For example, assessing sample suitability requires the ability to identify when the last preserved ring in a sequence will be useful in the site chronology. Sample selection also needs to consider how a timber relates to the construction or repair of a structure or the processes by which a potential sample come to be deposited in a specific place in an archaeological site. In standing buildings, for example, this could include a consideration of the potential that a timber has been re-used, perhaps given information in historic records.

Aside from highly specialised sample selection, dendrochronological samples require careful handling to ensure the preservation of the full ring sequence and, for waterlogged material, to ensure stable storage conditions. Waterlogged wood specialists and conservators as well as dendrochronologists should be consulted in these cases. To select suitable samples for dendrochronology will therefore require detailed consultation between a range of experts including dendrochronologists, wood specialist conservators, standing building specialists and field archaeologists.

What will the dendrochronologist sample?

Whether dendrochronological samples consist of cores, sections recovered with a chainsaw or whole timbers, there are some common considerations. First, long ring sequences will need to be recovered from individual timbers to increase the chance that the sequence matches. Secondly, a range of timbers will need to be sampled to construct a 'floating' site chronology. Thirdly, the delicate structures of a timber or tree need to be preserved. If any material is lost this must be noted in the sample documentation. Storage conditions are important to ensure the sample is not damaged after recovery.

If a section of wood or timber is removed with a chain saw, this will be $c.$ 50–150 mm thick. If the samples are to be recovered by coring, the bore size of the drill will limit the core diameter. Many corers produce a sample in the region of $c.$ 15 mm diameter. Whatever method is used, the section or core needs to be orientated so that the sample is perpendicular to the annual growth rings to achieve the clearest cross-section through the timber or tree.

The locations of sampling positions need to be clearly recorded so that any queries about the sample can be investigated subsequently. Because dendrochronological work is often undertaken on standing buildings or other structures of considerable aesthetic or historical significance, and which may be protected by statute or other conservation status, consideration of the visibility of any sample locations should be made in the project design by the dendrochronologist. The importance of minimising the impact of any destructive sampling on a structure may be a significant consideration in which locations are selected for sampling.

What will limit the value of a sample, and how to add value to your sampling
In standing buildings the potential for a complex history of construction, use, modification and repair necessitates discussion between project managers, buildings archaeologists and dendrochronologists to select samples that produce the maximum information to satisfy the research aims. In some cases, *termini post quos* measurements may be sufficient to answer research questions. However, if a dated event beyond a *terminus post quem* is required, measurements on samples with bark edge or other very young wood tissues need to be made. The preservation of these tissue structures may therefore be the limiting factor in addressing the project research aims. Combining dendrochronology and radiocarbon measurements in a wiggle matching approach (Chapter 2; Chapter 8) can improve precision and resolve sequences that do not 'date' by dendrochronology alone.

Sampling for luminescence measurements in the field

How to take samples, can I do this myself?
Accurate light-stimulated luminescence measurements require on-site background radiation measurements and water measurements as well as complex sample recovery techniques. It is therefore essential to commission a specialist to recover samples. To facilitate sampling of deposits sections need to be cleaned and recorded prior to the light-stimulated luminescence specialist's visit. Archaeological interpretations of context interfaces will be very important in deciding on the sample locations. Similarly, evidence for deposit formation, the presence of inhomogeneous deposits, truncation and changes in the site hydrology will be important for the specialist. For example, dumped deposits that might have been insufficiently 'bleached' should be avoided, so 'primary' fills or water-lain contexts may not represent ideal light-stimulated luminescence candidates. Consultation between the excavation team and the specialist is very important in these terms.

For samples of ceramic building material, a buildings archaeology assessment should be completed prior to sampling. The relationships between phases of structural modification need to be identified. Any evidence of repair needs to be recorded so that samples can be robustly associated with the sequence of construction. As with sediment sequences, sample locations need to be identified and recorded prior to sampling.

What will the luminescence specialist sample?
Sediment samples are often taken by the light-stimulated luminescence specialist from an open section. Tubes (*c.* 70 mm diameter and *c.* 300 mm long) will be pushed into the recorded section with as little disturbance as possible in order to minimise potential exposure to light. The tube will then be capped and wrapped in material such as black plastic to exclude light. The sediment sample positions can then be used to take *in situ* radiation measurements. Additional samples to measure the water content of the sediment need to be taken.

For ceramic building material sampling, material can either be taken as cores or whole items of undisturbed brick or tile can be removed. Samples can be as small as *c.*

50 × 100 mm although larger samples allow laboratories more scope. As with sediment samples, each sample location needs an *in situ* radiation measurement and samples of the surrounding mortar matrix or sediment need to be recovered to measure the water content.

What will limit the value of a sample, and how to add value to your sampling
Non-specialist recovery of light-stimulated luminescence samples will seriously limit the accuracy and usefulness of any measurements.

light-stimulated luminescence chronologies can be made more precise when the method is applied in combination with other chronometric measurements, for example, light-stimulated luminescence measurements made on a sequence of a ditch fills could be constrained by radiocarbon dates on a placed deposit within that sequence.

Sampling for archaeomagnetic directional measurements in the field
How to take samples, can I do this myself?
Archaeomagnetic samples need to be recovered by a specialist. Levelling the sample surface in the field and recording the orientation of the sample are critical. Selection of suitable deposits for sampling also requires specialist input. Local magnetic anomalies or disturbance resulting from the slumping or the truncation of a deposit can alter the accuracy and usefulness of any measurement.

What will the archaeomagnetic specialist sample?
Deposits suitable for archaeomagnetic samples are quite specific: a deposit needs to be homogeneous, well-fired, fine grained, consolidated and containing minerals capable of taking on a stable remanent magnetism. The deposit needs to have not been disturbed or subject to local changes in magnetic fields.

Depending on how compact and consolidated a deposit is the archaeomagnetic specialist will recover material using one of a range of different techniques (Chapter 5). The deposit will therefore have to be fully recorded for archaeological purposes prior to sampling. The specialist may need to make several sampling visits over the course of the excavation in order that deposits identified at different stages are sampled. A close discussion between the archaeomagnetic dating specialist and the site director will be needed to identify how and when deposits will be sampled to facilitate sample recovery in the context of overall site management.

What will limit the value of a sample, and how to add value to your sampling
Archaeomagnetic measurements are useful in providing an age estimate technique on fired deposits, a type of context common on many archaeological sites. Used in combination with radiocarbon measurements on short-life samples from the last firing of a feature, the two approaches provide estimates for different dated events that should be very closely related. Other techniques that lend themselves well to be used in combination with archaeomagnetic dating are luminescence techniques.

Because of the shape of the archaeomagnetic calibration curve (Chapter 5), it is possible that a calibrated age estimate may produce multi-modal distribution for the last firing of a deposit. In some cases, it is possible to refine estimates based on archaeological prior information – such as for example a broad understanding of the period of use based on the material culture. However, there may be cases where this poses challenges for interpretations.

Chapter conclusions

Scientific chronologies are created by the application of **sampling strategies** on site. These sampling strategies determine whether suitable material is recovered to effectively address research aims. Scientific dating strategies should be created by chronometric specialists **in consultation** with experts in ecofacts and material culture and the fieldwork director. A systematic approach to developing these strategies can be found in the 'A, B, C, D' approach. The strategy needs to be **communicated to the excavation team** clearly, with training that allows them to apply these strategies. In the most effective solutions to research questions, both the scientific dating aims and the site constraints are considered. Documenting the **process of sample recovery** is essential, especially on projects working with a range of specialists or large schemes working across many areas. Specialists in scientific dating need to be given time to revise sampling strategies over the fieldwork lifecycle and enough notice to get to site and to recover specialist scientific dating samples. Integrated sampling strategies for a **range of chronometric techniques** may achieve the most eloquent solutions, and result in the most unexpected research findings.

Bibliography

Bayliss, A. 2015. Quality in Bayesian chronological models in archaeology. *World Archaeology* 47, 677–700

Millard, A. 2014. Conventions for reporting radiocarbon determinations. *Radiocarbon* 56(2), 555–9

Jansma, E., Brewer, P. and Zandhuis, I. 2010. TRiDaS 1.1: The tree-ring data standard. *Dendrochronologia* 28(2), 99–130

Scott, E., Naysmith, P. and Cook, G. 2017. Should archaeologists care about ^{14}C intercomparisons? Why? A summary report on SIRI. *Radiocarbon* 59(5), 1589–96

8. Analysing datasets: Bayesian inference and archaeological chronometric data

Seren Griffiths and Richard Staff

In this chapter we think about groups of scientific dating measurements, how to present and interpret these and how we can relate them. We focus here on the use of Bayesian inference to work with groups of chronological data. Bayesian analysis allows us to relate groups of measurements formally. These approaches combine current archaeological knowledge with new data or observations to provide revised understandings that are expressed probabilistically are are termed 'posterior' expressions. The widespread application of Bayesian chronometric analysis using computer software has enabled sophisticated chronological analyses.

As well as these revised or posterior expressions the *process* of engaging critically with chronometric data can be very important in archaeological research. This process of analysis can produce important observations about a dataset – for example how robust a model is, how representative a group of chronometric results are of a form of practice, or perhaps systematic issues with the results themselves. These observations are as important as any results produced by an analysis. As part of Bayesian chronological analysis in archaeology we can:

- summarise groups of complex data,
- estimate the timing of key archaeological events of interest for which direct scientific dating measurements may not exist,
- think about how events are defined by their position in both time and space,
- sometimes produce more precise chronologies,
- combine different types of chronological information,
- write more critical narratives by thinking about the specificity of chronometric data and how data relate to narratives that are more or less generalising.

In this chapter we do three key things. We consider some of the underlying concerns and approaches in working with groups of data. Secondly, we consider the different types of relationships between groups of data and why these relationships are important. Thirdly, we work through some case studies that explore these different types of chronological relationships or models. In our case studies we use some of the examples we have introduced in the previous chapters.

As we have emphasised throughout this volume, to produce accurate scientific chronologies it is very important to think about the association between the chronometric measurement (the dated event) and the aspects of the archaeological record that you are trying to investigate (the archaeological events of interest). As we introduced in Chapter 2, it was the pioneering work of T.H. Waterbolk (e.g. 1971) that first started to explore these ideas in terms of building robust radiocarbon chronologies (Waterbolk 1971; Mook and Waterbolk 1985; Chapter 2).

Thinking critically about the association between the dated event and the archaeological event of interest becomes even more important when dealing with groups of data when we want to:

- produce a synthesis of the chronometric data from an individual site,
- produce a thematic chronology for
    - practices identified at many different sites, or
    - types of material culture recovered from many sites,
- produce chronologies using results from different scientific dating techniques.

In each of the previous chapters we have explored the underlying principles of a selection of the scientific dating methods used in archaeology. These principles provided the basis for thinking about how measurements relate to each other, and how we can use scientific dating measurements to build meaningful chronologies and considered narratives.

Approaches to archaeological chronometric data and Bayesian modelling

Over the last 30 years scientific dating in archaeology has changed dramatically as a result of the development and application of Bayesian chronological modelling. These approaches were first developed by Caitlin Buck (e.g. Buck *et al.* 1991; 1992; 1994; 1999; Buck and Christen 1998) and have been substantially developed by Christopher Bronk Ramsey (e.g. 1995; 1998; 2001; 2009). Andrew Millard (e.g. Millard 2002; Buck and Millard 2004) and Alex Bayliss (e.g. Whittle *et al.* 2011; Hines and Bayliss 2013; Bayliss 2015) have applied Bayesian approaches to large assemblages of data, undertaking complex chronological modelling.

Bayesian probability

Applications of Bayesian statistical analyses to help build chronological models are underpinned by the work of an 18th century Presbyterian minister, Rev Thomas Bayes. Bayes' Theorem, as it became known, was posthumously published in 1763.

Bayesian inference expresses our understandings of uncertainty in terms of probability. We have pre-existing understandings of the world – based on our experiences and knowledge – and as we learn new information we integrate that (e.g. chronometric measurement data) with existing information (e.g. stratigraphy and phasing) to revise our understandings.

In Bayesian terms, our pre-existing understandings are termed our *a priori* or prior beliefs. When we integrate our new information (or in Bayesian terms our 'likelihoods', in this case scientific dating measurements) and our prior beliefs, we develop our *a posteriori* or revised beliefs. So, given our previous understanding of the world, we can estimate the probability of some new observation given a specific set of conditions.

Archaeological prior beliefs

Archaeologists are very good at making new observations. These can include information about finds, sites, people from the past and so on. We are also very good at sorting, classifying and ordering these new observations so that we can relate them to our existing knowledge structures, for example, when we first recover an artefact we can think about the size, form, material type, find location and so on. These new observations are related and qualified according to our prior beliefs. When we think about residual, or intrusive or curated material culture on a site we are evaluating the material using our prior beliefs about the relative sequence in which things were produced. We do this instinctively. So, when fieldwalking, we can immediately identify a sherd of blue-and-white transfer ware as a particular type of artefact which has attached to it – what we understand to be – an appropriate currency or distribution in time and space. This same sherd would be considered intrusive in an assemblage of Bronze Age material culture because of what we understand to be appropriate to Bronze Age artefacts; in a Bronze Age assemblage this sherd would be matter out of place.

In some cases these prior beliefs can become unhelpful; new observations may mean that we should re-evaluate our prior beliefs but intellectually this can be very difficult. This is why the *process* of thinking critically about all aspects of chronometric data and what they mean in archaeological terms is an important part of chronological analysis. Our prior beliefs can constrain our attempts to arrive at revised understandings even when we are presented with new evidence. This can be the case when archaeologists use culture historical terms to describe conditions in the past as if they had a real validity rather than as a heuristic device. If someone tells you that they research 'the Neolithic' what they are actually telling you is how their thinking about the past has been conditioned by our discipline's history (see Chapter 9). In every chronometric analysis prior beliefs need re-evaluation as part of the iterative process of archaeological knowledge production.

There are lots of cases in archaeology where local knowledge structures have been shown to be inaccurate. The first radiocarbon revolution demonstrated the problems with some of these archaeological prior beliefs. In Chapter 1, Glyn Daniel was still reeling from the radiocarbon revolution some 30 years later. What is widely remembered about the early radiocarbon revolution is that it demonstrated how wrong Daniel's (and others') ideas were about the 'megalithic culture', for example. What is less widely remembered, but more important, is that essentially the same rationale of pattern recognition and ordering is still routinely applied in archaeological reasoning today. Today we have more evidence and more independent chronometric measurements but it would be arrogant to believe that all of the prior beliefs that we hold, inferred from the same sound archaeological reasoning, will endure. The archaeologist David Clarke (1972) recognised that lots of these ways of thinking about the time in archaeology become what he termed 'iconic models' – models that we have developed that we *should* use to test our understandings but that, instead, can become relatively inflexible frameworks. Such models are not independent of the circumstances in which they were developed. In the statistician George Box's terms, all models are wrong, some models are useful (Box 1976; cf. Bayliss *et al.* 2007).

How do we start to work with our prior beliefs to build *useful* chronological models? There are two very important themes in the process of archaeological chronological modelling:

- *Critical evaluation of prior beliefs*. It is very important that we have thought critically about our prior beliefs. What do we actually mean by the time models that we have developed? How have the classes of prior beliefs we are using been constructed? Which aspects of these models are we more-or-less confident in? Are there any inherent biases or structuring principles that we are making implicitly? When might we feel we have a weight of evidence to challenge our existing understandings?
- Consideration of the nature of archaeological observations. Prior beliefs that are developed from very specific and particular observations will probably be less wrong than more generalised prior beliefs. We may have more confidence in specific observations in contrast to more generalised understandings about the past. So, for example, stating that the British Bronze Age is earlier than the British Iron Age is a very generalising prior belief. It is a generalised culture historic model that refers to big packages of things and site types distributed over a wide region and developed over a long period of study. It might be true in some parts of Britain but not in others. It might be true of some types of 'Bronze Age' material culture but not others. It might be true of some types of 'Iron Age' sites but not others. Use of these kinds of generalising prior beliefs in model building is likely to produce very generalising interpretive narratives and explanations and is also likely to reinforce the existing knowledge structures within which these prior beliefs are constructed.

There are several ways in which we can develop more specific and particular observations. For example, rather than talking about all material culture from culture historic packages we might focus on our observations about the presence of different types of pottery; based on our understandings of the relative typological development, we might suggest that the Bronze Age pottery on site A is older than the Iron Age pottery on site B. In contrast to a generalising culture historic approach this model is more specific in time and space and, critically, in the material type under analysis.

One of the most useful ways of deriving specific observations in archaeology is by thinking about the laws of stratigraphy. In archaeology, using the law of stratigraphic superposition as the basis for our prior beliefs, we might expect a lower deposit in a sequence to have formed earlier than upper deposits. All other things being equal, material culture in the lower deposit should therefore be older than material culture in overlying deposits. However, to apply this approach usefully for the purposes of constructing robust scientific chronologies in archaeology we would need the *individual* stratigraphic relationships to be observed on a specific site and, moreover, we would need to engage critically with deposit formation processes and with sample taphonomy. While the generalising principle that 'lower deposits are older deposits' often holds true, there are many reasons why this might not be the case on a specific site, for example the excavation of more recent negative features into older deposits.

To establish really useful prior beliefs, therefore, we want specific and particular archaeological observations. Because scientific chronologies are often built during post-excavation work and may go through various iterations of chronology building, we also require these close observations to be evidenced in the site archive. Site records provide a means to simplify the physical form of the site and to rationalise stratigraphic relationships. These kinds of highly specific prior beliefs are powerful because many lines of evidence and detailed observation contribute to their formation, over an iterative process of excavation and recording that creates the logical scaffolding to underpin these knowledge claims (see Chapter 9).

Computer programs

A variety of computer programs exist to apply Bayesian modelling to chronometric datasets in archaeology. These include the OxCal program developed by Bronk Ramsey (1995) and the BCal program developed by Buck *et al.* (1999). Both programs can be run online and the OxCal program can be downloaded for offline use. BCal is available from https://bcal.sheffield.ac.uk (accessed May 2020) and OxCal is available from https://c14.arch.ox.ac.uk/oxcal.html (accessed May 2020). Another group of programs have been developed using the R statistical package. These include Bchron (Haslett and Parnell 2008; https://CRAN.R-project.org/package=Bchron) and rbacon (Blaauw and Christen 2011; https://CRAN.R-project.org/package=rbacon), both of which focus on age-depth modelling which allow palaeo-environmental reconstructions (Chapter 6). Bchron also allows relative sea-level estimation with time uncertainty attached (Parnell and Gehrels 2015).

In this volume, the OxCal package has been employed which also includes the ability to undertake age-depth modelling for palaeo-environmental reconstruction (Chapter 6), as well as the ability to apply Bayesian approaches to anthropogenic chronological data.

Why modelling is important

Many scientific dating techniques produce age ranges with associated uncertainties, that is to say, scientific age estimates are rarely precise to a single year but instead can be expressed in terms of likelihoods. In terms of calibrated radiocarbon measurements, these distributions have a shape determined by the structure of the calibration curve and the error term derived for that specific measurement.

With determinations obtained by Accelerator Mass Spectrometry, for example, radiocarbon 'dates' are actually measurements of ratios of carbon isotopes in a sample. The standard deviation that is quoted is estimated from repeat measurements on standards. By measuring known-age samples it is possible to ascertain an appropriate confidence envelope within which the known-ages of these samples lie. A certain imprecision therefore will be associated with scientific chronologies in these cases simply because of the measurement process. Even with a group of short-lived samples closely associated in time, this imprecision, together with the shape of the calibration curve, could mean that a group of results may appear smeared over a considerable period of time (cf. Baillie 1991).

Bayesian modelling can account for some of this imprecision by imposing a statistical distribution on a group of related measurements. Figure 8.1 shows a group of radiocarbon results. If we knew nothing more about the relationships between the samples that produced these measurements, we might look at them and suggest that they represented activity over a couple of centuries, say from the mid-15th through to the mid-17th century cal. AD.

Actually, these results are very closely related. In Figures 8.2–8.4 we look at different ways of relating these data and the effects on their distribution. In these figures the ways we have presented the data are indicted by the brackets down the left side and OxCal Chronological Query Language 2 (CQL2) terms (Bronk Ramsey 1995; 2009 and references therein). Here, for clarity, the CQL2 terms are shown in `Courier` font in the text. In each of these case studies outlined below, the underlying principles of the technique need to be considered. Only then can we think about how the relationships between the dated events and the archaeological events of interest are best expressed in a model. It is perfectly possible to construct models that are misleading or that take a very partial view of the relationships between data. Such models can bias output and prove unhelpful.

In OxCal, a relatively neutral relationship that we can express between results is that *the measurements are all related* but that we have no further understanding of the nature of this temporal relationship. This kind of relationship could be analogous to an archaeological 'phase' on a site. Figure 8.2 shows how this kind of relationship can be expressed in OxCal. Here we have imposed a statistical distribution of the radiocarbon measurements using the `Phase` command. In this case the radiocarbon data will be uniformly distributed across the `Phase` with the `Boundary` parameters expressing the belief that this activity started and ended at a specific point in time. These `Boundary` parameters provide estimates for the timing of the start and end of activity in this case and often correspond to the events that archaeologists are most interested in. There are other ways to program the distribution of data including, for example, exponential rise or fall of events in a group. In each modelling case study these prior beliefs need to be considered critically. They may not be the most appropriate or, to paraphrase George Box, they may not be the most useful models available.

Using this model we can estimate that the start `Boundary` for this activity occurred in *cal. AD 1480–1640 (95% probability, start related measurements*, Fig. 8.2). We can estimate that the end `Boundary` occurred in *cal. AD 1520–1660 (95% probability, end related measurements*, Fig. 8.2). These two estimates reflect our understandings of the

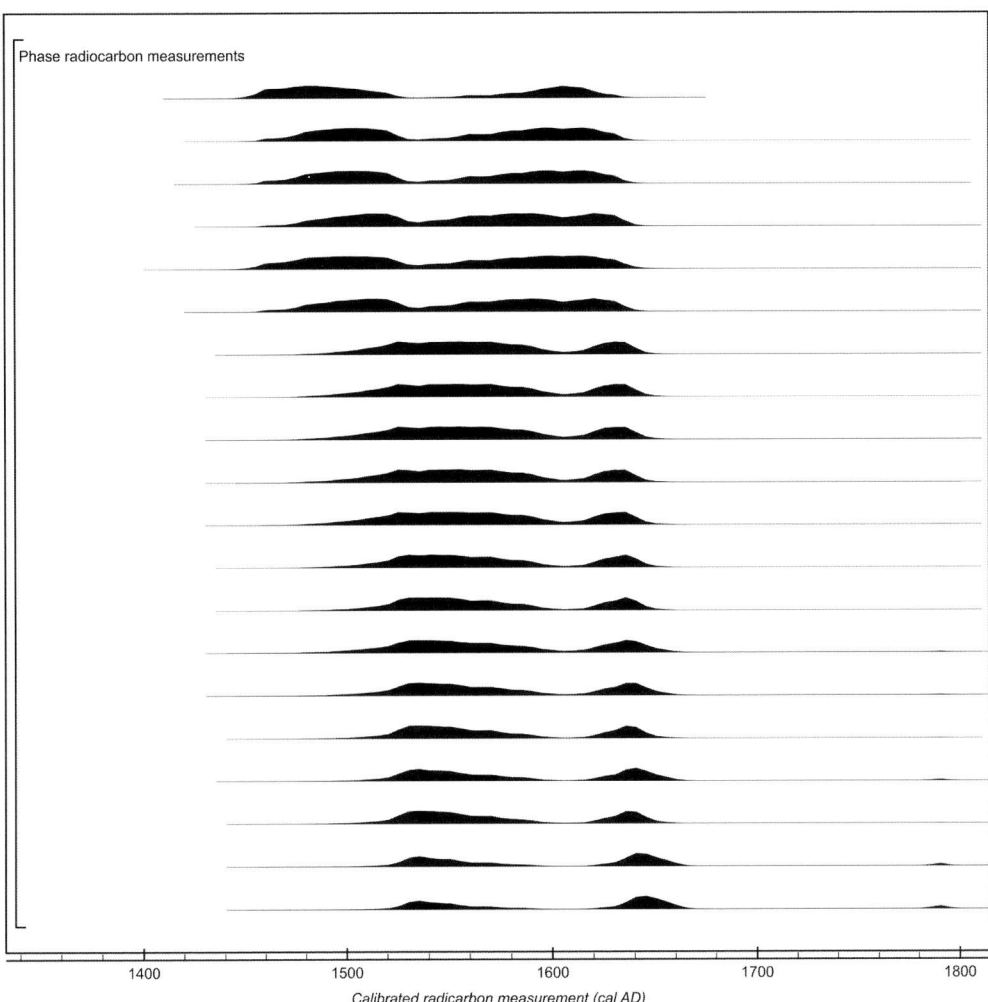

Figure 8.1. A group of calibrated radiocarbon results from the 16th century cal. AD. Copyright: Seren Griffiths.

relationships between the data and the new information provided by the radiocarbon data. Estimates that are produced from these models are usually quoted in italics to differentiate them from calibrated results or other forms of age estimates. For the models below we apply a standard approach to quoting model output. For example, for the start of activity associated with the Coneybury Anomaly we would quote the estimate in terms of the:

- Highest Posterior Density range: 3820–3660 cal. BC
- Posterior Density Interval: 95% probability
- Parameter Name: start_Coneybury_anomaly
- Figure in which Calculated: Figure 8.5

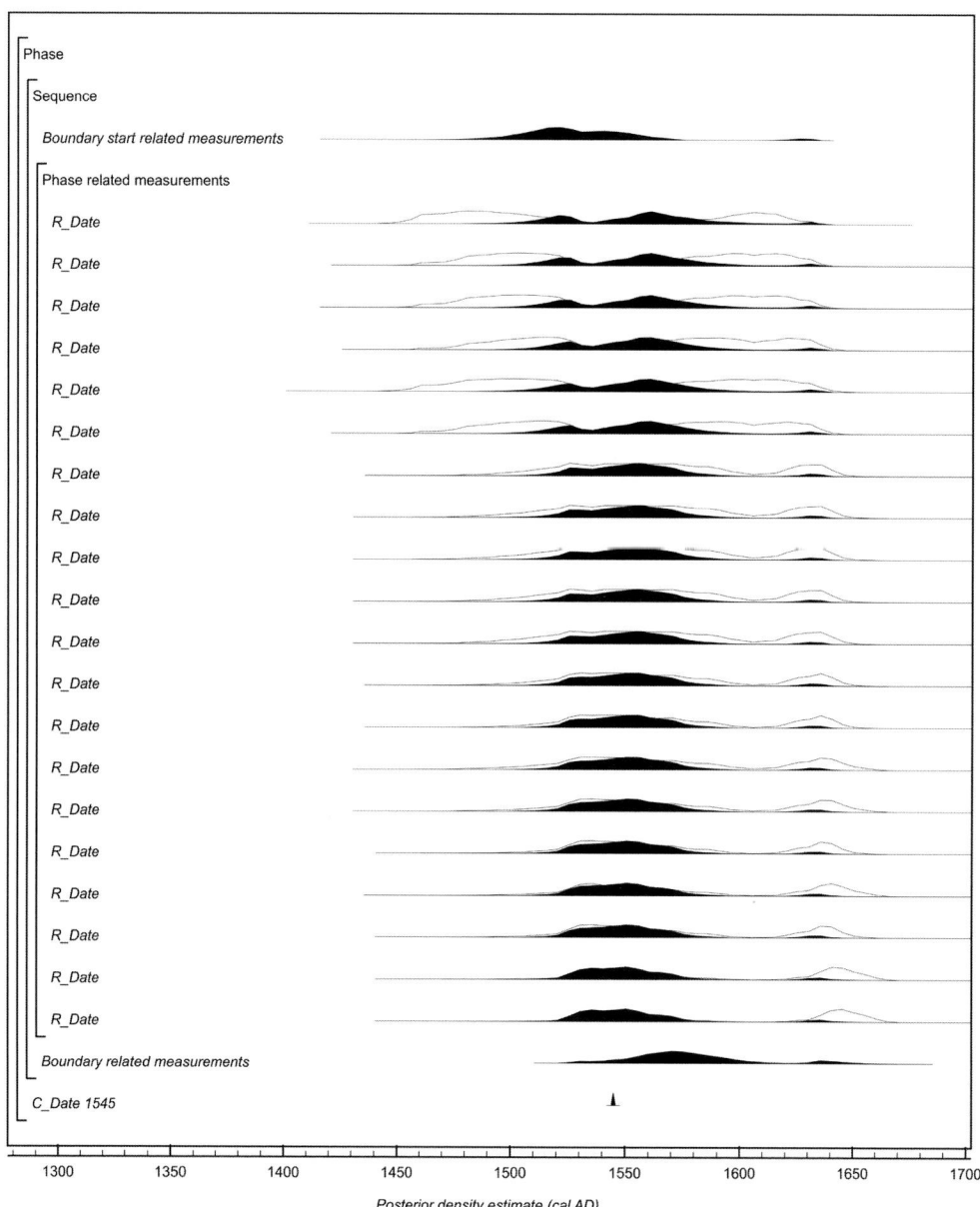

Figure 8.2. The radiocarbon results shown in Fig. 8.1 related in an OxCal Phase model defined by Boundary parameters. The large square brackets down the left-hand side of the figures, along with the OxCal CQL2 keywords, define the model. The results shown in outline are calibrated radiocarbon data, while those in black are posterior density estimates. Copyright: Seren Griffiths.

As well as simple models where results are presented in a single OxCal `Phase` of related activity, it is possible to build more complicated models, for example where one group of related activity is succeeded by another. This can be achieved in a modular fashion by using prompts in the OxCal menus. We develop increasingly complex case studies throughout this chapter. First, we work through the impacts of statistical scatter on the dataset shown in Figure 8.1.

For the data plotted in Figure 8.1 we actually know even more about the relationships between these different age estimates. The results have a much closer association than simply deriving from a coherent archaeological phase of activity. The results we are looking at here are all measurements on the same archaeological sample of bone. These measurements were all produced on a single sample of pig bone from the *Mary Rose*, the warship of English King Henry VIII, which sank in AD 1545 (Brock *et al.* 2007; see Chapter 3 for discussion of the dendrochronological results from the wreck). The pigs recovered from the wreck were taken on board as food sources. In this case therefore, the archaeological event of interest (when the pig died) and the dated event (when carbon isotope exchange ended) are very closely related. There is some difference between these two events because of the way bone tissue forms and we discuss this further below.

Because the measurements were all produced on the same skeletal element it would be appropriate to take a weighted mean using a Chi-squared test prior to calibration. This test determines whether results are statistically significantly different (in this case at the 5% confidence level) and can be applied to data in OxCal using the `R_Combine` function. In this case, if the measurements are accurate they should not be statistically significantly different because the results were all produced on the same skeletal element. The exception would be when an accurate measurement is one of the 5% that lie outside the quoted 95% range. In this case the results are not statistically significantly different; the T' value (T'=21.3) is below the 5% significance level (T'5%=30.1) for the number of results included in the Chi-squared test in this case (Ward and Wilson 1978). Since these results are not statistically significantly different we can quote the weighted mean as a better estimate for the death of this pig than the posteriors from the model outlined above. The weighted mean (317±6 years BP) produces the calibrated date range of AD 1510–1640 (95% confidence).

We can compare this weighted mean to the known date of the sinking of the *Mary Rose* in Figure 8.3. We can see that our weighted mean is both *accurate* (it includes the real point in time when we know that the pigs must have died, AD 1545) and is relatively *precise* (the date range is not very wide). An accurate estimate is correct, the precision refers to the range on that correct age estimate.

It is rarely the case that we know exactly the timing of an archaeological event that we are also seeking to investigate through scientific dating measurements. There are, however, lots of other forms of prior information that we can use to revise age estimates. Different types of prior information and different ways of incorporating these into models will result in different solutions. When we are thinking about which model we apply to a group of data it can be useful to evaluate how sensitive

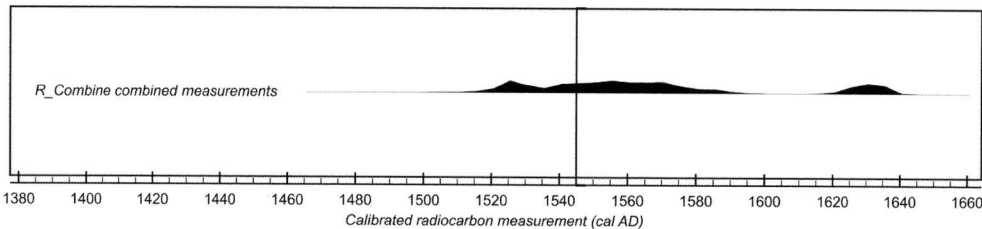

Figure 8.3. A weighted mean taken prior to calibration gives the date range cal. AD 1510–1640 (95% confidence; T'=21.3; T'5%=30.1; v=19; Ward and Wilson 1978). When we compare this to the known date of the sinking of the Mary Rose *we can see that this estimate is accurate. Copyright: Seren Griffiths.*

our outputs are to the prior information that we introduce. If we get very different results depending on our interpretations and our treatment of the data do we need to think critically about how confident we are in our prior beliefs? Do we need to think critically about the knowledge structures that underpin these prior beliefs? What biases might we be incorporating? Very precise age estimates (estimates with a short date range) can be very attractive in archaeological narratives but we need always to ensure that increases in precision are not at the expense of accuracy (estimates that actually incorporate the real point in time that the measurement relates to). If we had modelled our *Mary Rose* data so that we had a very precise date range of say cal. AD 1510–1530, our answer would be precise but inaccurate. In archaeology, because chronology structures many other aspects of knowledge creation, we want to achieve accurate chronologies above everything else; precision is good, but accuracy is much, much better.

Another way that we could think about these data might be with knowledge of the other material culture from the wreck. If we knew that the ship sank in the reign of King Henry VIII but we did not know exactly when we could use this very powerful historical information in our model. We can combine the estimates using a weighted mean as we did before, but in addition we could constrain the calculation to reflect our prior belief that the pig died before the death of Henry VIII in AD 1547. We do this in the estimate 'combined measurement with prior' in Figure 8.4. This revised calibrated date range suggests that the individual died in cal. AD 1514–1547 (95% confidence; rounded out to the nearest year). We can see that this estimate is much more *precise* than the one given above. In this case, because the sample is of known age, we happen to know the result is also *accurate*.

We can differentiate between modelling approaches that make use of 'informative' prior information and those less prescriptive models that use 'uninformative' prior information (Bayliss *et al.* 2007). The former might include highly structured stratigraphic sequences, for example. However, depending on the measurements and nature of the archaeological problem in question, even relatively uninformative prior information can be very helpful in chronology building.

We mentioned above that the *process* of modelling can also suggest unexpected patterns in data and should be valued as part of the analysis in itself. The preferred,

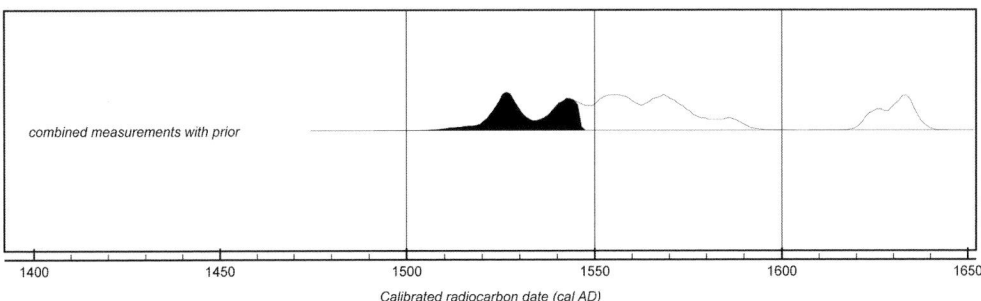

Figure 8.4. The weighted mean taken prior to calibration and constrained using the known-age of the death of King Henry VIII in AD 1547. We can see that this distribution is much more precise but remains accurate for the known age of the event. The result shown in outline is the weighted mean, that shown in black is this distribution modified with our historic prior information. Copyright: Seren Griffiths.

published outputs from Bayesian statistical analysis of chronometric measurements may well reflect only one of several possible interpretations of results. How do we know which model is the most appropriate solution for our problem? We can think about this in terms Alex Bayliss has used, of a model being *importantly* wrong (Bayliss *et al.* 2007). To think about how much impact our specific interpretations have on model outputs, it is worth comparing outputs from different types of models, as we started to explore with the example shown in Figure 8.3. If, given different interpretations of the prior information, the outputs for a group of estimates change by several centuries or in ways which will have significant impact on our interpretations, it is advisable to present a range of possible solutions to clarify which of our prior assumptions impact the model output to a greater or lesser extent. Certainly, we should acknowledge in our publications that our results are contingent upon a very specific series of interpretations (prior beliefs) that have been included within our models.

Types of models

We noted above that models can be defined as using informative or uninformative prior beliefs. Another way of thinking about our approaches can be in terms of the type of model employed. We can identify four broad types of chronological model that are routinely employed. Very sophisticated analyses can use these approaches in conjunction with one another. The different approaches are:

- Site-specific prior information models. These are based on closely observed relationships from an individual site. Often this might include a series of stratigraphic relationships or perhaps a model of archaeological phases of activity that followed one from another.

- Text-based prior information models. Scientific dating measurements offer an alternative to written sources in the construction of chronologies, however, there are lots of cases where text-based information might be useful. These can include, for example, where a site is identified in an historical document or inscription as being founded on a particular date. How does this relate to our independent scientific evidence?
- Culture historic models. These models are based on the identification of groups of related things and sites which have a temporal and spatial currency. Such models are often the legacy of long histories of archaeological research over large geographical areas. They can be used to suggest a relative order in any associated chronometric measurements.
- Known age interval models. In these cases, a sample itself provides a proxy for the passage of time that can be used as prior information. This type of model includes Bayesian dendrochronological wiggle matching (see Chapter 3). Less precisely defined growth of other living organisms can also be employed in wiggle matching approaches, as we shall see in the 'Ötzi' case study below.

Regardless of the prior information applied to an assemblage of chronometric data, all Bayesian chronological inference in archaeology rests on three critical considerations. These are:

- First, we need to think about how dated events relate to archaeological events of interest. To address this key idea we can think about the:
  - Nature of the sample. Given the underlying principles of the scientific dating method and the nature of the sample, what does the measurement mean? Does the nature of the sample compromise the utility of the result in terms of the underlying principles of the dating method?
  - Sample taphonomy. In biotic samples, do we have a clear understanding of how the measured sample entered the deposit from which it was recovered?
  - Deposit formation. Do we have a clear understanding of how the deposit from which the sample was recovered formed? Is it possible that a sample was redeposited, moved or otherwise disturbed so that there is a significant interval of time between the dated event and the parent deposit formation? Do the deposit formation processes compromise the association between a measurement and the archaeological event of interest?
- Secondly, we need to consider how all the measurements relate to each other There may be different considerations depending on types of data we are working with and the types of models we are hoping to build. This may be especially relevant in terms of multi-technique chronologies where different dated events are represented by different techniques.
- Thirdly, we need to consider what the scientific measurements represent in terms of a sample of activity from the past. Does the assemblage of scientific dating measurements comprise a representative sample of overall activity? Does the dataset in fact only represent a subset of this activity or is it in any other way biased? If 90% of data derive from one site can we hope to build a culture historic model or, realistically, is the dataset heavily skewed?

These three critical considerations need to be addressed as part of the model building process. They may relate to previous archaeological research including, for example, the production of legacy data from a region. If an 'A, B, C, D' approach to designing a scientific dating sampling strategy on site has been employed (Chapter 7) this can be used as a basis for analysis.

In the following section, we discuss a range of case studies and work through some of the modelling choices made in their construction. Code for selected case studies is included in the Appendix so that readers can compare the approaches that we have taken and reproduce or revise them.

Case studies

Site-specific prior information models

Excavation is a very involved process which includes the generation and revision of many datasets. During the process of excavation, stratigraphic relationships between deposits are identified. These observations are recorded in the site archive in section drawings, matrices, plans that show site phases and the stratigraphic narrative. These records are all effectively models for the passage of time. Because these time models are produced during processes of very close observation even seemingly relatively neutral models, such as archaeological phase models (where sites are split into different 'phases' of activity), can be really powerful in the creation of site-specific chronologies.

Case study: early Neolithic activity from the Coneybury Anomaly occupation
In Chapter 2 we introduced some of the radiocarbon measurements associated with the Coneybury Anomaly. At Coneybury we had relatively little informative prior information. The results all derived from a single fill of the feature. The nature of the archaeological material culture indicated at least two possible interpretations for the formation of the material culture assemblage recovered from the fill. The first was that this was dumped material which had been brought together over a very short period of time. The second was that it comprised material that had been stored or curated in some way prior to being deposited in the feature.

Twelve radiocarbon results were produced on samples from this fill. Two results on a beaver bone from the assemblage could have been affected by an inbuilt aquatic dietary offset. Further research might indicate if a reservoir offset should be applied to the beaver results. In Chapter 2 we therefore followed Barclay *et al.* (2018) in presenting these results as *termini post quos,* having also combined these repeat measurements on the same element using the `R_Combine` function. The results have been included in a simple `Boundary`-defined `Phase` (Fig. 8.5). This is a relatively neutral treatment of these results; it reflects our understanding that these results are *related* but that we have no further understanding of the relationships between the parent samples. In the model shown in Figure 8.5, we can estimate that this activity commenced in *3820–3660 cal. BC (95% probability; start_Coneybury_anomaly;* Fig. 8.5) or in *3780–3670 cal. BC (68%*

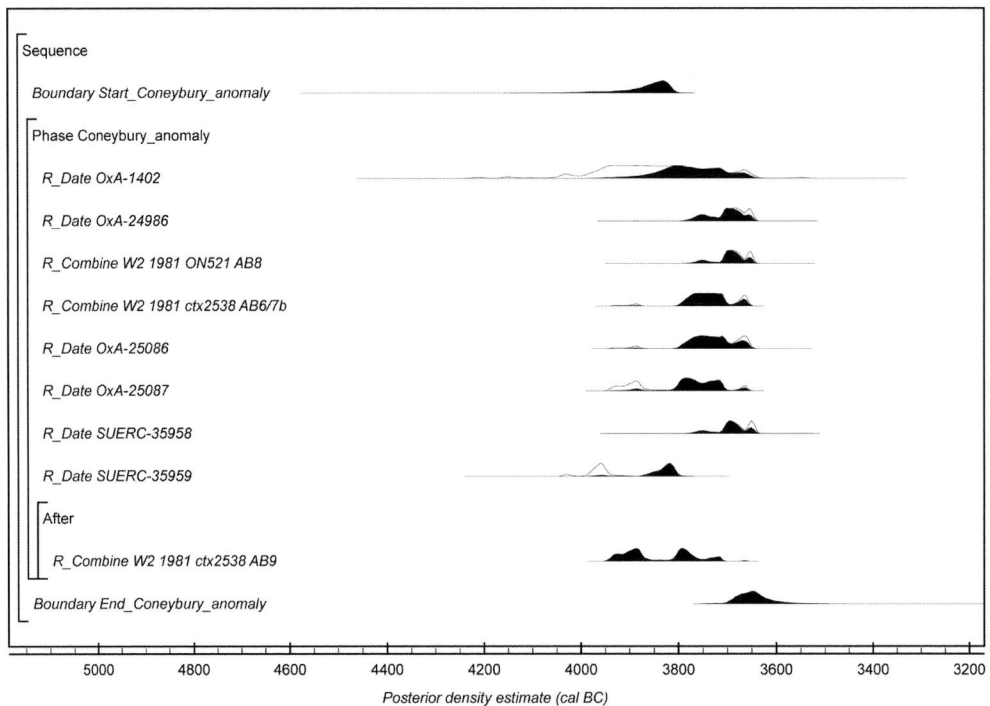

Figure 8.5. A simple `Boundary-defined Phase` *model for the results from the Coneybury Anomaly following Barclay* et al. *(2018). The large square brackets down the left-hand side of the figures, along with the OxCal keywords, define the model, as does the code (Appendix). The results shown in outline are calibrated radiocarbon results while those in black are posterior density estimates. Copyright: Seren Griffiths.*

probability). We can suggest that the end of this activity occurred in *3710–3600 cal. BC (95% probability;* or in *3690–3640 cal. BC 68% probability; end_Coneybury_anomaly;* Fig. 8.5). We can estimate the duration of this activity as occurring over *1–130 years (95% probability;* or *5–80 years 68% probability; duration_Conebury_primary_fill;* Fig. 8.6).

Even this relatively limited prior information allows us to usefully revise our understanding of the nature of the assemblage from this feature. The model applied here is **site-specific** but relatively **uninformative**.

Case study: Vaynor henge

The radiocarbon results from Vaynor henge (Chapter 2) were associated with a lot of informative prior information derived from the site stratigraphy. Because there was activity at Vaynor henge over several hundred years there was also a real possibility that ecofactual evidence might have been reworked or redeposited. On a site for which we have evidence for activity over a considerable period thinking about residual or intrusive material is very important. Scientific dating measurements on samples that were residual or intrusive would produce age estimates that could be misleading in

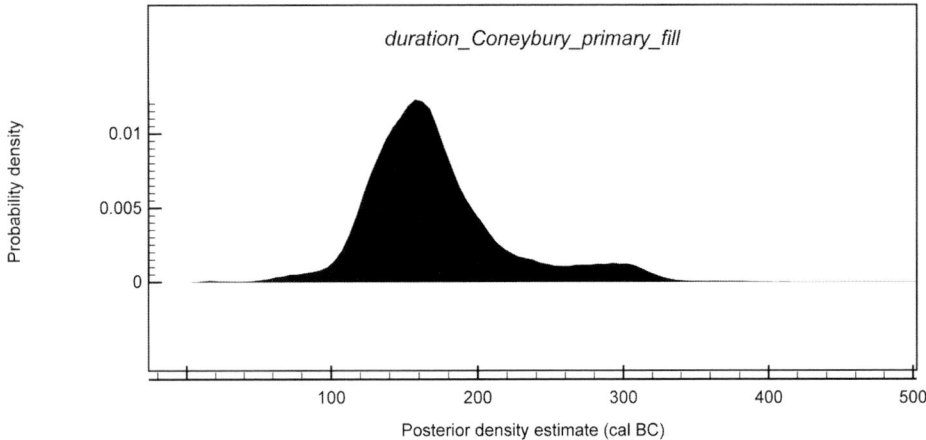

Figure 8.6. The duration of activity represented by the radiocarbon measurements from the fill of the Coneybury Anomaly (Fig. 8.5). The distribution is calculated as shown in the code (Appendix). Copyright: Seren Griffiths.

terms of chronology construction and we would want to try to identify these as part of the analysis and model building process.

There are a number of ways in which we can attempt to exclude the possibilities of misleading residual or intrusive age estimates in chronologies. This is important for informative chronological models that make use of stratigraphy because, if measurements were produced on samples that have been redeposited, are intrusive or are residual, then the measurements would not be consistent with each other or with the age of formation of their parent deposits. At Vaynor henge two approaches were taken to selecting samples for measurement and examining the results. First, a bulk sampling strategy had been developed such that large volumes of sediment were processed for the recovery of charred plant remains from lots of different deposits. This allowed an assessment of the frequency of ecofacts in any unit of soil and, therefore, a consideration of whether material might be representative of activity at particular stages in a site's history or might be more likely to represent intrusive or residual material.

Samples of charred plant remains and charcoals for radiocarbon measurements were selected from assemblages that were relatively rich; the interpretation was that these ecofacts might represent activity associated with the use of the monument. However, this still left the potential that some of the material in these assemblages was redeposited or intrusive. These samples did not have a *direct* relationship between the ecofacts and the event of interest but, based on the frequency of material and the multiple measurements from the same contexts, we believe that there is a relationship with activity.

In this case, at least two radiocarbon results were produced on different types of plant macrofossils from each of the deposits that was selected for scientific dating. The use of different species here is important. Material of different types and of different radiocarbon ages might enter a deposit by different taphonomic pathways. If charred plant material of different types (but of the same radiocarbon age) is recovered from a deposit we can suggest that it is more likely to result from anthropogenic activity associated with the use of the monument.

In the case of Vaynor henge, the post-excavation chronology building had multiple stages of radiocarbon work. This included the initial simulation modelling as part of a reflexive approach to implementing Bayesian chronologies in archaeology (Bayliss 2009). The simulation modelling was followed by two phases of radiocarbon sample submission, as part of an initial assessment phase of post-excavation work and then as part of the further analysis stage. After the first round of results the models were revised and rerun with the new data. This process of critical consideration allowed sample selection to be revised as new data were produced. The second round of sample submission meant that it was possible to identify that one result (SUERC-51706) was produced on residual material. As a consequence of this assessment this result was not included as a likelihood in the subsequent analysis model. In this case it was presented as an `Outlier`.

At Vaynor henge, ecofacts were selected for scientific dating to try and provide a representative sample of activity across the site stratigraphy. Using our stratigraphic observations we were able to identify three classes of radiocarbon results. The first was those from the sequence of deposits from the earlier ditch fills, where the site records suggested that there were two successive periods of infilling, perhaps occurring at different rates. The second class of results was those from a sequence of later ditch fills. The third class was those from post-settings inside the henge ditch which were not stratigraphically related to the ditch fill sequence. In Figure 8.7, we show results from the henge ditch fills that are stratigraphically related using several `Sequence` commands in OxCal. The two `Sequence` commands represent the two different early infilling episodes; these are then followed by successive phases of subsequent activity in the feature (which we represent using successive `Phase` commands). The interior features are stratigraphically unrelated to the ditch fill sequences so we have presented these results as part of a `Boundary`-defined `Phase` of activity which occurred on the site. Full details of the results and the site are found in Darvill *et al.* (2020) with the detailed descriptions of the modelling approaches in Barber and Hart (2015). The results in Figure 8.7 suggest that the henge was established in *2720–2460 cal. BC (Start early ditch fill, 95% probability,* Fig. 8.7).

The unexpected result from this project was that part of the henge was used in the post-Roman period. This chronological longevity would not necessarily have been identified without a sampling strategy that sought to be representative of the different features on the site. The model applied here is **site specific** and **informative** in terms of its use of stratigraphy.

Culture history models

Culture history models move beyond the observations made on individual sites and attempt to synthesise evidence from a number of sites, from a region or from groups of material culture. As these synthesis models often use legacy data from a range of projects

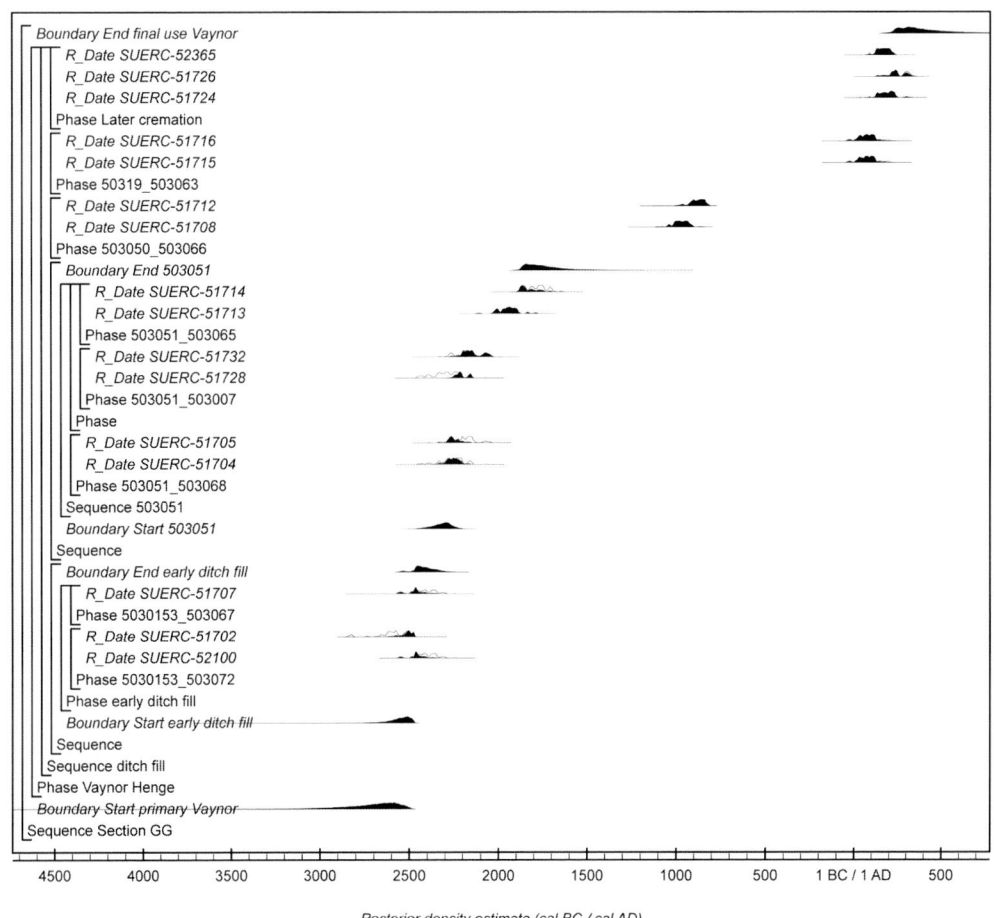

Figure 8.7. A site-specific, informative stratigraphic model applied to the results from Vaynor henge. The large square brackets down the left-hand side of the figures, along with the OxCal keywords, define the model, as does the code (Appendix). The results shown in outline are calibrated radiocarbon results, while those in black are posterior density estimates. Full details of the results are given in Darvill et al. *(2020), see Chapter 2 for further details. Copyright: Seren Griffiths.*

they can include the analysis of measurements produced using different techniques, for different purposes, and to different standards. In these cases, there may be challenges in combining such diverse datasets. This might include an absence of information in archival sources which might now be regarded as important for the interpretation of different measurements.

There are great benefits in culture historic models in terms of moving archaeological narratives beyond individual sites. However, to produce the most effective analysis there needs to be a detailed quality assurance assessment of every measurement and construction of appropriate site-specific models prior to moving into more generalising culture history interpretations. When moving further and further beyond the closely observed evidence from individual sites, archaeologists need to be clear about the increasingly generalisations that occur in interpretations. Generalising models can result in sweeping research findings and there can be great advantages in trying to maintain specificity in these bigger analyses.

Case study: the Mesolithic–Neolithic transition in Britain
Recent chronological work in Britain has explored the currency of Mesolithic and Neolithic culture historic packages. In these analyses, Mesolithic people are defined as hunter-gatherer-fisher communities who existed in Britain after the end of the last glaciation. Mesolithic people used characteristic microlithic technology. Neolithic assemblages are characterised by new lithic technology including polished stone axes and the first introduction to Britain of pottery, monuments, house structures of new forms and some domesticated plants and animals.

A series of publications in the early 21st century explored the temporal currency of individual types of Neolithic artefacts and sites, and the 'Neolithic package' more broadly. These include the innovative wide-ranging applications of Bayesian statistical modelling by Alasdair Whittle and Alex Bayliss (for example Whittle *et al.* 2011; Whittle 2018). As part of this work, it is possible to compare differences in the timing of the regional appearance of Neolithic material culture and practices (for example Griffiths 2014; 2021; Fig, 8.8).

Constructing these bigger culture historic analyses from legacy results requires considerable data cleaning and an examination of the qualities of each measurement and the degree to which any measurement is associated with any archaeological event of interest. Following data cleaning, site-specific models can be constructed and, following this, an analytical model can be constructed that reflects the ways in which groups of data from different sites are related as part of a whole cultural complex. Culture historic models run in OxCal can take many hours or days to resolve.

By producing such synthetic culture historic models we can start to think about the broad tempo of change and, from this evidence, archaeologists can start to think about the *processes* which brought about these patterns. What is critical in such models is that the culture historic groupings are clearly defined in terms of material culture and site type and that they are *not* defined in terms of time or space. This is essential to allow different types of cultural packages or activities to overlap and thus exist at the same time. For example, in the case of the British Neolithic examples discussed here, one of the interesting aspects of this research is the evidence for overlap that has been identified in the north of England between Mesolithic material culture and Neolithic material culture (Griffiths 2014; 2021). Mesolithic practices in Britain did not cease everywhere at the same time to be succeeded by Neolithic practices. By recognising that events are defined in time as well as in space, these types of analysis allow us to produce more nuanced narratives than those which present a 'block' model of time, with different culture historic traditions succeeding each other.

The model that produced the results shown in Figure 8.8 is **culture historic** and includes both **informative** elements derived from the site-stratigraphic models, and relatively **uninformative** prior information derived from the culture historic

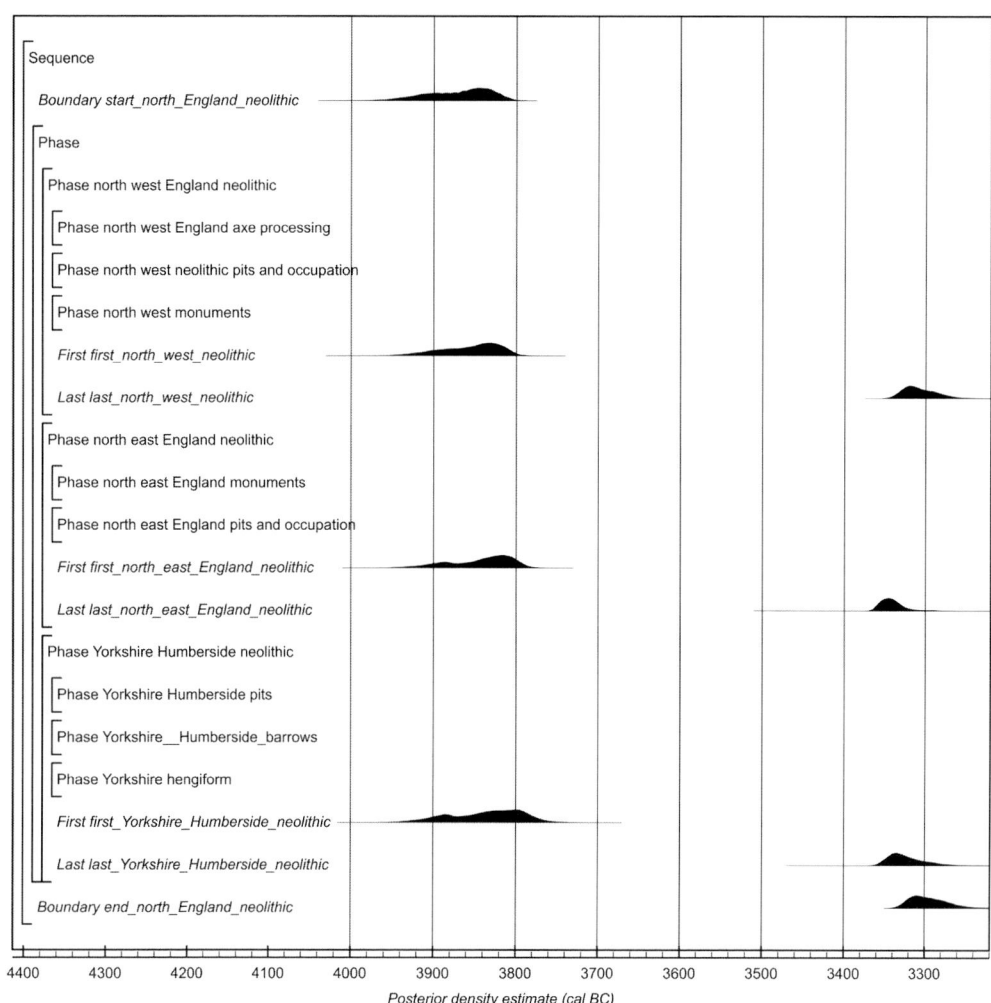

Figure 8.8. Posterior density estimates from a culture historic model for activity associated with Neolithic practices, material culture and sites from northern England. Estimates have been produced for the start and end of Neolithic activity. Full details are given in Griffiths (2021). Copyright: Seren Griffiths.

associations. In this case study, both the site-specific informative prior information, and the culture historic uninformative prior information prove very powerful archaeological knowledge claims. Here, the culture historic uninformative prior information is powerful because of the size of the dataset and because of the way these generalising prior beliefs structures our understanding.

Case study: Bronze Age metalwork in Britain

An even more informative approach to culture history packages than that shown in the previous example can be developed by using the relative chronological information that material culture typologies or seriations afford. Typologies or, more formally expressed, seriation analyses provide the basis for relative temporal classifications. Typological analyses are based on the principles that some forms of material culture start to be used before others, that styles of material culture change or develop over time and that the frequency of the presence of these different types also changes over time.

In a famous early example, in the 19th century Oscar Montelius produced some of the first important relative chronologies by creating typological studies on features with a clearly understood 'closing' event (such as assemblages from graves). In the 20th century a famous analysis by Edwin Dethlefsen and James Deetz (1966) focused on the frequency of different burial motifs on headstones in Colonial cemeteries in eastern Massachusetts from the 1680s–early 19th century.

Work led by Stuart Needham (Needham *et al.* 1998) applied a typological model to radiocarbon results associated with British Bronze Age metalwork. In this case, the analysis included radiocarbon results produced by Needham and colleagues for their project as well as legacy data from other projects. For the legacy data, the British Bronze Age Metalwork project made a detailed assessment of different sample types (including the presence of preservatives, wood offsets and so on) and the association with metalwork. For the new measurements Needham *et al.* produced, short-life samples (<30 years inbuilt age offset) that were selected from organic materials adhering to diagnostic bronze artefacts.

Needham *et al.* (1998) grouped the radiocarbon measurements by association with four groups of metalwork identified by their forms, decoration and styles. These are: Acton/Taunton types, Penard, Wilburton, and Ewart Park types. Based on assessment of the contexts and styles, it is possible to suggest a broad model of typological change over time from Acton and Taunton>Penard>Wilburton>Ewart Park.

However, it is possible to represent this broad temporal model in a number of different ways. In Figure 8.9 we show the outputs of some of these:

- as different groups of activity that were chronologically independent,
- as related, overlapping phases,
- as successive phases as part of a sequence of metalwork traditions, and
- as phases of successive traditions in terms of the first use of different styles but recognising that these styles may have overlapped during their currency.

Each of these models combines prior information (in terms of the temporal relationships between all the data) which are then expressed in the OxCal CQL2 keywords and brackets shown in Figure 8.9. In this case we make use of the Phase, Sequence and Boundary commands and we relate the data within these models to reflect the different interpretations we have outlined above. The code for the models presented in Figure 8.9 is given in the Appendix.

By comparing the results from these different modelling approaches in Figure 8.9 we can start to think about the impact of our interpretation of the prior information (and our modelling choices) have on the model outputs. In most cases we can see that the outputs for the different parameters are broadly similar in both the medians and the posterior distributions. These results do not appear very sensitive to our modelling choices. However, there are some important distinctions. We can see that

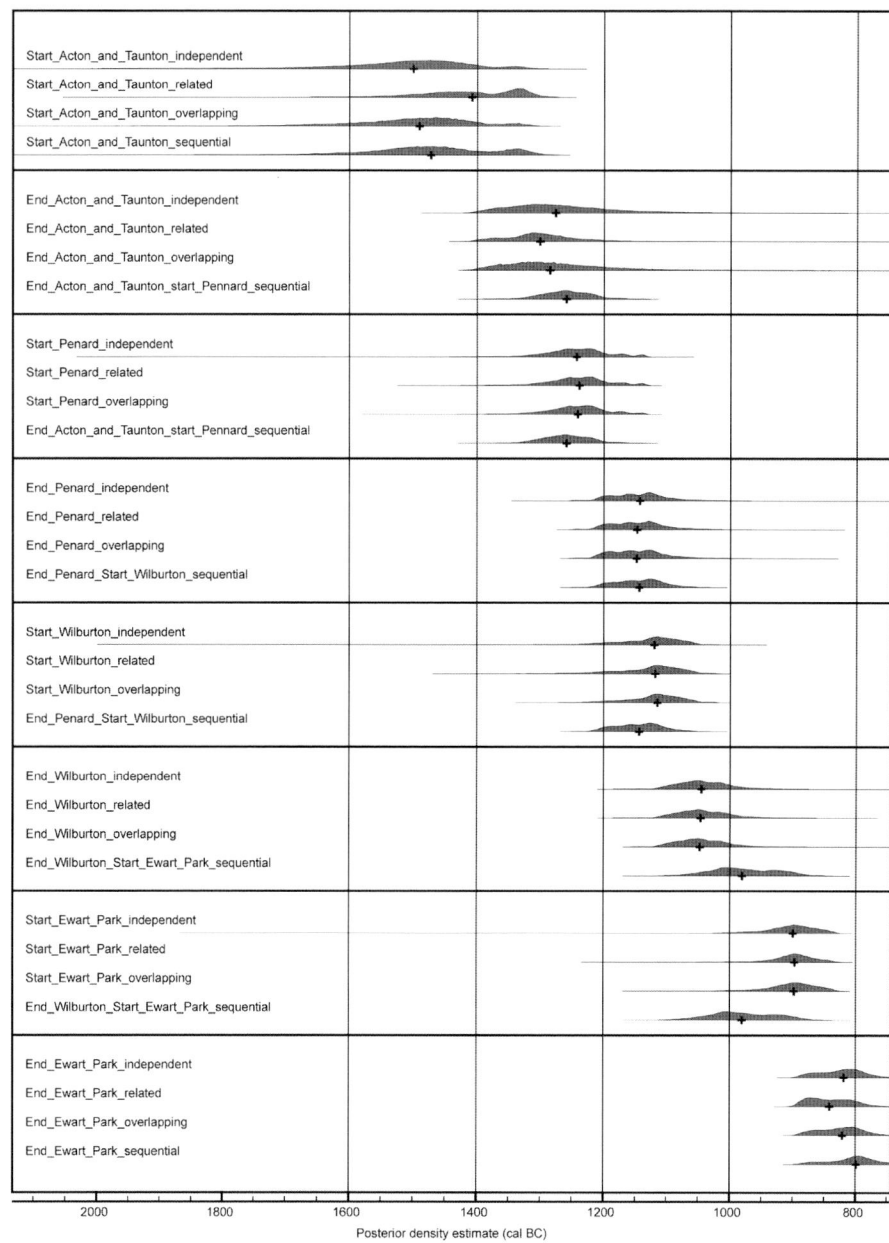

Figure 8.9. Posterior density estimates from different approaches to the chronological modelling of radiocarbon results associated with Bronze Age styles of metal axehead from Britain. The data can be found in Needham et al. (1998). The different modelling approaches compare how our outputs change when we express different prior information. This process of model construction and comparison is critical in the analysis and interpretation of data. The code for these different approaches is included at the end of this chapter. Copyright: Seren Griffiths.

the parameter *Start_Acton_and_Taunton_related* has quite a distinct distribution from the equivalent parameters produced from the other models. What is this telling us? In this case the parameter *Start_Acton_and_Taunton_related* was calculated in a model where all the activity was related and was constrained within an overall Boundary-defined Phase. Because all the other activity in this model occurs later, because there are relatively few radiocarbon measurements in the Acton and Taunton Phase, and because we have constrained the data in each of the Phase in the model to be related together, this estimate has been shifted later. The susceptibility of this parameter to move is highlighting that we have probably under-sampled this phase of activity; we do not have enough data in this part of the model. If it were possible to get more radiocarbon measurements on samples well-associated with Acton and Taunton axeheads that would be a sensible thing to do. Failing that, this part of our output might be emphasising that we might want to express hesitancy in our understanding of the timing of the start of the Acton and Taunton axehead currency.

Does this variation matter? Well, it depends on our research question and what we want to know. It depends how precisely we need our chronology to be expressed. It depends if we are evaluating competing interpretations; all of these models are possible. So, which of these models is 'best'? Again, it depends. We suggested above that the Acton and Taunton Phase probably does not have enough data to be fully representative of this activity. So, all these models could be improved. Archaeologically speaking, perhaps the sequential model appears least satisfactory. The idea that everywhere across Britain people simultaneously stopped using one type of artefact and started using another does not seem to match what we know about human society. As we noted in Chapter 7, events are *spatially* as well as temporally defined. Even on a single site, some people may continue to use certain material culture for periods of time after things drop out of the general currency of use. Archaeologically speaking, the model that we regard as the most applicable is the one that indicates that all this activity is related and that there is some relative ordering to the events indicated by the typology of axeheads but that these different phases of activity may well have overlapped. We therefore prefer the results from the overlapping model but with our caveat about the estimate for the start of the Acton and Taunton phase as expressed above.

All the models applied here are **culture historic** and, because they use the relative, typological sequence, they are **informative**. Comparing the outputs from models using different prior beliefs is a form of **sensitivity analysis** and is very useful in starting to think critically about our data and our prior beliefs. As we have seen here the *process* of modelling data in different ways can be a very important part of the analysis. We can see that the different choices impact on our output in slightly different ways. We need to think about whether these differences are meaningful for our analysis and about which model is the least partial and least wrong representation of what we, as archaeologists, think that we know about an individual case study.

Text-based prior information

One of the most exciting ways of working with scientific chronologies in archaeology can be combining evidence from a range of dating techniques with historically attested events.

These could include the ascent of monarchs, the establishment of cites or territories, the end of periods of rule or the destruction of buildings or sites. There is a wide range of different text-based sources that archaeologists might want to work with. These could include inscriptions on monuments or memorials as well as a variety of written sources and a range of different calendrical systems. Historically attested climate or weather events can also be compared with multi-proxy evidence for palaeo-environmental responses.

Scientific chronologies might be usefully compared with text-based chronologies for a variety of reasons. In terms of dynastic or political narratives, people in the ancient world were as prone to exaggerating their achievements as people are today. As a result, there are lots of cases where ancient equivalents of public relations agents created partial impressions of the past. This is especially true where there are questions of patronage. In Britain, in the 7th and 8th centuries AD, the monk and early historian Bede is famously selective in his subject matter (e.g. Higham 2006), while the historical documents that form the *Anglo Saxon Chronicle* have notable bias in favour of the achievements of Alfred the Great and other West Saxons (e.g. Davis 1971; see below).

Part of the value in comparing scientific dating chronologies with text-based sources is that these are independent types of dating evidence. An estimate for the establishment of a town, the date of a plague or of a battle provided by radiocarbon measurements is unlikely to be biased in the same ways that textual sources will be. When working with these types of problems we need to consider the precision of scientific dating evidence, the social context in which text-based sources were produced and why there might be tensions between these different types of evidence. If text-based sources and the scientific dating chronologies are in disagreement the tension can still be very instructive. Written sources, whether the king lists of ancient Egypt, Roman memorials to successful military campaigns or the written histories of Saxon rulers, may often be produced in particular political contexts and may omit or over-inflate events in the past, or be misread or mistranslated in the present.

Case study: Saxon Stafford
Figure 8.10 shows the chronometric results produced from excavations at Tipping Street and other results from Saxon Stafford (see Dodd *et al.* 2015 and Hamerow *et al.* 2020 for details). We first introduced these results in Chapter 2 and Chapter 5. From the work at Tipping Street, eight radiocarbon measurements and one archaeomagnetic measurement were produced on samples of charred plant remains and burnt clay from Saxon pottery kilns. In this case, during the analysis of these results we identified that some of the radiocarbon fuel measurements were slightly older than the archaeomagnetic result. This could reflect the storage of fuel prior to use in the kilns with the result that the date of the last firing would be slightly later than the age of the fuel. In the model presented here (Fig. 8.10), we have included the fuel measurements from Kiln GRP 4308 in a `Sequence` model in OxCal to reflect this prior belief.

From the site stratigraphy we have other dated events that we can relate to kiln GRP3408. Kiln GRP3401 is stratigraphically later than GRP3408. We can then suggest that the fuel assemblage from the later kiln, GRP3401, should be later than the use of the earlier one, GRP3408. We have therefore used the `Sequence` to indicate that we believe all the activity associated with GRP3401 occurred *after* all of the activity associated with GRP3408.

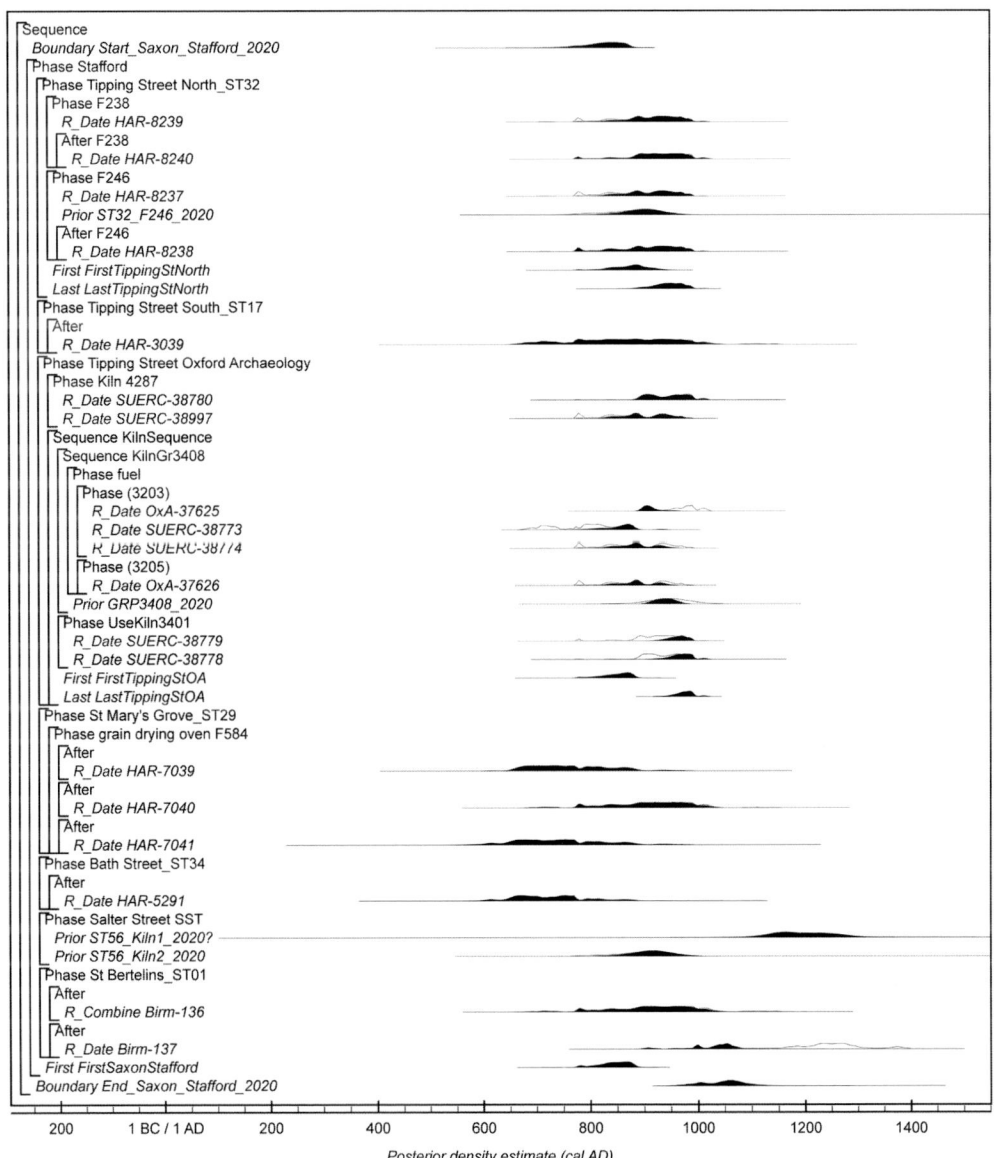

Figure 8.10. Outputs from a model incorporating archaeomagnetic and radiocarbon results associated with Saxon activity at Stafford. See Dodd et al. (2014), Hamerow et al. (2020) and Chapters 2 and 5 for further details. Copyright: Seren Griffiths.

The work at Tipping Street is part of a long history of investigation of Saxon Stafford. Other archaeomagnetic and radiocarbon results are available from different sites in the town. We can use these to construct a currency model for Saxon activity in Stafford. In the model presented here (Fig. 8.10) we have included these other results for activity and adapted the model developed in Dodd *et al.* (2015); in the rest of the model beyond Tipping Street there is relatively little *stratigraphic* prior information beyond the association of results with different archaeological sites or phases of work. What this model does do is include radiocarbon results produced on samples including potential 'old wood' as *termini post quos* using the `After` function. Bronk Ramsey (2009) provides other approaches to including 'old wood' results in analyses. In the currency model for Saxon Stafford shown in Figure 8.10 we have also excluded one archaeomagnetic result from the calculations, that from the kiln excavated at Slater Street, ST56 Kiln 1. Samples from this deposit behaved poorly during measurement (Dodd *et al.* 2015) and the result is inconsistent with the radiocarbon results from the same feature. We think that this archaeomagnetic measurement was an inaccurate age estimate for the firing of that hearth.

All the age estimates shown in Figure 8.10 are associated with diagnostic culture historic Saxon activity; for example, the production of Saxon Stafford Ware and activity associated with a Saxon church. We can therefore use all of these results to estimate that the start of Saxon activity at Stafford occurred in cal. *AD 735–890* (*Start_Saxon_ Stafford_2020; 95% probability*; Fig. 8.10), and most probably in cal. *AD 800– 875 cal.* (*68% probability*). This estimate can be compared with historic sources which attest to Saxon presence at Stafford. The Mercian Register of the *Anglo Saxon Chronicle* indicates that Stafford was established as a burh – or a defended settlement – in AD 913 by Æthelflæd, daughter of the West Saxon King Alfred the Great.

We can compare the timing for our estimate for the start of Saxon activity at Stafford with this key date in the history of the burh. We can do this using the `Order` function in OxCal, a command which compares the probability that different parameters occurred in a relative order. From our calculations it is highly probable (*99.6% probable*), that the start of Saxon activity at Stafford occurred before the establishment of the burh in 913. Moreover, it is highly probable (*94% probable*), that the start of the Saxon activity we have sampled also occurred before another key event, the Viking raids documented in 874.

There are important things to consider about what this sample signifies though. This dataset may not provide a *representative* sample of all Saxon activity at Stafford. It arguably emphasises the last part of the sequence as the archaeological development work may have only sampled the upper (later) part of the sequence. Secondly, in addition, for archaeomagnetic measurements, it is the *last* firing that is sampled as the dated event. This sample of data therefore could well under-estimate the earliest Saxon presence in Stafford. This example may be one of the cases where the history of a place is more complicated than that reported in documentary sources. Comparing the archaeological evidence with historic sources is therefore an important way of evaluating such evidence.

The model applied here includes **site-specific** information, deriving from the **stratigraphic** information from the Tipping Street site. It is **informative** because of the use of stratigraphy. It also includes a text-based analysis because of the comparison of the output with **historically** attested events.

Case study: Richard III

The famous discovery of King Richard III of England under what was then a car park in Leicester, county town of Leicestershire in central England, provides another comparison case study between scientific dating and text-based chronologies. The now famous 'King in the car park' was successfully identified as the last Plantagenet King of England, Richard III, on the basis of ancient DNA evidence (King *et al.* 2014). However, the radiocarbon measurements from this individual are instructive in thinking about text-based models.

In 2012 an excavation was undertaken on the former site of the Grey Friars friary in Leicester (Buckley *et al.* 2013). The site was suspected to be the location of the medieval church of the convent of the Grey Friars where the deposed king had been buried in the same year, 1485, as Richard's defeat and killing by King Henry VII at the Battle of Bosworth. The historical veracity of this date is established by multiple written sources, for example the early 16th century *Historiae Anglicae* by Polydore Vergil, even if the precise location of the battlefield is less-well understood.

The 2012 excavations identified the Grey Friars church and different structural elements within it. The burial identified as that of King Richard III was in the south-western section of the church choir but was not marked in any way and so the positive identification of the burial as that of the king was determined from the ancient DNA evidence. A range of complementary data also suggested that the burial represented King Richard III including skeletal evidence consistent with battle trauma. How would scientific dating evidence compare with the very precise, historically attested date of death for King Richard III in 1485?

Four results were commissioned on a sample of rib bone (Hamilton and Bronk Ramsey 2012; Cook *et al.* 2015). These were not statistically significantly different at the 5% significance level (T'=3.8; T'5%=7.8; v=3; SUERC-42896 434±18 BP; SUERC-42902 440±17 BP; OxA-27182 478±25; OxA-27183 480±25; Ward and Wilson 1978; Fig. 8.11), and a weighted mean (calculated using the R_Combine function in OxCal as outlined above) provides a date range of cal. AD 1430–1460 (95% confidence). How can any individual with this date of death be identified as King Richard III, who, we know from historical records, died in 1485?

Different skeletal elements form or turnover at different rates and at different points in life (Sealy *et al.* 1995). Teeth are formed in childhood and, therefore, can provide information about the chemical constituents of diet during this period. Dense bones such as femurs may form over the *c.* 10-year period before a person dies though this varies given the age and sex of a person and potentially a range of environmental and genetic factors (Hedges *et al.* 2007); we return to this point with the example of the ice mummy 'Ötzi' below. Rib bones are reformed over an individual's life cycle and represent an averaged carbon signal from only the last few years of an individual's life; measurements on ribs should thus not be the source of this difference between the radiocarbon measurements and the known historical date of Richard's death.

Looking at the stable isotope measurements provides important additional information. Stable isotope information from Richard's later life (Lamb *et al.* 2014) suggests that he had a rich diet which included significant contributions from fish. Hamilton and Bronk Ramsey (2012) estimated from the stable isotope values of a rib sample that Richard ate a diet with 27.6%±10% marine contribution.

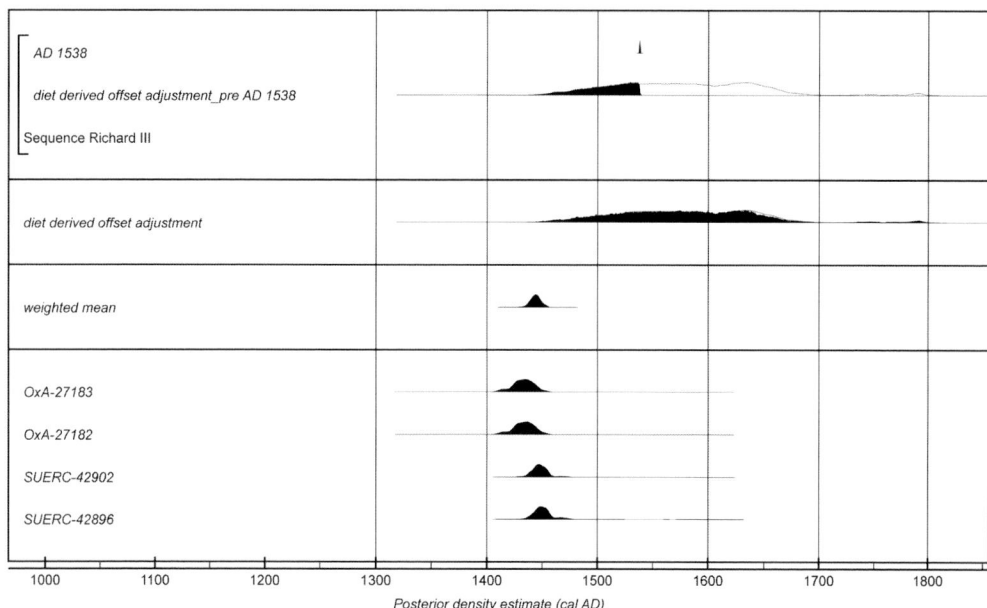

Figure 8.11. Radiocarbon results from the individual identified as Richard III. The lower part of the figure shows the calibrated results. The upper parts show various ways of revising these results by taking a weighted mean to reduce scatter, applying an appropriate diet-derived offset to produce an accurate estimate and, finally, constraining the result based on prior information about historical events. Copyright: Seren Griffiths.

As discussed in Chapter 2, marine and other aquatic reservoirs have a higher proportion of infinitely old carbon isotopes than in terrestrial reservoirs. Because of the lower proportion of radiocarbon isotopes, measurements on samples with marine contributions will appear erroneously old if they are calibrated using a terrestrial calibration dataset. Samples with such diet-derived offsets need to be calibrated with a special calibration dataset to produce accurate age estimates. Marine calibration curves exist and they are most effective if combined with local knowledge of the marine reservoir effect, because the mixing of carbon isotopes can be very variable within oceans and seas. In this case, Hamilton and Bronk Ramsey (2012) thus also applied a local marine reservoir offset of –29±51 years based on research into the reservoir conditions around Britain.

To produce an accurate age estimate for the death of this individual we need to calibrate the result to reflect the 27.6%±10% of the diet that derived from marine sources and with a local reservoir offset of –29±51 years. We can do this by selecting both the marine and terrestrial calibration curves using the `Curve` function in OxCal. We can then apply a local marine reservoir offset using the `Delta_R` function within the program and weighting the proportion of the diet that was sourced from marine and terrestrial resources. As we can see in Figure 8.11, the impact of the marine resources on the age estimates are significant; we can see how much younger the distribution is after we have corrected it for the diet-derived offset.

This corrected distribution is much less precise, because of the uncertainty associated with the diet-derived reservoir offset. However, we now believe it to be an *accurate* estimate for the timing of the archaeological event in question, the death of King Richard III. The corrected radiocarbon age range is AD 1465–1645 (at 95% confidence), which includes the point in time – AD 1485 – when King Richard III was killed.

As with lots of archaeological sites, the team investigating this burial had additional prior information. They knew that the Grey Friars chapel in which Richard had been buried was demolished, probably in 1538, when the Dissolution of the monasteries by King Henry VIII took effect in Leicester. Given that all burials must have occurred before this date it is possible to revise the age estimate for the death of the individual even further. This person must have died prior to 1538, and we can use this to constrain the age estimate further in the distribution 'diet derived offset adjustment_pre AD 1538' (Fig. 8.11). This distribution suggests that at 95% confidence this individual died in 1460–1540, which is entirely in keeping with the date of death of King Richard III in AD 1485.

The calibration work applied here uses prior information from dietary reconstruction to produce **accurate** age estimates. It uses information from **text-based** sources to examine the result. The constraint from the historical date of dissolution of the chapel is highly **informative** in terms of its impact on the resulting date range.

Known-age interval models

In many of the examples we have looked at here we have good understandings of the *relative* chronological relationships between a group of samples that have been measured by scientific dating techniques. Even using an uninformative and neutral single `Phase` model for an archaeological site our prior information allows us to relate measurements and to make them more precise in some cases. However, it is much less common on archaeological sites that we have very specific information about the time intervals between measurements.

As introduced in Chapter 3, Bayesian dendrochronological wiggle matching is one example where we have independent evidence about the specific time intervals between samples measured by scientific dating techniques. In dendrochronological wiggle matching, radiocarbon measurements are produced on individual annual tree rings or on blocks of rings representing known growth periods (for example of 5 or 10 years). In a wiggle match, multiple measurements are produced at points over the ring sequence of the piece of timber or wood. The number of rings between each radiocarbon sample is therefore known and can be included in the analysis to indicate that the dated events are separated by a specific number of years. These known-age intervals can therefore be used to produce more precise age estimates for the radiocarbon results. As well as increasing precision, adding radiocarbon results to a sequence can be used to wiggle match or 'date' a dendrochronological sample that will not match against regional dendrochronological curves on its own. In addition, it is possible to estimate other aspects from a dendrochronological sequence based on what is known from the structure of the wood or timber sample.

Bayesian dendrochronological wiggle matching is perhaps the best-known example of using known-age intervals between samples measured by scientific dating to improve archaeological chronologies. There are other examples where annually formed increments can be used to constrain measurements such as, for example, those found in varves, corals or shells (with additional marine in-built offsets if appropriate; e.g. Helama and Hood 2011).

While wiggle matching of samples with well understood, known-age intervals is relatively commonly applied, the potential of the technique has not been fully recognised for samples where the age interval is less well understood. We explore one such example below.

Case study: medieval standing building wiggle matching
In Britain, wiggle matching is often used as part of the conservation process to explore which elements of a wooden structure belong to different phases of construction or repair, as well as more generally to explore a structure's history.

The Church of St Peter, West Liss, Hampshire, UK is a complicated structure that has evidence for many phases of modification (Arnold *et al.* 2020; see Chapter 3). Understanding which elements were built when was critical for conservation and management of the structure. Several timbers were dated by conventional dendrochronology but several important timbers could not be matched to regional ring-width master chronologies. Sub-samples were taken from the same timbers for radiocarbon dating and all the results were analysed using a Bayesian dendrochronological wiggle match using the D_Sequence function in OxCal. Figure 8.12 shows a wiggle match sequence from one of the timbers at St Peter's. In this model, we have incorporated the radiocarbon results and the known-age interval based on the number of rings between the dated samples using the Gap function.

In this case we are working with oak timbers. This species has very specific cell structures in different tissues which allows a differentiation between the much older heartwood and the much younger sapwood. Depending on climate and local growing conditions (see Chapter 3) different numbers of sapwood rings will be present in a tree before these are converted to heartwood. In the absence of 'bark edge', the presence of the 'transition' between the heartwood and the sapwood is therefore very important in building chronologies. Using a Bayesian dendrochronological wiggle match it is possible to estimate the date of the heartwood/sapwood transition. In Figure 8.12 we have estimated the heartwood/sapwood transition using the interval between the last radiocarbon measurement and the known number of rings. We estimate that the heartwood/sapwood transition formed in *cal. AD 1285–1310* (*95% probability*; or *cal. AD 1290–1305 68% probability*; *LSS_A37_h_s*; Fig. 8.12).

In addition, if we have the heartwood/sapwood transition we can further estimate the *felling* date of a timber if we have a good knowledge of the average sapwood ring count from that region. For the purposes of this timber we have used an estimate for British native oak trees for the sapwood rings after the heartwood/sapwood transition (for further details see Bayliss and Tyers 2004; Arnold *et al.* 2020). In this example we

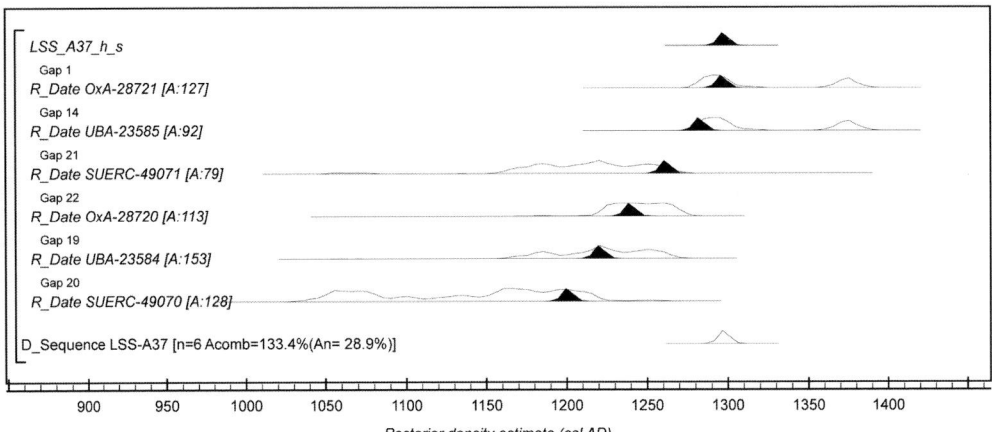

Figure 8.12. A Bayesian wiggle match for radiocarbon results from a timber from the Church of St Peter, West Liss. The results shown in outline are calibrated radiocarbon results, while those in black are posterior density estimates. Because the intervals between the radiocarbon samples are known from dendrochronology, this prior information can be expressed in the analysis. Here we calculate the timing of the heartwood/sapwood transition which is preserved in the timber. Full details are given in Arnold et al. (2020). The OxCal CQL2 keywords and brackets define the model. Copyright: Seren Griffiths.

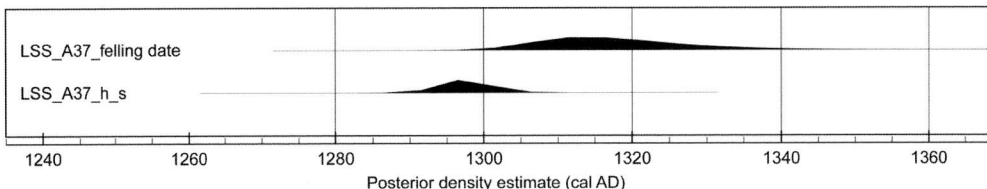

Figure 8.13. An estimate for the felling date of the timber using the heartwood/sapwood transition estimate calculated in Fig. 8.12. This estimate has been produced using local knowledge about the average number of sapwood rings oak trees produce. Full details are given in Arnold et al. (2020). Copyright: Seren Griffiths.

have used the Shift function in OxCal to estimate the felling date using an average sapwood count for the region. We estimate that the felling date was in *cal. AD 1295–1340* (95% probability; or *cal. AD 1305–1325* 68% probability; *LSS_A37_felling*; Fig. 8.13). The most appropriate estimate for the number of sapwood rings will depend on the local growing conditions and, in undertaking this kind of analysis, it is always a good idea to contact dendrochronologists who have worked in the study area to achieve the most appropriate estimate.

The Bayesian wiggle matching work applied here uses **known-age intervals**. It is highly **informative** because of the way the multiple measurements and well understood relationships between the dated events fit the measurements to the calibration dataset.

Case study: 'Ötzi'

As mentioned when we discussed the dating of the body thought to be King Richard III, different tissues in the human body (and those of other animals) have different radiocarbon ages. This is due to the times at which they form and whether tissues turn-over during the life cycle. Because of this, skin will exhibit a younger apparent radiocarbon age than bone from the same organism. The ice mummy 'Ötzi' was discovered on the Austrian–Italian border (46.7739926296481 N, 10.8371631758747 E (WGS84)) in 1991 by hikers. His body had been preserved in ice and because of the cold and anoxic conditions his remains (including soft tissues) were extremely well preserved. Lots of radiocarbon measurements were produced on different samples from 'Ötzi' which were recognised to be of different ages (Hedges *et al.* 1992). Indeed, it was the different radiocarbon ages of these measurements that led to the development of the earliest version of the OxCal program (Bayliss and Bronk Ramsey 2004; Chapter 2).

We have modelled measurements from 'Ötzi' in a variety of ways to explore the impacts of different interpretations of carbon cycling and tissue turn-over in the human body. In Figure 8.14, we can see results on samples of skin and samples of bone from the Oxford and Vienna radiocarbon laboratories (see Hedges *et al.* 1992; Rom *et al.* 1999 for full details). The results on the bone samples are statistically consistent (ETH-8342; OxA-3419; OxA-3371; OxA-3372; OxA-3420;T'=3.3; T'5%=9.5; $v=4$; Ward and Wilson 1978). Taking a weighted mean of these results using the `R_Combine` function in OxCal gives us a radiocarbon age for the bone samples of 4567±27 BP, which calibrates as 3380–3110 cal. BC (85.9% confidence, or 3500–3460 cal. BC 9.5% confidence).

The measurements on the skin samples are also statistically consistent (OxA-3373; OxA-3374; OxA-3421; OxA-3375; OxA-3376; ETH-8345.la; ETH-8345.lb; ETH-8345.1; ETH-8345.2; T=4.7; T5%=15.5; $v=8$; Ward and Wilson 1978). A weighted mean of these results gives us a radiocarbon age of 4522±23 BP for the skin, which calibrates as 3360–3260 cal. BC (29% confidence) or 3240–3110 cal. BC (66% confidence).

However, we know more about the relative radiocarbon ages of these samples because of our understanding of carbon cycling in the body. The bone measurements should be, in isotopic terms, 10–15 years older than the skin. In Figure 8.14, we have presented this using the `Sequence` model in OxCal. We have constrained the bone weighted mean to be 15 years older than the tissue weighted mean, with a normally distributed uncertainty of 5 years using the `Interval` function. This is probably appropriate as the sampled bone was a pelvis, a robust and dense element that probably takes a reasonably long time to turn-over, and because the individual was *c.* 45 years old and bone turn over slows with age (Hedges *et al.* 2007; see Chapter 2). We have also included an `Interval` function to reflect the potential difference between the measurements on the skin tissues, and the date of death. This `Interval` function has been set to 1 month, with a very small normally distributed uncertainty of a couple of weeks to reflect some variation in the turn-over of skin tissue. We have then estimated the date of death using the `Date` function within OxCal. Using these prior beliefs, we estimate that 'Ötzi' most probably died in *3360–3320 cal. BC (64% probability, or 3215–3175 cal. BC 21% probability, or 3145–3110 cal. BC 11% probability,*

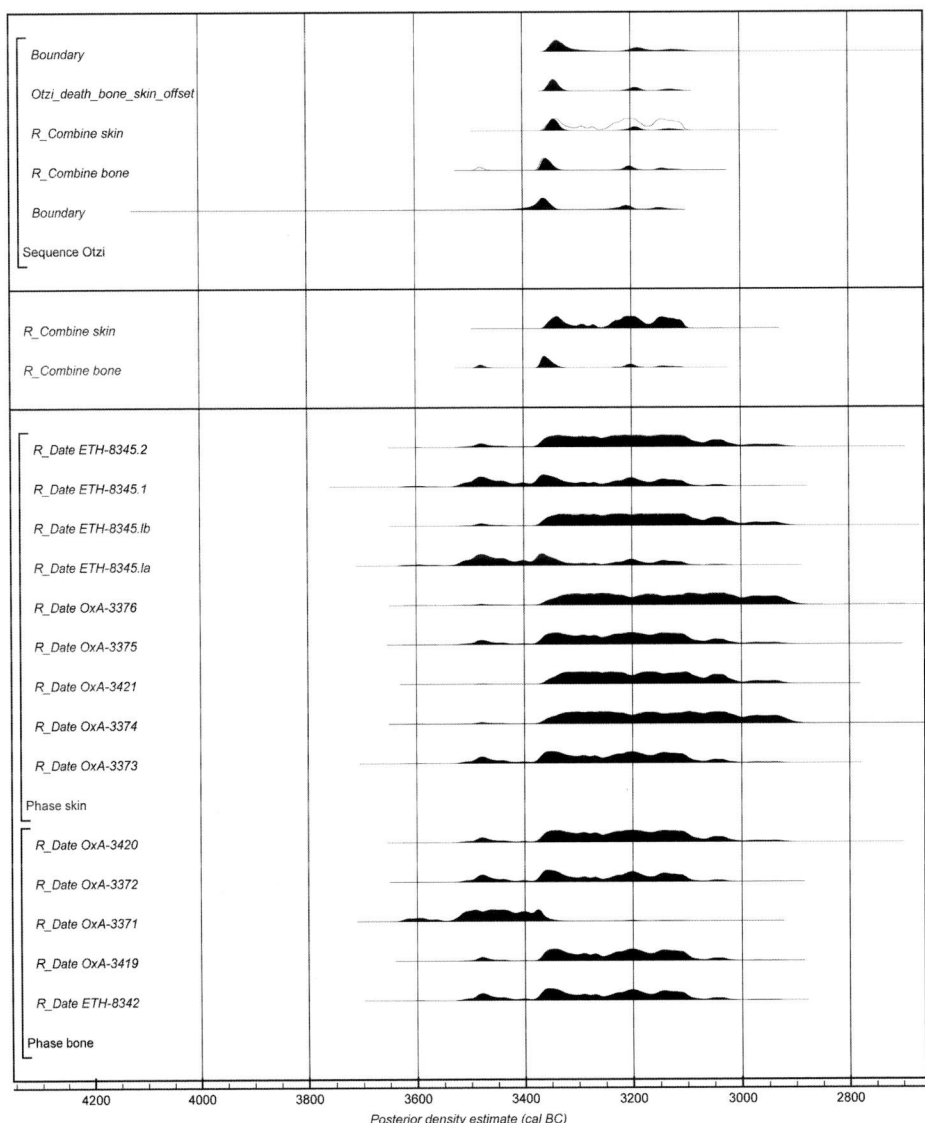

Figure 8.14. Radiocarbon results produced on samples of skin and samples of bone from the ice mummy 'Ötzi' (see Hedges et al. 1992; Rom et al. 1999 for full details). At the bottom of the figure are calibrated results from the different types of tissue samples. In the middle are the weighted means on these results by tissue type. At the top is an example of how these weighted means could be further constrained based on our understanding of the relative ages of the parent samples. We have used these relative ages to provide an estimate for the date of death, in this part of the figure posterior density estimates are given in solid plots with the weighted means in outline. Using this model, it is most probable that 'Ötzi' died in the 34th century cal. BC. There are many other ways to model these data but the exercise demonstrates the potential for wiggle matching on osteological or other tissue sample. The code is included in the Appendix. Copyright: Seren Griffiths.

Otzi_death_bone_skin_offset, Fig. 8.14). The age intervals here include more uncertainty than the dendrochronological wiggle matching example; human tissue turn-over can vary between individuals and unfortunately the tissue turn-over which we measure does not preserve annual increments like certain tree species. However, the underlying approach is the same. We are using our prior beliefs about the temporal associations between the different dated events to wiggle match these results to the shape of the calibration dataset.

In Figure 8.15, we can see some of the posteriors from this model on the calibration curve. The shape of the calibration dataset is very important in thinking critically about

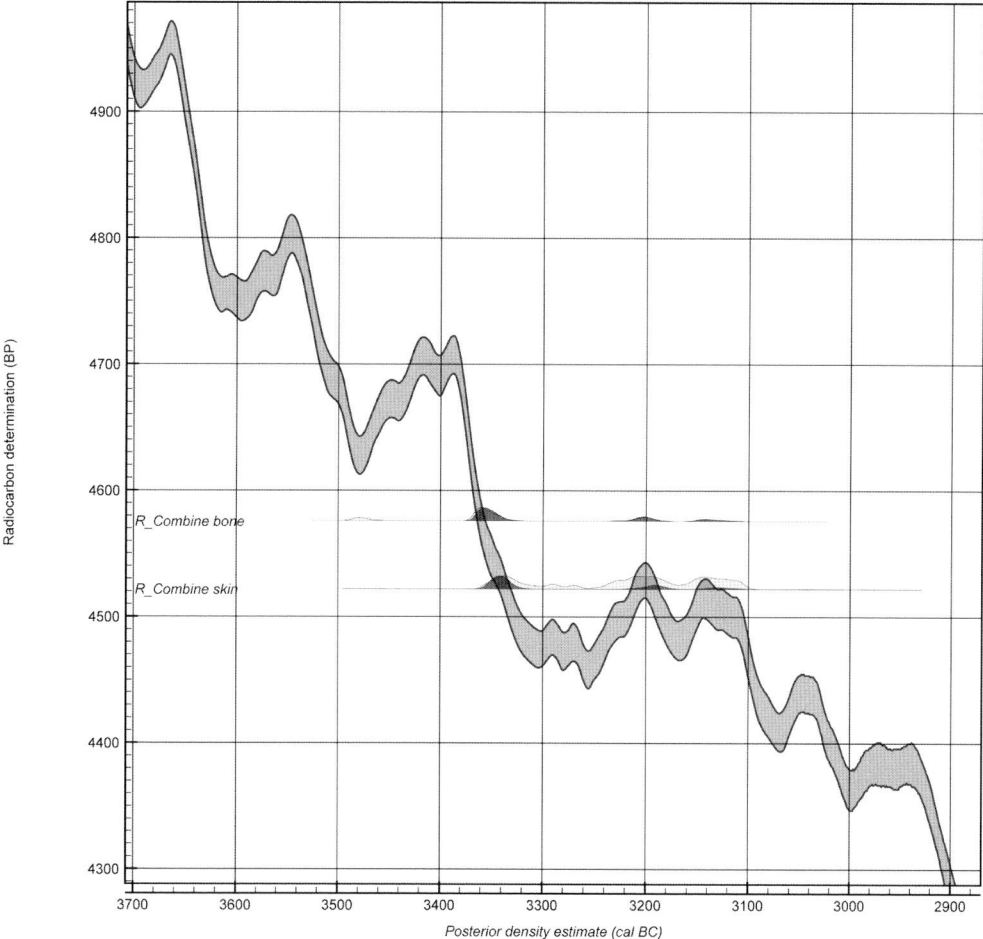

Figure 8.15. The posterior density estimates calculated in the model shown in the upper part of Fig. 8.14 as plotted against the calibration curve. The impact of relating the measurements on the two sample types with an estimate reflecting the interval between the formation of the different tissues is apparent. These distributions and the shape of the calibration curve suggest a date of death in the 34th century cal. BC. Copyright: Seren Griffiths.

our outputs. In this case, the available data suggest that 'Ötzi' could have died in the 34th century cal. BC, but better understanding of the carbon cycling in his tissues would help refine this.

The outputs presented here have explored the potential for biologically-derived **known-age intervals** and are highly **informative**. Different models of bone turn-over might produce very different age estimates. We have included this example to highlight the potential for other forms of wiggle matching beyond dendrochronology as a very productive potential research avenue.

Case study: quasi-continuous sediment deposition
The examples included in the discussion above focus on anthropogenic activity. As we saw in Chapter 6, archaeologists are often interested in the relationships between human activity and palaeo-environmental events. Palaeo-environmental cores, monoliths or other sequences of samples include important prior information about the relative ordering of different palaeo-environmental events defined by proxies. In these cases, chronometric measurements produced on samples from these sequences are associated through their relative positions and the order of the sediment sequence provides an indication of the passage of time.

In certain depositional environments continuous accumulation of sediment can be assumed over time. Such (quasi-)continuous accumulation is more likely in the 'natural' environment (for example lake or marine sediment deposition, peat accumulation and so on) than soil formation processes which include anthropogenic inputs (for example manuring or other agricultural practices). Chronological information from such sequences may be very important in the modelling and interpretation of anthropogenic sites.

In the West Liss dendrochronological wiggle matching example above, the D_ Sequence command was used to constrain results produced on dendrochronological sequences which were separated by distinct numbers of annual tree-rings. In the case of continuous sedimentary deposition we do not have the same clearly-defined 'known-age' intervals between samples – with the arguable exception of 'varved' (annually laminated) deposits. However, we *can* use the accumulated sediment depth as a proxy for the passing of time. On a very simplistic level, given quasi-continuous deposit formation we might anticipate that sedimentary deposits twice as thick might have taken twice as long to accumulate. In such a simplified case where sedimentation rate is constant, a U_Sequence ('uniform sequence') can be applied in OxCal (Bronk Ramsey 2008).

However, in nature, a truly constant sedimentation rate rarely occurs with fluctuations in sedimentation rate far more likely through time. In OxCal such variation is accounted for through the application of a P_Sequence model, which implements an underlying Poisson-process mathematical model and thus provides a more realistic representation of authentic, complex sedimentation processes (Bronk Ramsey 2008). The rigidity (i.e. linearity) of a P_Sequence is defined in OxCal using a parameter, 'k', where a higher value of k gives an increasingly linear deposition rate, while a lower value of k allows increasing flexibility (or 'wiggliness'). The k parameter can be specified *a priori* but it is also possible to allow the program to apply a model averaging approach to determine the optimal value of k (i.e. optimal `P_Sequence` rigidity) based upon the initial age/depth relationship of samples from the unmodelled data (Bronk Ramsey and Lee 2013). For example, if the unmodelled ages of the dated samples fall close to a straight line, OxCal will utilise this information to infer that the same relationship holds for the interpolated/extrapolated depths in the `P_Sequence` and produce a relatively precise, modelled uncertainty envelope for the interpolated/extrapolated depth range. Conversely, if the unmodelled ages of the dated samples imply more variable sedimentation rates, OxCal will produce broader uncertainty envelopes for the interpolated/extrapolated depth range to account for this.

One recent example of this type of work was undertaken at Cerro Benitez (51.55 S, 72.583333 W (WGS84)), southern Patagonia. The site is important in furthering our understanding of the relationships between environmental change, faunal extinctions and the early peopling of southern Patagonia. Because of the location of this site, the southern hemisphere calibration dataset SHCal20 (Hogg *et al.* 2020) was used to calibrate the results.

A detailed palynological record was produced (McCulloch *et al.* 2021) from an 11 m long sediment core extracted from a closed basin mire at Cerro Benitez with accompanying chronological data provided by nine radiocarbon dates and two geochemically-identified tephra (i.e. volcanic ash) layers, themselves previously radiocarbon dated elsewhere. A `P_Sequence` model was constructed (Fig. 8.16), applying the model averaging approach to objectively determine the optimal rigidity, k. Formal outlier analysis was also applied using the notation `Outlier_Model("General",T(5),U(0,4),"t");` and applying the prior belief that each measurement had a 1/20 chance of being an outlier (`Outlier(0.05);`). This approach objectively down-weights the influence of any 'spurious' radiocarbon determinations deemed to be inconsistent with the others (Bronk Ramsey *et al.* 2010). The age-depth model produced (Fig. 8.16) shows the classic 'string of sausages' plot with chronological uncertainties being greater in between the dated core depths. In this case study, the interpolated uncertainty envelopes are relatively imprecise since the dated samples imply a somewhat variable sedimentation rate down the core profile. For detailed implications of the pollen-derived environmental record on the local archaeological excavations, see discussion by McCulloch *et al.* (2021).

The results presented here use **sample depth** and understandings about **deposit formation** as prior information. Depending on the distribution of the measurements through the sequence, such models can be **highly informative**, certainly in contrast to the relatively neutral associations that we began looking at in terms of OxCal `Phase` models.

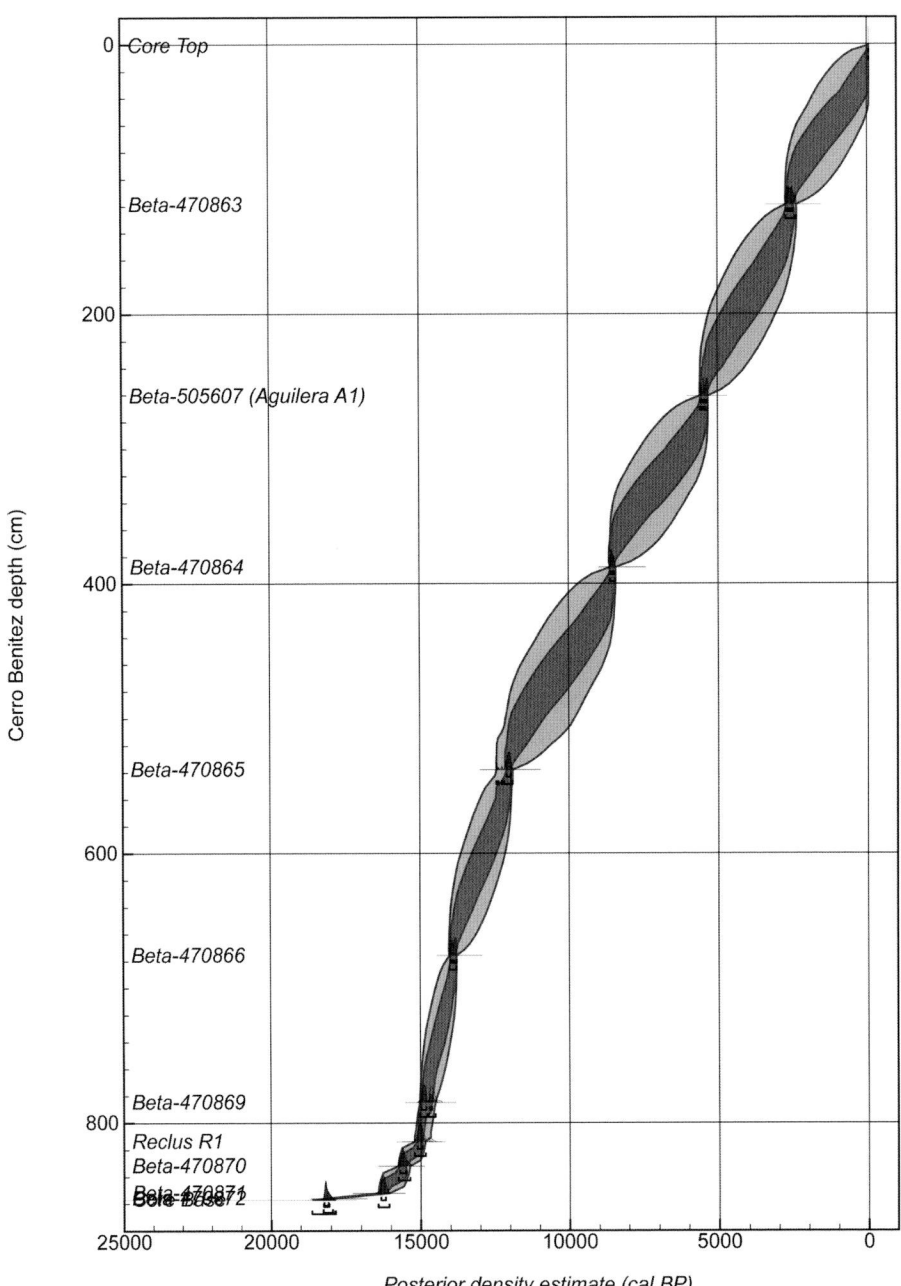

Figure 8.16. The age-depth model from the palynological core from Cerro Benitez. The depth of radiocarbon measurements, together with the rigidity of the model and, in this case, the outlier analysis also applied, constitute the prior beliefs applied here. From this model it is also possible to estimate the timing of other palaeo-environmental events of interest even if we do not have direct dating for these events (see Chapter 6). Copyright: Richard Staff.

Chapter conclusions

The case studies in this chapter highlight the importance of limiting any uncertainty in the **association** between the dated event and the archaeological event of interest; this includes ensuring **accurate** measurement techniques, thinking about sample **taphonomy**, **deposit formation** and the use of multiple or **repeat measurements**. Needless to say, significant improvements in the **precision** as a result of modelling can be accompanied by a diminution in the **accuracy** of resultant ranges. It is very important to ensure that increased precision is not achieved at the expense of accuracy.

The application of **Bayesian inference** in archaeological chronological modelling has been identified as the latest significant development in scientific dating in archaeology. Using Bayesian inference should provide an opportunity to think critically about how we incorporate archaeological prior information and expert knowledge into our narratives. In this sense, it should prompt important epistemological questions in our discipline. We develop discussion of the importance of critical thinking in chronologies in Chapter 9, along with other considerations about how we write about time in archaeology.

Bibliography

Arnold, A., Bronk Ramsey, C., Cook, G., Griffiths, S., Reimer, P. and Marshall, P. 2020. Church of St Peter, West Liss, Hampshire. Tree-ring analysis and radiocarbon wiggle matching of the nave, south aisle and porch roof. Portsmouth: Historic England Research Report Series 69-2015 (online) [https://historicengland.org.uk/research/results/reports/69-2015]

Baillie, M. 1991. Suck-in and smear. Two related chronological problems for the 90s. *Journal of Theoretical Archaeology* 2, 12–16

Barber, A. and Hart, J. 2015) South Wales Gas Pipeline Project. Site 503. Archaeological excavation. Kemble: unpublished Report Cotswold Archaeology Project 9150, Cotswold Archaeology Report 13328, Dyfed Archaeological Trust Event Number 102846

Barclay, A., Bayliss, A. Bronk Ramsey, C., Cleal, R., Cook, G., Healy, F., Higbee, L., Marshall, P., Pelling, R. and Stevens, C. 2018. Dating the Earliest Neolithic Ceramics of Wessex. Historic. Portsmouth: England Research Report Series no. 63–2018

Bayliss, A. 2009. Rolling out revolution: using radiocarbon dating in archaeology. *Radiocarbon* 51(1), 123–47 doi:10.1017/S0033822200033750

Bayliss, A. 2015 Quality in Bayesian chronological models in archaeology. *World Archaeology* 47, 677–700

Bayliss, A. and Bronk Ramsey, C. 2004. Pragmatic Bayesians: a decade integrating radiocarbon dates into chronological models. In Buck and Millard (eds) 2004, 25–41

Bayliss, A. and Tyers, I. 2004. Interpreting radiocarbon dates using evidence from tree rings. *Radiocarbon* 46(2), 957–64 [doi:10.1017/S0033822200036018]

Bayliss, A., Bronk Ramsey, C., van der Plicht, J. and Whittle, A. 2007. Bradshaw and Bayes: towards a timetable for the Neolithic. *Cambridge Archaeological Journal* 17(1, supplement), 1–28

Blaauw, M. and Christen, J. 2011. Flexible paleoclimate age-depth models using an autoregressive gamma process. *Bayesian Analysis* 6(3), 457–74. [doi:10.1214/11-BA618] [https://projecteuclid.org/euclid.ba/1339616472]

Box, G. 1976. Science and statistics. *Journal of the American Statistical Association* 71(356), 791–99 [doi:10.1080/01621459.1976.10480949]

Brock, F., Bronk Ramsey, C. and Higham, T. 2007. Quality assurance of ultrafiltered bone dating. *Radiocarbon* 49(2), 187–92

Bronk Ramsey, C. 1995. Radiocarbon calibration and analysis of stratigraphy: the OxCal program. *Radiocarbon* 3(2), 425–30

Bronk Ramsey, C. 1998. Probability and dating. *Radiocarbon* 40(1), 461–74

Bronk Ramsey, C. 2001. Development of the radiocarbon calibration program OxCal. *Radiocarbon* 43(2A), 355–63

Bronk Ramsey, C. 2008. Radiocarbon dating: revolutions in understanding. *Archaeometry* 50, 249–75 [doi:10.1111/j.1475-4754.2008.00394.x]

Bronk Ramsey, C. 2009. Bayesian analysis of radiocarbon dates. *Radiocarbon* 51(1), 337–60

Bronk Ramsey, C. and Lee, S. 2013 Recent and planned developments of the program OxCal. *Radiocarbon* 55, 720–730. https://doi.org/10.2458/azu_js_rc.55.16215

Bronk Ramsey, C., Dee, M., Lee, S., Nakagawa, T. and Staff, R. 2010 Developments in the calibration and modeling of radiocarbon dates. *Radiocarbon* 52(3), 953–61

Buck, C. and Christen, J. 1998. A novel approach to selecting samples for radiocarbon dating. *Journal of Archaeological Science* 25(4), 303–10

Buck, C. and Millard, A. 2004. *Tools for Constructing Chronologies: crossing disciplinary boundaries.* London: Springer

Buck, C., Litton, C. and Scott, E. 1994. Making the most of radiocarbon dating: some statistical considerations. *Antiquity* 68, 252–63

Buck, C., Litton, C. and Smith, A. 1992. Calibration of radiocarbon results pertaining to related archaeological events. *Journal of Archaeological Science* 19, 487–512

Buck, C., Kenworthy, J., Litton, C. and Smith, A. 1991. Combining archaeological and radiocarbon information: a Bayesian approach to calibration. *Antiquity* 65, 808–21

Buck, C., Christen, J. and James, G. (1999). BCal: an on-line Bayesian radiocarbon calibration tool. *Internet Archaeology* 7 [https://doi.org/10.11141/ia.7.1]

Buckley, R., Morris, M., Appleby, J., King, T., OSullivan, D. and Foxhall, L. 2013. The king in the car park: new light on the death and burial of Richard III in the Grey Friars church, Leicester, in 1485. *Antiquity* 87, 519–38

Clarke, D. (1972). *Models in Archaeology*. London, Methuen.

Cook, G., Ascough, P., Bonsall, C., Hamilton, W. D., Russell, N., Sayle, K., Scott, E. and Bownes, J. 2015. Best practice methodology for ^{14}C calibration of marine and mixed terrestrial/marine samples. *Quaternary Geochronology* 27, 164–71

Darvill, T., David, A., Griffiths, S., Hart, J., James, H. and Rackham, J. 2020. *Timeline. The Archaeology of the South Wales Gas Pipeline: Excavations between Milford Haven, Pembrokeshire and Tirley, Gloucestershire*. Kemble: Cotswold Archaeology Monograph 13

Davis, R. 1971. Alfred the Great: propaganda and truth. *History* 56, 169–82

Dethlefsen, E. and Deetz, J. 1966. Deaths heads, cherubs, and willow trees: experimental archaeology in Colonial cemeteries. *American Antiquity* 31(4), 502–10

Dodd, A., Goodwin, J., Griffiths, S., Norton, A., Poole, C. and Teague, S. 2015. Excavations at Tipping Street, Stafford, 2009–10. *Transactions of the Stafford Archaeology and History Society* 47, 1–115

Foard, G. and Curry, A. 2013. *Bosworth 1485: a battlefield revisited.* Oxford: Oxbow Books

Griffiths, S. 2014. A Bayesian radiocarbon chronology of the early Neolithic of Yorkshire and Humberside. *Archaeological Journal* 171, 2–29

Griffiths, S. 2021. The last hunter of a wise race: evidence for Neolithic practices in northern England. In G. Hey (ed.), *New Light on the Neolithic of Northern England*, 31–51. Oxford: Oxbow Books

Hamerow, H., Bogaard, A., Charles, M., Forster, E., Holmes, M., McKerracher, M., Neil, S., Bronk Ramsey, C., Stroud, E. and Thomas, R. 2020. An integrated bioarchaeological approach to the medieval 'Agricultural Revolution': a case study from Stafford, England, c. AD 800–1200. *European Journal of Archaeology* 23(4), 585–609

Hamilton, W.D. and Bronk Ramsey, C. 2012. Grey Friars, Leicester 2012: Radiocarbon dating of human bone from Skeleton 1, the, since confirmed, remains of Richard III, Leicester: unpublished report, University of Leicester Archaeological Services

Haslett, J. and Parnell, A. 2008. A simple monotone process with application to radiocarbon-dated depth chronologies. *Journal of the Royal Statistical Society. Series C (Applied Statistics)* 57(4), 399–418

Hedges, R., Clement, J., Thomas, C. and O'Connell, T. (2007). Collagen turnover in the adult femoral mid-shaft: modelled anthropogenic radiocarbon tracer measurements. *American Journal of Physical Anthropology* 133, 808–16

Hedges, R., Housley, R., Bronk Ramsey, C. and Van Klinken, G. 1992. Radiocarbon dates from the Oxford AMS system. Archaeometry datelist 15. *Archaeometry* 34(2), 337–57

Higham, N. 2006. *(Re-)reading Bede: the Historia Ecclesiastica in context*. London: Routledge

Helama, S. and Hood, B. 2011. Stone Age midden deposition assessed by bivalve sclerochronology and radiocarbon wiggle matching of *Arctica islandica* shell increments. *Journal of Archaeological Science* 38(2), 452–60

Hines, J. and Bayliss, A. 2013. *Anglo-Saxon Graves and Grave Goods of the 6th and 7th Centuries AD: a chronological framework*. Oxford: The Society of Medieval Archaeology

Hogg, A., Heaton, T., Hua, Q., Palmer, J., Turney, C., Southon, J., Bayliss, A., Blackwell, P., Boswijk, G., Bronk Ramsey, C., Pearson, C., Petchey, F., Reimer, P., Reimer, R. and Wacker, L. 2020 SHCal20 Southern Hemisphere calibration, 0–55,000 years cal. BP. *Radiocarbon* 62(4), 759–78

King, T., Fortes, G., Balaresque, P, Thomas, M., Balding, D., Maisano Delser, P., Neumann, R., Parson, W., Knapp, M., Walsh, S., Tonasso, L., Holt, J., Kayser, M., Appleby, J., Forster, P., Ekserdjian, D., Hofreiter, M. and Schürer, K. 2014. Identification of the remains of King Richard III. *Nature Communications* 5, 5631 [https://doi.org/10.1038/ncomms6631]

Lamb, A., Evans, J., Buckley, R. and Appleby, J. 2014. Multi-isotope analysis demonstrates significant lifestyle changes in King Richard III. *Journal of Archaeological Science* 50, 559–65

McCulloch, R., Mansilla, C., Martin, F., Borrero, L., Staff, R. and Tisdall, E. 2021. The nature and timing of landscape change in the region of Cerro Benítez, Última Esperanza, southern Patagonia (52°S): new insights into the history of megafaunal extinctions and human occupation. *Quaternary International* 6(1), 116–29

Millard, A. 2002. Bayesian approach to sapwood estimates and felling dates in dendrochronology. *Archaeometry* 44(1), 137–43

Mook, W. and Waterbolk, T.H. 1985. *Handbook for Archaeologists. No 3. Radiocarbon Dating*. Strasbourg: European Science Foundation

Needham, S., Bronk Ramsey, C., Coombs, D., Cartwright, C. and Pettitt, P. 1998. An independent chronology for British Bronze Age metalwork: the results of the Oxford Radiocarbon Accelerator Programme. *Archaeological Journal* 154, 55–107

Parnell, A. and Gehrels, W. 2015. Using chronological models in late Holocene sea-level reconstruction from saltmarsh sediments. In I. Shennan, A. Long and B. Horton (eds), *Handbook of Sea-Level Research*, 500–13. Hoboken NJ: Wiley-Blackwell

Reimer, P., Austin, W., Bard, E., Bayliss, A., Blackwell, P., Bronk Ramsey, C., Butzin, M, Cheng, H., Edwards, R., Friedrich, M., Grootes, P., Guilderson, T., Hajdas, I., Heaton, T., Hogg, A., Hughen, K., Kromer, B., Manning, S., Muscheler, R., Palmer, J., Pearson, C., van der Plicht, J., Reimer, R., Richards, D., Scott, E., Southon, J., Turney, C., Wacker, L., Adolphi, F., Büntgen, U., Capano, M., Fahrni, S., Fogtmann-Schultz, A., Friedrich, R., Köhler, P., Kudsk, S., Miyake, F.,

Olsen, J., Reinig, F., Sakamoto, M., Sookdeo, A. and Talamo, S. 2020. The IntCal20 Northern Hemisphere radiocarbon age calibration curve (0–55 cal. kBP). Radiocarbon 62(4), 725–57

Rom, W., Gosler, R., Kutschera, W., Priller, A., Steier, P. and Wild, E. 1999. AMS ^{14}C dating of equipment from the icemen and of spruce logs from the prehistoric salt mines of Hallstatt. *Radiocarbon* 41(2), 183–97

Sealy, J., Armstrong, R. and Schrire, C. 1995. Beyond lifetime averages – tracing life-histories through isotopic analysis of different tissues from archaeological human skeletons. *Antiquity* 69, 290–300

Ward, G. and Wilson, S. 1978. Procedures for comparing and combining radiocarbon age determinations: a critique. *Archaeometry* 20, 19–31

Waterbolk, T.H. 1971. Working with radiocarbon dates. *Actes du VIIIe congrès international des sciences préhistoriques et protohistoriques* 1, 11–25

Whittle, A. 2018. *The Times of Their Lives. Hunting History in the Archaeology of Neolithic Europe*. Oxford: Oxbow Books

Whittle, A., Bayliss, A. and Healy, F. 2011. *Gathering Time: Dating the Early Neolithic enclosures of southern Britain and Ireland*. Oxford: Oxbow Books

9. Scientific dating and narrative

Seren Griffiths

This volume has focused on the role that scientific dating plays in archaeology. We have introduced some of the key methods of scientific dating and the underlying principles in Chapter 2–5, followed by some consideration of practical applications on site in Chapters 6–7, and ways of analysing datasets in Chapter 8. In Chapter 9 I will focus the nature of chronometric data and the ways in which scientific dating relates to the practice and theory of archaeological work more broadly.

In the opening chapter we encountered Glyn Daniel still reeling, some 30 years later, from the impact of the first radiocarbon revolutions. The introduction of scientific dating to archaeology provided arguably the only paradigmatic revolution the discipline has seen. In Daniel's terms, scientific dating generally and radiocarbon dating specifically, defined the start of Modern archaeology. In this sense, archaeology is a very young discipline and arguably we have not yet resolved some of the tensions that derive from our attempts to incorporate scientific chronologies in archaeological narratives.

The first applications of radiocarbon dating had a profound impact on archaeologists, demonstrating the incompatibility of current intellectual frameworks with these new data. The profound impact of having *independent* evidence for the first time cannot be under-estimated. These new datasets were so challenging that some archaeologists regarded the method as profoundly flawed, not that their intellectual frameworks for the past might be imperfect. This distrust of radiocarbon occurred in part because some of the fundamental principles of the radiocarbon method were still being established (see Neustupný 1970 for details of the recognition of these developments).

However, in some cases, the new radiocarbon measurements were treated with suspicion because archaeologists were not critical enough about their own approaches to the past. This is what happened for example when the eminent British prehistorian Stuart Piggott declared his issues with radiocarbon dating as results were '… archaeologically unacceptable …', with the '… Durrington Walls radio-carbon date … roughly a millennium too high!' (Piggott 1959, 288–9). Piggott was right in this instance, the radiocarbon results were not accurate estimates for the use of the henge at Durrington Walls as the results came from an old land surface under the bank, but he was right for the wrong reasons. He had not thought critically enough about what the results might represent. Piggott declared the result archaeologically unacceptable because he thought the henge was associated with Beaker pottery, which should be much younger based on '... chronologies constructed by archaeological means ...' (Piggott 1959, 289).

Piggott was not unique in finding the radiocarbon revolution a challenge to make sense of. Because our disciplinary knowledge structures are so conditioning it can be difficult even to identify such tensions because we are habituated to thinking about the past in very specific ways. Trying to do this should be an essential part of archaeology. There are two useful ways that researchers can start to do so. In pre-text or 'prehistoric' contexts, it may be useful to think about scientific chronometric results as estimates for activity defined in time and space, rather than by culture-historic terms. In cases with written records, it might be useful to think critically about the veracity of the timescapes outlined in these sources.

An early example of this approach was taken by the influential Czech archaeologist Evžen Neustupný who stated that we '... shall assume that all the archaeological periods in different places of the Earth are contemporary if they produce identical radiocarbon dates' (Neustupný 1968, 50–1). The apparent simplicity of this statement belies its profundity. Neustupný is having to make the point explicit that independent dating techniques might provide more accurate chronologies than received relative culture historic chronologies. This tension – between how we use chronology as a tool to think *with* and how we make new knowledge claims – still exists in archaeology. In part because of this tension in the discipline, and in part because of the legacy of the positivism of the 1970s, scientific dating measurements are often treated as if they have a special innate status in archaeological narratives. When this process occurs, chronometric measurements have taken on the status of 'science facts'.

'Science facts' are a specific type of archaeological knowledge claims. They have an existence which is different from the normal processes of knowledge production and transmission that occur in archaeology. When people talk about 'absolute dates' in archaeology they are identifying the nature of these measurements as 'science facts'. Hopefully the preceding chapters in this volume have demonstrated that there is no such thing as an 'absolute date' in archaeology. These measurements are created as part of a whole series of complex processes. To use them effectively in chronology construction we need to think about the underlying principles, the nature of the dated event, the archaeological event of interest and the association between these two key ideas. But we also need to think about how the *process* of chronology construction exists as a form of situated knowledge, created, presented and incorporated into narratives within existing knowledge structures, and often through a series of complex data journeys.

Neustupný was perhaps the clearest earliest researcher to recognise the importance of the integrated and interdependent nature of chronologies, practice and narratives. For example, in 1969 he noted that:

> ... chronology as a reconstruction of temporal coordinates of archaeological finds should be independent of the interpretation of the finds. It should also be independent of our knowledge of the way of living of prehistoric groups. These principles should be observed especially in building the chronology. However, once being constructed, chronology cannot remain indifferent to all the other branches of archaeology ...' (Neustupný 1969, 61).

As noted in Chapter 1, part of the challenge of dealing with chronologies is that time is both an axis against which we assemble sequences, and a way of thinking about the past that we are investigating. In order to tackle these issues archaeologists have employed a range of approaches to the 'time dimensions'. Over the last few decades we have seen focuses on experiential time and 'thick' description (e.g. Edmonds 1999) and the temporality of experience (often taking Ingold (2000) as a point of departure). We have seen Big Data studies where exhaustive approaches to sampling attempt to capture the entirety of human experience (e.g. Bevan et al. 2017). We have seen the discussion of unit issues and scalar approaches where the analytical frameworks and epistemological approaches are emphasised (e.g. Ramenofsky 1998; Bailey 2008). However, despite Neustupný's foresight it is only occasionally that we see the critical consideration of the ways in which scientific chronological data are integrated into wider theoretical approaches in archaeology (e.g. Murray 1999; Lucas 2008; Wylie 2020).

In the rest of this last chapter, we look more broadly at some of the ways in which 'science facts' are created and consumed through the process of data journeys. It we do not think critically about the data journeys which take place in chronology construction and narrative creation we may simply replicate existing understandings. It is at this intersection of data, practice and understanding that we have potential to make space for new narratives and interpretations.

'Science facts' and archaeological narratives

In archaeology chronological data and, to a lesser extent, other scientific measurements can be treated as if they are 'neutral' or will 'speak for themselves'. Chronometric data are especially susceptible to this treatment because they hold dual positions as both constituents of the sequences against which we assemble archaeological knowledge and are the subjects of archaeological investigations. When chronometric data become science facts they are essentialised. This happens when they are stripped of all the processes that brought them into being and they are presented as if existing outside the intellectual structuring principles with which archaeologists interpret these chronometric data. The science factinesses are some of the most difficult aspects with which to engage when creating narratives. This is because chronometric science facts are used to underpin our discipline's language, approaches and hierarchies.

The powerful potency of chronometric data as science facts in archaeological narratives results from several contributing factors. Chronometric data represent new evidence. They are empirical. They are demonstrable. They are expressed within a clearly defined scale. They are expensive. They have to be produced through a combination of very specialised procedures or data journeys including using powerful machines that sometimes go 'ping'. They are verifiable, either through repeated measurements or, in the cases of radiocarbon measurements, through the measurement of known-age samples or laboratory intercomparisons. They can be directly related to the time axis that frames all our other knowledge claims. They are associated with the paradigm shift that created Modern archaeology. Perhaps also, at some level, many archaeologists find the authenticity of an independent 'answer' amid our compromised understandings highly seductive.

This combination of criteria means that chronometric measurements have a unique status as science facts in archaeology. The innateness and inalienability of ancient DNA measurements may mean that these data approach a similar status but I would suggest that chronometric data – as science facts in archaeology – are quite distinct because of the ways they occupy the dual location as subject of inquiry and, simultaneously, as they produce the temporal sequence.

The assumption of the essentialised, atheoretical nature of chronometric data as science facts is encapsulated by the Lewis Binford quote (Taylor 2000, 15) we introduced in Chapter 1. In this Binford expressed the belief that, after the development of the radiocarbon method, the activities of archaeologists could suddenly be directed 'towards theory building rather than towards chronology building' as if these aspects of our work could be elegantly divorced. In this chapter we follow Neustupný in maintaining that, on the contrary, chronologies are always theoretically charged; chronologies are created through practices in the field, in the laboratory and in the interpretation and creation of narratives which refer to existing knowledge structures.

Perhaps the most obvious examples of chronometric data becoming science facts are when results are reported as 'the first' or 'the oldest' example of a site or type of material culture. These reports often include uncritical and atheoretical uses of chronological data in the production of archaeological narratives and are often reported in the popular press as if there is peculiar merit or authenticity in identifying the oldest example of some thing or other. This kind of approach owes much to the attitude outlined in the Binford quote above. These approaches also belie a peculiar kind of use of science facts in the creation and development of professional standing in the archaeological discipline. In these cases, claims for 'the first' or 'the oldest' are often deployed for career advancement and are often associated with a peculiar machismo that can still permeate archaeological practice.

To embrace the full potential of scientific dating in archaeology, and not simply to reproduce current understandings, we need to resist the temptation to deploy chronometric data as science facts. This requires consideration of how we create chronological sequences and the structures that facilitate knowledge claims. Critical to these approaches is how groups of data are used in concert and how we incorporate these data into archaeological narratives.

Warrants, reversibility, close observation and Big Data

Alison Wylie (2020) has discussed the interpretation of chronometric data in terms of the logical 'scaffolding' associated with how knowledge claims are transformed and occluded across the life cycle of scientific data. Wylie argues that radiocarbon data are the conclusions of extended practical arguments that depend upon a great deal of contingent local scaffolding (Wylie 2020, 291). To make these knowledge claims we build on all the inherent expertise from the recovery of samples in the field upwards. In this volume, we have tracked the stages on the journeys of various chronometric data. We can distinguish these processes in terms of: sampling in the field; the definition, identification and representation of archaeological events of interest; the associations between the event of interest and the dated event; the underlying physical and chemical principles that provide the basis for accurate or inaccurate measurements; and the analysis and modelling that accompany the presentation of data.

Wylie terms such supporting evidence the 'warrants' for chronometric data. In Chapter 8, we described these warrants in terms of the 'closeness' of the observations that are used to interpret specific temporal attributes or relationships. We differentiated for example between a 'close' site-specific series of observations and records, and the much more abstracted, but highly situated, observations that underpin culture historic models.

In Chapter 7, we outlined a way to think up from the very small individual chronometric samples to approaches to interpretation using our 'A, B, C, D' of scientific dating. We construct the best scientific dating chronologies when there is an integrated approach to all the processes that accompany the production and analysis of these measurements.

We argued in Chapter 8 that specific observations were the basis for more robust Bayesian models (see below). In Bruno Latour's terms site-based observations are generally also more 'reversible' (Latour 1999, 61), with knowledge transformations less black-boxed and the basis for knowledge claims more specific. The manipulations and transformations that occurred can be more easily reconstructed, and the partialness of these interpretations explored by other workers.

A different series of warrants or observations occur when chronometric results are related using much more abstracted culture historic packages. Here when we relate groups of chronometric data in terms of packages the underlying warrants that structure this knowledge will probably have been through many more transformations than the individual site-derived close observations. These associations are therefore much more abstracted.

Because culture historic or other abstracted concepts will have been developed from across a wider range of sites and over decades of research, such concepts can take on the status of David Clarke's (1972) 'iconic models'. These are apparently neutral concepts that should be tested by research but can become established knowledge structures which instead delineate debates and narratives.

Perhaps the most abstracted use of chronometric measurements as science facts occurs in some Big Data analyses. The definition of Big Data is not determined by the *scale* of datasets but the nature of the datasets and what they are suggested to represent. The social scientist and Big Data specialist Rob Kitchin (2014) has written about how we define such Big Data studies. This is important in terms of thinking about the research aims of Big Data studies in archaeology, in terms of how chronometric data are employed in some archaeological narratives, and how chronometric data are essentialised in some of these processes. Kitchin defines Big Data using a variety of qualities, including projects which are:

- Huge in volume,
- Huge in velocity (being created in or near real-time),
- Exhaustive in scope, striving to capture entire populations or systems (n=all),
- Fine grained in resolution,
- Relational in nature, containing common fields that enable the conjoining of different datasets,
- Flexible, holding traits of extensionality (can add rapidly) and scale-ability (can expand in size rapidly).

Here, supporting warrants or close observations that would otherwise be used to validate knowledge claims are abstracted in preference for a very different analytical approach. In these cases, the scale and nature of scientific datasets are used to leverage resultant knowledge claims. Because of the ways that Big Data analyses are undertaken the underpinning warrants are often elided so that data become, in effect, entirely irreversible. Generalising statistical treatments of lots of chronometric data undertake this leveraging, and we can see this approach in some uses of Sum analyses of radiocarbon measurements (see Contreras and Meadows 2014; Bronk Ramsey 2017; Crema and Bevan 2021 for discussion).

Big Data projects in archaeology tend to be significantly smaller than in other disciplines such as computer science or contemporary population studies. However, if we think of Big Data in terms of Kitchin's qualitative definitions, we can see that in archaeology large-scale chronometric research projects have these Big Data qualities. Many large-scale chronometric projects seek to be exhaustive in scope, capturing all the evidence that exist. And the scope of this is often *everything* – the entirety of human existence. In many of these cases, data journeys are made redundant because chronometric data have become something else – science facts. When dealing with legacy data in Big Data approaches where the underlying warrants are unclear or data journeys not reversible, it can be helpful to apply several different forms of analyses. This can be used to try and help us to think more critically about the underlying distributions of data and so to think in several ways about what they represent (e.g. Griffiths *et al.* 2022).

Chronological knowledge structure and sequence

Having thought about the qualities of chronometric data and how chronometric data are used in temporal sequences, we now want to look at the ways these sequences related to our knowledge structures. As noted in Chapter 1, the creation and deployment of culture historic terms continues the tradition of 19th century codification that we see for example in the work of Christian Jurgensen Thomsen and Jens Jacob Asmussen Worsaae in Denmark, John Lubbock in Britain and Edouard Lartet in France. All such schemes attempt to resolve one of the most insurmountable issues in archaeology, whichever period or place, things or sites you happen to be researching. Prior to the development of scientific dating, all classificatory systems, typologies and culture historic schemes are attempts to create the structure for narratives by defining a particular material signature in time and space. We can think about these approaches as the first level of theorising a discipline – classification and generalisation – in terms of a history of science approach. Culture historic schemes are ways of thinking that seek to move beyond the very particular signature from a site to allow us to talk more generally. These processes are one of the ways in which archaeological knowledge structures are developed but it is also important to engage critically with this process of generalisation when we are working between chronological data and producing narratives.

The terms that we use to write our histories influence the kinds of stories that we tell. Intellectually, narratives that privilege received chronological knowledge structures tend to valorise specific types of underlying causal mechanisms – often that invoke 'cultural' change – to patterns observed in datasets. We can see this tendency in Britain from at least the 1960s when Grahame Clark (1966) discussed the importance of the 'Invasion Hypothesis' (and we have seen lots of these themes repeated again in the light of recent aDNA evidence). In these kinds of studies there is often a single causal mechanism for change while messiness and complexity, as well as limitations in the available evidence, are downplayed.

Critiquing the culture historic terms traditionally used to structure the past is not just an academic discussion of a 'terminology trap'. It is the logical conclusion of the first radiocarbon revolution. I argue that the full potential of the first radiocarbon revolution can only be achieved if we recognise the importance of moving beyond these classificatory models which should enable us to work in different ways with evidence from material culture, chronometric techniques and existing knowledge structures, to create a more nuanced and impressionistic representation of the past. Bayesian approaches should allow us the potential to do just this; the radiocarbon revolution will only be fully achieved if we move beyond these disciplinary inheritances and write comparative *international* histories. If we cannot, we may be failing to realise that our habits of interpretation and explanation that owe more to convenient modes of thought that is our disciplinary inheritance.

In the late 1960s Daniel and Neustupný were both attempting to come to terms with exactly the same question. As noted in Chapter 1, Daniel was resigned '… the old labels should be abolished and people should talk in chronological periods … but I expect that we shall go on using terms like Neolithic and Bronze Age' (Daniel 1968, 346). As we saw above, Neustupný made a more optimistic and foresighted argument.

As a profession we are still to resolve this issue and to synthesise the various aspects of the time dimensions in archaeology. If archaeology started again in the 1950s we are still a very young discipline with much work to do. The tendency to treat chronometric measurements as science facts and the overbearing legacy of our culture historic intellectual inheritance are significant contributions in our failure to resolve this fundamental issue. The imprecision of chronometric results has also hampered attempts to move away from traditional models of the past and to use time, defined in years, decades and centuries, to structure our narratives. Bayesian statistical modelling may provide increased precision and analytical processes with which we can counter these traditional approaches. However, such an undertaking will require determined and radical work to not simply repeat the narrative structures, tropes and causal mechanisms that we have inherited. The real Bayesian 'revolution' will be if we can write histories that only make use of culture historic terms as descriptive qualities of the past rather than as structuring principles which pre-determine the scope of archaeological enquiry. Seventy years after archaeology started again can we harness all these new developments to create a new type of archaeological narrative outside the confines of our culture historic inheritance? Only if we treat chronometric data, chronologies, material culture, sites and ecofacts with equal philosophical status and critical consideration when we produced our narratives.

Chapter conclusions

In this chapter, I have attempted to think critically about how we write histories or archaeological **narratives** using chronometric data. Narratives start to be built in the time **models that we apply on site**, as part of our excavation and sampling strategies, and in our classifications and interpretations of things. Even when we are working at the level of recovering ecofacts from an individual context on site, we are part of the **process of knowledge creation** that leads to the production of scientific chronologies and their eventual employment in archaeological narratives. As Ian Hodder (1997) once famously observed, archaeological interpretation starts at the trowel edge. Wherever we work, chronology building is a highly situated process. Chronometric science facts are powerful pieces of evidence, and they are created and deployed in inherently political contexts.

The most effective scientific dating programmes are probably those where there is a **close curation of knowledge** about how samples are recovered, what they represent in terms of the archaeological event of interest and how they relate more widely beyond an individual site. To go beyond the production of accurate measurements and precise chronologies from individual sites and move into the creation of narratives that critically address wider archaeological research questions we need to do several things. We need good chronometric data. I suggested an 'A, B, C, D' approach (Chapter 7) to the production of chronometric data based on the underlying principles of these methods (Chapters 2–5). We also need to **track the data journeys** and the observations with which we can analyse these measurements (Chapter 8). But overall, we need to more **integrated approaches to the time dimensions in archaeology**.

The cover of this volume features the heavily restored passage tomb at Bryn Celli Ddu as the sun rise on a summer solstice. It matters at Bryn Celli Ddu that this location was the focus of over 1000 years of monument building and that when the sun rises on the longest day it still shines down the stone passage to illuminate the chamber within. The story of this site combines both evidence for deep-time history, its role in the history of our discipline (as part of Glyn Daniel's megalithic culture for example) and as a contemporary site for pagan worship and archaeological fieldwork (both arguably forms of reverence). The richest narratives about people, places, things and other beings are not those that take abstracted approaches, they are those that use granularity to challenge conventions and new data to test the structuring principles of our subject. As a relatively young discipline we have still not come to terms with the full implications of the paradigm shift the started with the introduction of radiocarbon dating in the 1950s. To resolve these continuing tensions we need to recognise that chronological data never speak for themselves.

Bibliography

Bailey, G. 2008. Time perspectivism: origins and consequences. In S. Holdaway and L. Wandsnider (eds), *Time in Archaeology: time perspectivism revisited*, 13–30. Salt Lake City UT: Utah University Press

Bevan, A., Colledge, S., Fuller, D., Fyfe, R., Shennan, S. and Stevens, C. 2017. Holocene fluctuations in human population demonstrate repeated links to food production and climate. *PNAS*. 114, 49, E10524–E10531

Bronk Ramsey, C. 2017. Methods for summarizing radiocarbon datasets. *Radiocarbon* 59, 1809–33 [https://doi.org/10.1017/RDC.2017.108]

Clark, G. 1966. The invasion hypothesis in British archaeology. *Antiquity* 40, 172–89 [doi:10.1017/S0003598X00032488]

Clarke, D. 1972. *Models in Archaeology*. London: Methuen

Contreras, D. and Meadows, J. 2014. Summed radiocarbon calibrations as a population proxy: a critical evaluation using a realistic simulation approach. *Journal of Archaeological Science* 52, 591–608

Crema, E. and Bevan, A. 2021. Inference from large sets of radiocarbon dates: software and methods. *Radiocarbon* 63(1), 23–39 [doi:10.1017/RDC.2020.95]

Daniel, G. 1968. *The First Civilizations: the archaeology of their origins*. London: Thames and Hudson

Edmonds, M. 1999. *Ancestral Geographies of the Neolithic Landscapes, Monuments and Memory*. London: Routledge

Griffiths, S., Johnson, R., May, R., McOmish, D., Marshall, P., Last, J. and Bayliss, A. 2022. Dividing the land: time and land division in the English north Midlands and Yorkshire. *European Journal of Archaeology* 25(2), 216–37 [doi:10.1017/eaa.2021.48]

Ingold, T. 2000. *The Perception of the Environment. Essays in Livelihood, Dwelling and Skill*. Abingdon: Routledge

Kitchin, R. 2014. Big Data, new epistemologies and paradigm shifts. *Big Data & Society* 1(1) [doi: 10.1177/2053951714528481]

Latour, B. 1999. Circulating reference. Sampling the soil in the Amazon Forest. In B. Latour, *Pandora's Hope: Essays on the Reality of Science Studies*, 24–79. Cambridge MA: Harvard University Press

Lucas, G. 2008. Time and the archaeological event. *Cambridge Archaeological Journal* 18(1), 59–65

Murray, T. 1999. A return to the 'Pompeii premise'. In T. Murray (ed.), *Time and Archaeology*, 8–27. London; Routledge

Neustupný, E. 1968. Absolute chronology of the Neolithic and Aeneolithic periods in Central and South Eastern Europe. *Slovenská Archaeológia* 14(1), 19–56

Neustupný, E. 1969) Economy of the Corded Ware Cultures. *Archeologické Rozhledy* 21(1), 43–68

Neustupný, E. 1970. A new epoch in radiocarbon dating. *Antiquity* 44, 38–45

Piggott, S. 1959. The radio-carbon date from Durrington Walls. *Antiquity* 33, 289–90

Ramenofsky, A. 1998. The illusion of time. In A. Ramenofsky and A. Steffen (eds), *Unit Issues in Archaeology. Measuring Time, Space and Material*, 74–84. Salt Lake City UT: University of Utah Press

Taylor, R. 2000. The contribution of radiocarbon dating to New World archaeology. *Radiocarbon* 42(1), 1–21

Wylie, A. 2020. Radiocarbon dating in archaeology: triangulation and traceability. In S. Leonelli and N. Tempini (eds), *Data Journeys in the Sciences*, 285–301. Dordrecht: Springer Open

Appendix: Code for selected case studies in Chapter 8

Code for Figure 8.5. The Coneybury Anomaly (after Barclay et al. *2018)*
```
Plot()
 {
  Sequence()
  {
   Boundary("Start_Coneybury_anomaly");
   Phase("Coneybury_anomaly")
   {
    R_Date("OxA-1402", 5050, 100);
    R_Date("OxA-24986", 4925, 30);
    R_Combine("W2 1981 ON521 AB8")
    {
     R_Date("OxA-24987", 4941, 32);
     R_Date("SUERC-35960", 4900, 30);
    };
    R_Combine("W2 1981 ctx2538 AB6/7b")
    {
     R_Date("OxA-24988", 4952, 32);
     R_Date("OxA-24989", 4997, 31);
    };
    R_Date("OxA-25086", 4966, 31);
    R_Date("OxA-25087", 5003, 30);
    R_Date("SUERC-35958", 4905, 30);
    R_Date("SUERC-35959", 5135, 30);
    After()
    {
     R_Combine("W2 1981 ctx2538 AB9")
     {
      R_Date("OxA-25766", 5149, 32);
      R_Date("SUERC-35964", 4905, 30);
     };
    };
    Span("duration_Coneybury_primary_fill");
   };
   Boundary("End_Coneybury_anomaly");
  };
 };
```

Code for Figure 8.7. The Vaynor henge (after Barber and Hart 2015; Darvill et al. *2020)*
```
Plot()
 {
  Sequence("Section GG")
  {
```

Appendix: Code for selected case studies in Chapter 8

```
Boundary("Start primary Vaynor Farm Henge");
Phase("Vaynor Henge")
{
 Sequence("ditch fill")
 {
  Sequence()
  {
   Boundary("Start early ditch fill");
   Phase("early ditch fill")
   {
    Phase("5030153_503072")
    {
     R_Date("SUERC-52100", 3928, 30);
     R_Date("SUERC-51702", 4057, 33);
    };
    Phase("5030153_503067")
    {
     R_Date("SUERC-51706", 8429, 33)
     {
      Outlier();
     };
     R_Date("SUERC-51707", 3939, 33);
    };
    First("FirstEarlyDitchFill");
    Last("LastEarlyDitchFill");
   };
   Boundary("End early ditch fill");
  };
  Sequence()
  {
   Boundary("Start 503051");
   Sequence("503051")
   {
    Phase("503051_503068")
    {
     R_Date("SUERC-51704", 3815, 33);
     R_Date("SUERC-51705", 3777, 33);
    };
    Phase("")
    {
     Phase("503051_503007")
     {
      R_Date("SUERC-51728", 3836, 33);
      R_Date("SUERC-51732", 3754, 35);
```

```
   };
   Phase("503051_503065")
   {
    R_Date("SUERC-51713", 3589, 33);
    R_Date("SUERC-51714", 3464, 33);
   };
  };
 };
 Boundary("End 503051");
};
Phase("503050_503066")
{
 R_Date("SUERC-51708", 2820, 33);
 R_Date("SUERC-51712", 2742, 33);
};
Phase("50319_503063")
{
 R_Date("SUERC-51715", 1947, 33);
 R_Date("SUERC-51716", 1947, 33);
};
Phase("Later cremation")
{
 R_Date("SUERC-51724", 1851, 33);
 R_Date("SUERC-51726", 1805, 33);
 R_Date("SUERC-52365", 1877, 26);
};
};
Sequence()
{
 Boundary("Start henge post alignment");
 Phase("Henge posthole alignment")
 {
  Phase("50366")
  {
   R_Date("SUERC-51735", 3972, 33);
   R_Date("SUERC-51727", 3904, 33);
  };
  Phase("503150")
  {
   R_Date("SUERC-51722", 3906, 33);
   R_Date("SUERC-51723", 3851, 33);
  };
  First("FirstHengePostAlignment");
  Last("LastHengePostAlignment");
  Span("DurationHengePostAlignment");
 };
 Boundary("End henge post alignment");
};
First("FirstUse");
Last("LastUse");
Span("DurationUse");
```

};
 Boundary("End final use Vaynor Farm Henge");
 };
};

Code for Figure 8.9. Comparative ways of presenting the results associated with British axeheads data presented in Needham et al. *(1998).*
Independent model
Plot()
{
 Sequence()
 {
 Boundary("Start_Acton_and_Taunton_independent");
 Phase("independent Acton_and_Taunton")
 {
  R_Date("independent OxA-5948", 3225, 65);
  R_Date("independent OxA-4651", 3220, 80);
  R_Date("independent OxA-5949", 3110, 50);
  R_Date("independent OxA-6177", 3055, 50);
  R_Date("independent OxA-5196", 3035, 40);
 };
 Boundary("End_Acton_and_Taunton_independent");
 };
 Sequence()
 {
 Boundary("Start_Penard_independent");
 Phase("independent Penard")
 {
  R_Date("independent OxA-5187", 3045, 55);
  R_Date("independent OxA-1526", 3030, 100);
  R_Date("independent OxA-5953", 3015, 45);
  R_Date("independent OxA-5951", 2980, 45);
  R_Date("independent OxA-4504", 2965, 65);
  R_Date("independent OxA-5952", 2965, 45);
  R_Date("independent OxA-5959", 2965, 45);
  R_Date("independent OxA-5183", 2930, 40);
  R_Date("independent OxA-4653", 2910, 55);
  R_Date("independent OxA-5950", 2910, 45);
  R_Date("independent OxA-5954", 3025, 55);
  R_Date("independent HAR-2940", 3020, 70);
 };
 Boundary("End_Penard_independent");
 };
 Sequence()
 {

```
Boundary("Start_Wilburton_independent");
Phase("independent Wilburton")
{
 R_Date("independent OxA-4656", 3005, 75);
 R_Date("independent OxA-4503", 2930, 55);
 R_Date("independent OxA-4502", 2925, 50);
 R_Date("independent OxA-5036", 2920, 50);
 R_Date("independent OxA-5197", 2910, 50);
 R_Date("independent OxA-5955", 2900, 45);
 R_Date("independent OxA-5035", 2900, 45);
 R_Date("independent OxA-5034", 2890, 45);
 R_Date("independent OxA-5956", 2850, 50);
 R_Date("independent OxA-5198", 2820, 70);
};
Boundary("End_Wilburton_independent");
};
Sequence()
{
Boundary("Start_Ewart_Park_independent");
Phase("independent Ewart_Park")
{
 R_Date("independent OxA-5957", 2810, 45);
 R_Date("independent OxA-4716", 2780, 50);
 R_Date("independent OxA-4654", 2765, 45);
 R_Date("independent OxA-5976", 2740, 45);
 R_Date("independent OxA-4652", 2720, 45);
 R_Date("independent BM-798", 2704, 50);
 R_Date("independent OxA-5962", 2685, 60);
 R_Date("independent OxA-6176", 2655, 50);
 R_Date("independent OxA-5977", 2620, 45);
};
Boundary("End_Ewart_Park_independent");
};
};
```

Related model
```
Plot("related")
{
 Sequence()
 {
  Boundary("Start_related");
  Phase()
  {
   Sequence()
   {
```

```
 Boundary("Start_Acton_and_Taunton_related");
 Phase("related Acton_and_Taunton")
 {
  R_Date("related OxA-5948", 3225, 65);
  R_Date("related OxA-4651", 3220, 80);
  R_Date("related OxA-5949", 3110, 50);
  R_Date("related OxA-6177", 3055, 50);
  R_Date("related OxA-5196", 3035, 40);
 };
 Boundary("End_Acton_and_Taunton_related");
 };
 Sequence()
 {
  Boundary("Start_Penard related");
  Phase("related Penard")
  {
   R_Date("related OxA-5187", 3045, 55);
   R_Date("related OxA-1526", 3030, 100);
   R_Date("related OxA-5953", 3015, 45);
   R_Date("related OxA-5951", 2980, 45);
   R_Date("related OxA-4504", 2965, 65);
   R_Date("related OxA-5952", 2965, 45);
   R_Date("related OxA-5959", 2965, 45);
   R_Date("related OxA-5183", 2930, 40);
   R_Date("related OxA-4653", 2910, 55);
   R_Date("related OxA-5950", 2910, 45);
   R_Date("related OxA-5954", 3025, 55);
   R_Date("related HAR-2940", 3020, 70);
  };
  Boundary("End_Penard_related");
 };
 Sequence()
 {
  Boundary("Start_Wilburton_related");
  Phase("related Wilburton")
  {
   R_Date("related OxA-4656", 3005, 75);
   R_Date("related OxA-4503", 2930, 55);
   R_Date("related OxA-4502", 2925, 50);
   R_Date("related OxA-5036", 2920, 50);
   R_Date("related OxA-5197", 2910, 50);
   R_Date("related OxA-5955", 2900, 45);
   R_Date("related OxA-5035", 2900, 45);
```

```
  R_Date("related OxA-5034", 2890, 45);
  R_Date("related OxA-5956", 2850, 50);
  R_Date("related OxA-5198", 2820, 70);
  };
  Boundary("End_Wilburton_related");
 };
 Sequence()
 {
  Boundary("Start_Ewart_Park_related");
  Phase("related Ewart_Park")
  {
   R_Date("related OxA-5957", 2810, 45);
   R_Date("related OxA-4716", 2780, 50);
   R_Date("related OxA-4654", 2765, 45);
   R_Date("related OxA-5976", 2740, 45);
   R_Date("related OxA-4652", 2720, 45);
   R_Date("related BM-798", 2704, 50);
   R_Date("related OxA-5962", 2685, 60);
   R_Date("related OxA-6176", 2655, 50);
   R_Date("related OxA-5977", 2620, 45);
  };
  Boundary("End_Ewart_Park_related");
 };
 };
 Boundary("End_related");
 };
};
```

Overlapping model
```
Plot("overlapping")
{
 Phase()
 {
  Sequence()
  {
   Boundary("Start_Acton_and_Taunton_overlapping");
   Phase("overlappingActon_and_Taunton")
   {
    R_Date("overlapping OxA-5948", 3225, 65);
    R_Date("overlapping OxA-4651", 3220, 80);
    R_Date("overlapping OxA-5949", 3110, 50);
    R_Date("overlapping OxA-6177", 3055, 50);
    R_Date("overlapping OxA-5196", 3035, 40);
   };
```

```
 Boundary("End_Acton_and_Taunton_overlapping");
};
Sequence()
{
 Date("=Start_Acton_and_Taunton_overlapping");
 Boundary("Start_Penard_overlapping");
 Phase("overlapping Penard")
 {
  R_Date("overlapping OxA-5187", 3045, 55);
  R_Date("overlapping OxA-1526", 3030, 100);
  R_Date("overlapping OxA-5953", 3015, 45);
  R_Date("overlapping OxA-5951", 2980, 45);
  R_Date("overlapping OxA-4504", 2965, 65);
  R_Date("overlapping OxA-5952", 2965, 45);
  R_Date("overlapping OxA-5959", 2965, 45);
  R_Date("overlapping OxA-5183", 2930, 40);
  R_Date("overlapping OxA-4653", 2910, 55);
  R_Date("overlapping OxA-5950", 2910, 45);
  R_Date("overlapping OxA-5954", 3025, 55);
  R_Date("overlapping HAR-2940", 3020, 70);
 };
 Boundary("End_Penard_overlapping");
};
Sequence()
{
 Date("=Start_Penard_overlapping");
 Boundary("Start_Wilburton_overlapping");
 Phase("overlapping Wilburton")
 {
  R_Date("overlapping OxA-4656", 3005, 75);
  R_Date("overlapping OxA-4503", 2930, 55);
  R_Date("overlapping OxA-4502", 2925, 50);
  R_Date("overlapping OxA-5036", 2920, 50);
  R_Date("overlapping OxA-5197", 2910, 50);
  R_Date("overlapping OxA-5955", 2900, 45);
  R_Date("overlapping OxA-5035", 2900, 45);
  R_Date("overlapping OxA-5034", 2890, 45);
  R_Date("overlapping OxA-5956", 2850, 50);
  R_Date("overlapping OxA-5198", 2820, 70);
 };
 Boundary("End_Wilburton_overlapping");
};
```

```
Sequence()
{
 Date("=Start_Wilburton_overlapping");
 Boundary("Start_Ewart_Park_overlapping");
 Phase("overlapping Ewart_Park")
 {
  R_Date("overlapping OxA-5957", 2810, 45);
  R_Date("overlapping OxA-4716", 2780, 50);
  R_Date("overlapping OxA-4654", 2765, 45);
  R_Date("overlapping OxA-5976", 2740, 45);
  R_Date("overlapping OxA-4652", 2720, 45);
  R_Date("overlapping BM-798", 2704, 50);
  R_Date("overlapping OxA-5962", 2685, 60);
  R_Date("overlapping OxA-6176", 2655, 50);
  R_Date("overlapping OxA-5977", 2620, 45);
 };
 Boundary("End_Ewart_Park_overlapping");
 };
 };
};
```

Sequential model
```
Plot()
{
 Sequence()
 {
  Boundary("Start_Acton_and_Taunton_sequential");
  Phase("sequential Acton_and_Taunton")
  {
   R_Date("sequential OxA-5948", 3225, 65);
   R_Date("sequential OxA-4651", 3220, 80);
   R_Date("sequential OxA-5949", 3110, 50);
   R_Date("sequential OxA-6177", 3055, 50);
   R_Date("sequential OxA-5196", 3035, 40);
  };
  Boundary("End_Acton_and_Taunton_start_Pennard_sequential");
  Phase("sequential Penard")
  {
   R_Date("sequential OxA-5187", 3045, 55);
   R_Date("sequential OxA-1526", 3030, 100);
   R_Date("sequential OxA-5953", 3015, 45);
   R_Date("sequential OxA-5951", 2980, 45);
   R_Date("sequential OxA-4504", 2965, 65);
   R_Date("sequential OxA-5952", 2965, 45);
   R_Date("sequential OxA-5959", 2965, 45);
```

```
  R_Date("sequential OxA-5183", 2930, 40);
  R_Date("sequential OxA-4653", 2910, 55);
  R_Date("sequential OxA-5950", 2910, 45);
  R_Date("sequential OxA-5954", 3025, 55);
  R_Date("sequential HAR-2940", 3020, 70);
 };
 Boundary("End_Penard_Start_Wilburton_sequential");
 Phase("sequential Wilburton")
 {
  R_Date("sequential OxA-4656", 3005, 75);
  R_Date("sequential OxA-4503", 2930, 55);
  R_Date("sequential OxA-4502", 2925, 50);
  R_Date("sequential OxA-5036", 2920, 50);
  R_Date("sequential OxA-5197", 2910, 50);
  R_Date("sequential OxA-5955", 2900, 45);
  R_Date("sequential OxA-5035", 2900, 45);
  R_Date("sequential OxA-5034", 2890, 45);
  R_Date("sequential OxA-5956", 2850, 50);
  R_Date("sequential OxA-5198", 2820, 70);
 };
 Boundary("End_Wilburton_Start_Ewart_Park_sequential");
 Phase("sequential Ewart_Park")
 {
  R_Date("sequential OxA-5957", 2810, 45);
  R_Date("sequential OxA-4716", 2780, 50);
  R_Date("sequential OxA-4654", 2765, 45);
  R_Date("sequential OxA-5976", 2740, 45);
  R_Date("sequential OxA-4652", 2720, 45);
  R_Date("sequential BM-798", 2704, 50);
  R_Date("sequential OxA-5962", 2685, 60);
  R_Date("sequential OxA-6176", 2655, 50);
  R_Date("sequential OxA-5977", 2620, 45);
 };
 Boundary("End_Ewart_Park_sequential");
 };
};
```

Code for Figure 8.14. Comparison for some of the data from the ice mummy 'Otzi', from data presented in Hedges et al. (1992) and Rom et al. (1999).

```
Options()
{
 Resolution=1;
};
```

Appendix: Code for selected case studies in Chapter 8   213

```
Plot()
{
 Phase("bone")
 {
  R_Date("ETH-8342", 4560, 65);
  R_Date("OxA-3419",4540,55);
  R_Date("OxA-3371",4660,55);
  R_Date("OxA-3372",4565,60);
  R_Date("OxA-3420",4530,70);
 };
 Phase("skin")
 {
  R_Date("OxA-3373",4550,70);
  R_Date("OxA-3374",4460,80);
  R_Date("OxA-3421",4480,55);
  R_Date("OxA-3375",4530,70);
  R_Date("OxA-3376",4450,80);
  R_Date("ETH-8345.1a", 4605, 65);
  R_Date("ETH-8345.1b", 4500, 70);
  R_Date("ETH-8345.1", 4585, 70);
  R_Date("ETH-8345.2", 4515, 70);
 };
 Line( );
 R_Combine("bone")
 {
  R_Date("ETH-8342", 4560, 65);
  R_Date("OxA-3419",4540,55);
  R_Date("OxA-3371",4660,55);
  R_Date("OxA-3372",4565,60);
  R_Date("OxA-3420",4530,70);
 };
 R_Combine("skin")
 {
  R_Date("OxA-3373",4550,70);
  R_Date("OxA-3374",4460,80);
  R_Date("OxA-3421",4480,55);
  R_Date("OxA-3375",4530,70);
  R_Date("OxA-3376",4450,80);
  R_Date("ETH-8345.1a", 4605, 65);
  R_Date("ETH-8345.1b", 4500, 70);
  R_Date("ETH-8345.1", 4585, 70);
  R_Date("ETH-8345.2", 4515, 70);
 };
 Line( );
 Sequence("Otzi")
```

```
{
Boundary();
R_Combine("bone")
 {
  R_Date("ETH-8342", 4560, 65);
  R_Date("OxA-3419",4540,55);
  R_Date("OxA-3371",4660,55);
  R_Date("OxA-3372",4565,60);
  R_Date("OxA-3420",4530,70);
 };
Interval(N(15,5));
R_Combine("skin")
 {
  R_Date("OxA-3373",4550,70);
  R_Date("OxA-3374",4460,80);
  R_Date("OxA-3421",4480,55);
  R_Date("OxA-3375",4530,70);
  R_Date("OxA-3376",4450,80);
  R_Date("ETH-8345.la", 4605, 65);
  R_Date("ETH-8345.lb", 4500, 70);
  R_Date("ETH-8345.1", 4585, 70);
  R_Date("ETH-8345.2", 4515, 70);
 };
Interval(N(0.083,0.038));
Date("Otzi_death_bone_skin_offset");
Boundary();
};
};
```